Food Combining
for Vegetarians

Dedication

To Doris Grant

whose doughty and enthusiastic championship of the Hay
system over many years has enabled countless people to
regain health and happiness.

Food Combining for Vegetarians

Jackie Le Tissier

Thorsons
An Imprint of HarperCollins*Publishers*

Thorsons
An Imprint of HarperCollins*Publishers*
77-85 Fulham Palace Road,
Hammersmith, London W6 8JB

Published by Thorsons 1992
This edition published 1992
3 5 7 9 10 8 6 4

A catalogue record for this book
is available from the British Library

ISBN 0 7225 2763 2
Typeset by Harper Phototypesetters Limited,
Northampton, England
Printed in Great Britain by
HarperCollinsManufacturing Glasgow

Contents

Acknowledgements

I wish to extend my appreciation to the following, who collectively have made this book possible:

Doris Grant and Jean Joice, without whom the idea for *Food Combining For Vegetarians* would never have existed. Their enthusiasm, encouragement and support throughout have been tremendous, and a great inspiration to me in writing this book. Special mention is due to Jean who so efficiently and patiently edited the entire draft prior to completion – her guidance and sound advice were invaluable.

Rose Elliot, for so kindly writing a foreword; Doctor MHS Bound, MD, FRCGP, and Doctor TW Parsons, MD, FRCP (Glas), who read the first section of this book, and offered their advice. Also, to Dr Bound for approaching the British Medical Association Library on my behalf to secure out-of-print works by Dr Hay; my two employers, Craig Alexander and Jay Hagger, for their patient understanding of my absences from the office while writing this book, and for making office facilities available for my use; Fresh Guernsey Herbs, for the generous supply of beautifully fresh herbs for trial recipes; Penny Davenport and Jeannette Lahr, Green Farm Nutrition Centre, for their expert nutritional guidance; the Librarian and Staff at the Guille-Alles Library, Guernsey; Joan Hodgson, for putting me in touch with Doris Grant during the initial stages of this project; my mother, who painstakingly helped me to adapt each recipe to American measurements; The Vegetarian Society, Vegan Society, *Here's Health* magazine, *Health Guardian* and *Health Now*, for their research into articles on the Hay System.

Special thanks must also go to Betty and John Middlebrook. They have supported me from the first wobbly steps in vegetarianism and the Hay System to becoming my trusted and expert 'tasters' for each recipe I developed – 'meals on wheels' took on a whole new meaning, as I subjected them, often daily, to strange-looking dishes! A further mention must be made to

John, who so carefully and patiently proof-read the manuscript, and amended any awful grammatical errors, before allowing me to submit it into the hands of Jean Joice.

My gratitude also goes to all family and friends who have patiently endured my involvement with this book, and offered encouragement throughout.

Foreword by Rose Elliot

Doris Grant says that she thinks this is a book which all food-combiners, not just vegetarians, will enjoy; and I'd like to add to that by saying that I think this is a book which all *vegetarians*, not just food-combiners, will enjoy!

Although I'd read the occasional article about the Hay diet, my first real contact with it came in the early 1980s, through my father. Having battled with a weight problem all his life, he eventually managed to lose weight successfully using the Beverly Hills diet. He then went on to discover the Hay system, which is based on the same principle of separating proteins and starches, but allows for a much greater variety of combinations of fruits and vegetables within those groups. I watched as, for the first time in his life, he was not only able to keep his weight steady and stay slim, but also enjoyed wonderful meals. He, like other followers of the Hay system, discovered that meals à la Hay are extremely good. So continuing to eat that way, as I have shown in my own book, *Vegetarian Slimming*, unlike trying to follow almost any other diet, is a pleasure rather than a pain. No wonder that advocates of Dr Hay's system prefer to call it a 'way of eating' rather than a diet.

Since witnessing my father's success, I've met many more people who have benefited greatly from changing to the Hay system. Usually they do so hoping that it will improve one particular ailment, and then they continue because they find not only does that condition clear up, but they feel so much better generally. In fact the results of the Hay diet are so impressive that I think it deserves to be taken seriously in scientific circles and the successes studied and the mechanism by which these are achieved properly researched.

Like most people who give the Hay way of eating a fair trial, I found that, after trying it for a week or so, I, too, became an enthusiast. I now like to eat the Hay way most of the time, and *Food Combining for Health*, by Doris Grant and Jean Joice has been amongst my most valued cookbooks since it appeared in

1984. I am therefore delighted that Jackie Le Tissier, in close consultation with Doris and Jean, has now continued where they left off, as far as vegetarians are concerned, and written Food Combining for Vegetarians. This book answers all the questions vegetarians might want to know about such things as pulses and peanuts, coconut, carob, chestnuts and tofu, not to mention kuzu, mirin and seitan, and is useful not only to vegetarians but to vegans also, whose needs are considered throughout. The tables showing the classification of foods into starch, protein and neutral, also alkaline and acid, are particularly helpful and comprehensive.

A strange fact I've discovered, when cooking Hay meals, is that the restriction imposed through not mixing protein and starch at the same meal, instead of being frustrating, stimulates creativity. It certainly seems to have had that effect on Jackie. Her recipes are delicious, with an imaginative use of ingredients which makes me want to go straight into the kitchen and start cooking – one of the hall-marks of a good cookbook. Recipes such as the Creamy Walnut and Coconut Dressing; the Pine kernel Sauce; and Leek, Mushroom and Pine kernel Lasagne are really tempting, or try Asparagus Dip, using fresh asparagus; or the intriguing Apple Tofu 'Cheesecake' and the Tofu Custard. Jackie's use of nuts to thicken sauces and make 'pastry' and crackers is particularly imaginative and will be invaluable to all food-combiners.

I wish Jackie and *Food Combining for Vegetarians* every possible success.

Rose Elliot

Introduction

It was a fortunate day for Hay enthusiasts when Jackie Le Tissier asked us to read the thesis she had prepared for the Cordon Vert Diploma of the Vegetarian Society. Her subject was the Hay system which she had discovered through reading our book *Food Combining for Health* and it was immediately apparent that here was someone who had not only extensively researched Dr Hay's teachings but had put them into practice in her own life with remarkable results.

A dedicated vegetarian, Jackie Le Tissier had so successfully adapted the system for her own use that when our publishers, Thorsons, asked us to suggest someone who could prepare a book of recipes for the fast growing number of vegetarian Hay dieters, we immediately put them in touch with Jackie. The result will be a blessing not only for vegetarians but for all followers of the Hay system. Quite apart from her extensive recipe section, the account of her remarkable restoration to health and escape from the threat of life in a wheelchair, her chapters on Hay precepts and their successful adaptation, make absorbing reading.

She is particularly good when stressing 'the gentleness' of embarking on the Hay lifestyle and it certainly involves no deprivation as her menus and recipes are unusual, imaginative and delicious.

For those who are determined to overcome health problems and get the very best out of life, this book will prove an inspiration.

Doris Grant and Jean Joice

1
Dr William Howard Hay —
the man and his life

William Howard Hay was born in Pennsylvania, USA, in 1866. After gaining his medical degree at New York University in 1891 he practised for sixteen years, until ill health made him doubt not only his training, but the whole system of conventional medical treatment and its application. He concluded that freedom from disease lay not in relieving symptoms, but in treating the underlying causes.

One hundred years later, this very same principle is being increasingly upheld by practitioners of our day supportive of what is now termed 'holistic', or 'complementary', medicine.

So how did Dr Hay's enlightened view actually come about? Aged forty and weighing sixteen stones, one pound (102kg/225 lbs), he decided that exercise was needed to help him lose weight. He began playing tennis daily, but waited until the end of the season to measure the extent of his success. To his horror, on weigh-in day, he discovered he had lost only one pound! Unfortunately, his increase in stamina had also resulted in an increase in appetite! He stopped exercising, but didn't curtail his eating habits which resulted, just over a year later, in a serious breakdown in health with Bright's disease, high blood pressure and a badly dilated heart.

Having been told by colleagues that the outlook was bleak, he decided that his health, or rather lack of it, lay in his own hands. He turned all his attention to study what was causing and influencing his illness.

He analysed, and subsequently changed, his eating and living habits, managing to reduce his weight to an ideal twelve stones and three pounds (78kg/171 lbs) in three months! To the immense surprise of himself and his physicians, his disease symptoms first slowly diminished – then disappeared! He became healthier than ever before.

His experience convinced him that his case was by no means an exceptional one and that too many members of the medical profession were inclined to treat symptoms rather than investigate the underlying cause of their patients' complaints.

His personal suffering and subsequent research resulted in his discovery that a balanced diet, with foods eaten in a combination so as to avoid a mixture of starch and protein at any one meal, leads to the alleviation of numerous symptoms of disease, and offers renewed health. This then led him to establish two further principles of his system of eating; the necessity of balancing the alkali to acid ratio of the body and ensuring regular and efficient waste food elimination.

He concluded that 'as we eat so we are', and: 'one can be as well as desired'. In over thirty years of professional practice, he was able to cure countless patients by advising them to improve their dietary habits.

His successful approach to health problems earned Dr Hay world wide professional acclaim.

He went on to develop and meticulously define his principles of eating, establishing what has become known as the 'Hay System'. This has been excellently expanded upon in *Food Combining for Health* by Doris Grant and Jean Joice, the publication of which has been of tremendous benefit to sufferers of ill-health or dietary problems, and many thousands, including the rich and royal, now openly admit to being firm converts to the Hay System. Adaptations of the Hay System can also be found in the 'Beverley Hills Diet', 'The Wright Diet' and 'Fit for Life'.

Dr William Howard Hay died in 1940. In many ways he was ahead of his time and without doubt pioneered a dietary revolution with his radical ideas.

Many of us are indebted to this man who perceived the body as a whole, putting sensible eating before medical prescription, and prevention before cure.

I hope this book will enable many more people to benefit from his guidelines for renewed health, vitality and enthusiasm for living.

2

My experience

Dr Hay's diet quite literally changed my life. In 1983, aged twenty-two, and full of the joys and challenges of life and a new career, I little realized that my happiness was about to topple. Over a period of months I became progressively stricken with burning and crippling pains in my feet (this was later to progress to my left knee), along with swelling to such an extent that my feet almost doubled in size – resulting in my looking rather like Mickey Mouse from the knees down! I had never experienced such physical distress before, and imagine my feeling of insult, on consulting a doctor, to be told to change my style of footwear! – knowing full well that the shoes I wore were in no way contributory to such acute discomfort.

Needless to say the pain did not lessen. After several visits to another doctor I was eventually sent for blood tests. These indicated that I was suffering from an inflammatory condition. Anti-inflammatory medication was prescribed, which, although having an initial effect in reducing the pain, soon wore off, resulting in repeat prescriptions – but for stronger drugs.

The intensity of the pain at this time was such that I admit to being reduced to tears on several occasions, and literally crawling on my hands and knees, rather than having to suffer the agony of standing up.

As the symptoms worsened so the drug doses changed and increased until I was referred to a specialist in an attempt to discover the true nature of my affliction. It was then that the diagnosis of a form of ankylosing spondylitis – an arthritic condition – was made. The reason for my contracting this was unclear. Vague mentions of a 'virus' were given, although it was also established that my particular tissue type is susceptible to this form of disease.

My relief at finally discovering what was wrong was soon dispelled, however, when prognosis was made. I was told that I might never be wholly well enough to maintain full-time employment, and might even end up in a wheelchair. I received this news with horror, and being by nature someone who does not give up easily, I resolved to look more closely at what alternatives to drugs were open to me in the way of treatment.

I had by now been forced to give up my job and return home to convalesce, making intermittent trips back to the specialist, before my case was passed over completely to a local doctor specializing in this field of inflammatory illnesses. Drug treatment continued, but it was in 1984, following intense study of alternative 'diets', and my determination to rid myself of medication, that a friend suggested I read her copy of the then recently published *Food Combining for Health* by Doris Grant and Jean Joice (Thorsons 1984). This book confirmed my feelings that disease and food are the closest of neighbours or the strongest of enemies, depending on our nutritional habits, and that because our bodies are so very often full of toxic accumulants, a vital and 'wholesome' manner of eating is essential to achieve a fresh and detoxified internal condition.

After reading *Food Combining for Health* my dietary interests took on a whole new slant. I realized that I ought to consider modifying not only the *types* of food I was eating, but also the various ways in which they were combined.

Less than twelve months later I was able to resume full-time work, and progressively regained my energy and enthusiasm for living, taking on new projects and living life to the full.

I now teach part-time, as well as holding a responsible and demanding job, and fit as much as I possibly can into every spare moment. I am frequently scolded for running around and doing too much! A far cry from the person once destined for the wheelchair!

I can also say, without exaggeration, that I never feel even a twinge of pain in my poor long-suffering feet or knee – the only visible reminder of the past being ten rather crooked and sorry-looking toes!

While following the Hay System, I decided to adopt a vegetarian lifestyle, and went on to adjust the Hay concepts to accommodate a meatless diet. As a result of my interest in vegetarian cookery, I undertook the Cordon Vert Diploma Course with The Vegetarian Society, for which the submission of a thesis on a vegetarian-related subject was required. I selected 'Eating the Hay Way – A Study of the Hay System of Eating with Reference to the Vegetarian/Vegan Diet'. This led me to contact Doris Grant and Jean Joice who suggested that my work on this topic be published. The result of this advice now follows.

The 'Hay Diet' has made a tremendous change not only to my health but also to my way of life. For it *is* a way of life – a simple set of guidelines to follow without any sense of abstemiousness or deprivation from the pleasures of eating. I hope too it will provide many people – not only vegetarians/vegans, but also those wishing to follow a more healthy style of eating – with a fresh approach to their existing dietary habits, and lead to the exuberant health and general harmony that I now experience.

Happy Food Combining!

Jackie Le Tissier

3

The Hay system and the vegetarian/vegan

Although Dr Hay was not a vegetarian or vegan, his regime does call for greatly reduced amounts of flesh foods, and for this reason the Hay System is easily adapted to a meat-free diet.

Dr Hay actually viewed vegetarianism as the ideal diet, a theory which, so far as the West is concerned, has become widespread only over the last few decades. He drew attention to the laws laid down by God to Adam and Eve in the Garden of Eden 'Eat of every herb that is upon the face of the whole Earth, and of every herb-bearing seed (vegetables, greens, grains) and of the fruit of every tree, in which there is the seed of a tree-bearing fruit'. His belief was that these are 'complete and specific directions for feeding . . . No mention was made of flesh of animal or fish, nor was the intention implied that these were ever to be used'.

He criticized meat as being a useless and unnecessary food, saying that: 'if we wish a concentrated protein then nuts are better than meat, not containing the usual toxins of the animal flesh'. This was an amazing comment considering that at the time vegetarians were considered 'of erratic mind' or 'under suspicion of madness'.

Further evidence for a vegetarian Hay System comes from the Essene Gospel of Peace – a third-century manuscript. This states: 'Kill neither men, nor beasts, nor yet the food which goes into your mouth. For if you eat living food, the same will quicken you, but if you kill your food, the dead food will kill you also . . . For everything which kills your foods, kills your bodies also . . . And your bodies become what your foods are . . .' Curiously apt in these days of food scares amid concerns about additives and BSE.

Indeed this manuscript must surely be the first known reference to the importance of care in food combining for it goes on to say: 'Cook not, neither mix all things one with another, lest your bowels become as steaming bogs . . . For I tell you truly, if you mix together all sorts of food in your body, then the peace of your body will cease, and endless war will rage in you.' Stirring stuff – and like so many early scripts, founded on sound common sense.

So, the Hay System and its principles are natural to vegetarianism/veganism and it is possible to adapt its concepts to fit these styles of eating. Indeed, with its emphasis on fruit, vegetable and salad foods, the basis of the Hay System is essentially vegetarian/vegan anyway.

It has been necessary to classify ingredients not found in Dr Hay's original listings. In most cases these foods – soya products for example – were not readily available in his day, though they form an important part of the vegetarian/vegan diet. Their inclusion, along with more obscure ingredients such as sea vegetables, will provide a comprehensive vegetarian/vegan food reference and enable you to build a 'store cupboard' to fit in with the principles of the regime, as well as your own dietary ideals.

For ease of reading, the term 'vegetarian/vegan' in this book will be written as 'vegetarian', and 'vegetarianism' will cover the dietary implications of both the vegetarian and vegan unless otherwise specified.

4

What is food combining? — the Hay System explained

The Hay System is an inspiring and enlightening look at food and the manner in which we use it. It involves a whole new way of life and living and, if followed faithfully, can lead to levels of vitality and vivacity not previously experienced. So do you feel like kicking the ceiling when you wake up each morning? If the answer is 'No!', then you are not as well as you could be – and I hope that this book will provide the impetus and guidance to a 'new healthy you'.

Quite simply there are Five Basic Rules to remember. These are:

1 starchy foods and sugars (carbohydrates) should not be eaten with proteins or acid fruits at the same meal
2 fruit, vegetable and salad foods should form the major part of the diet
3 starchy foods and sugars (carbohydrates), proteins and fats should be eaten in small amounts only
4 only wholegrain, unrefined carbohydrates should be eaten: all refined, processed foods – in particular white flour, white sugar and their by-products; highly processed fats; sweetened foods; foods containing unnaturally-occurring additives, preservatives and colourings – should be eliminated
5 there should be an interval of four to four-and-a-half hours between meals of different types

> The separation of protein and starch foods at each meal is the *most* important concept of the Hay System, simply encapsulated by Doris Grant and Jean Joice in the phrase **Don't mix foods that fight.**

In the words of Dr Hay 'To separate the incompatible foods is to continue to eat just the same things as formerly, but in different groupings, that is all. This is no difficult program, and entails no real self-denial, so should be undertaken easily by anyone, even the confirmed devotee of the table.'

The easiest way recommended by Dr Hay to include starch and protein foods in our diet and yet not mix them at the same meal is to base one meal a day on starchy foods with a healthy balance of vegetable and salad ingredients, and similarly another meal based on protein foods accompanied by fruit, vegetable and salad foods. The third meal, known as the Alkaline Meal (see page 66 for further explanation) will then provide the necessary food balance.

What are the starch and protein foods?

Starchy foods and sugars: (carbohydrates) are those which contain a carbohydrate concentration of 20 per cent or more, and are made up of:

* all types of cereals/grains (wheat, oats, barley, rye, rice etc) and cereal/grain products (breads, cakes, biscuits, pastas, etc)
* all types of sugar and sugar products (cakes, biscuits, puddings, confectionery, etc)
* starchy vegetables – potatoes, etc
* sweet fruits – dates, bananas, etc

Protein foods: are those which contain a protein concentration of 20 per cent or more, and include:

* dairy products
* eggs
* soya and soya products
* most nuts

Point 1, the importance of food separation, is explained on pages 21-24 (comprehensive starch and protein food charts are tabulated for your use: pages 61-65).

Points (2)-(4) above are self-explanatory, but point (5) is a new concept.

A time lapse between meals of different types (starch, protein or alkaline) is recommended to allow our digestive system to cope efficiently with one meal at a time and not throw it into confusion by too quickly demanding the assimilation of yet another meal before an earlier one has been digested. Treating digestion as a conveyor belt system should be avoided, for just as we ourselves require rest from continual motion to avoid fatigue and 'wear and tear', so too does this function of our body, a need which should always be respected.

The time lapse of four to four-and-a-half hours is not unreasonable when the usual meal breakdown of a day is considered – breakfast, say, at eight o'clock, lunch at one, and dinner at six – it does mean, though, that if you rise late and eat breakfast at ten you should not be thinking of tucking into lunch at one!

This break between meals does *not* mean that 'morning coffees' and 'afternoon teas' are taboo – eating and drinking between meals are allowed – provided it is in moderation! (See notes on snacking, page 97.)

From a more scientific point of view – the Hay System is essentially the practice of combining foods in such a way as to separate starches and proteins to ensure their complete and efficient digestion.

At the same time the system calls for: (1) the maintenance of the delicate, but vital, balance of alkaline and acid levels in the body and (2) the efficient elimination of accumulated food waste. These two further concepts are discussed in greater detail later in this chapter.

The Hay System is a style of eating which takes account of the body's natural functions. By applying to the total concept of digestion the preparation, combination, metabolism and elimination of foods, it illustrates that disease is often a result of incorrect feeding and the body's inability to rid itself of its accumulated food residues. To this end, therefore, we actually *feed our diseases*.

If this *is* the case, it follows that in the words of Dr Hay: *We create our own ills and for this reason we alone can effect a cure.*

The basic concepts of the Hay System are:

- to eat at each meal only foods which can be correctly combined
- to balance the alkali: acid ratio of the body
- to ensure efficient elimination of food waste

By keeping to these three principles you too can achieve a healthier body, mind and spirit, alive and alert to living.

The Hay System bases these hypotheses on the principle that not all foods are 'happy' with each other from a digestive point of view, and should therefore be kept apart. This Dr Hay showed by explaining that starchy foods and sugars (carbohydrates) and protein foods require diametrically opposite conditions of digestion. Simply separating into different meals those foods requiring protein breakdown and those requiring starch breakdown removes the pressure placed on our digestive system to act upon a mixture of all sorts of different foods – at the same time!

This stimulates a healthy body, offering relief from the numerous 'grumbles' of everyday living – indigestion, headaches and fatigue – and builds up resistance – our alkaline reserve – to more serious diseases such as heart trouble, strokes, high blood pressure and obesity, of which the lesser symptoms are often precursors. At the same time the regularity and efficiency of waste elimination from the body is enhanced.

'Eat at each meal only foods which can be correctly combined.'

The basis of food combination rests on the principle that there are three main food groups:

- Starchy Foods and Sugars (Carbohydrates) — must not be eaten with Protein Foods
- Protein Foods — must not be eaten with Starchy Foods and Sugars (Carbohydrates)
- Acid Fruits — must not be eaten with Starchy Foods and Sugars (Carbohydrates) — BUT — can be eaten with Protein Foods

Full lists of these are given in the food charts on pages 61-69.

I find it helpful to think of the following phrase when trying to remember to separate protein and starch:

'Mind your P's and S's!'

It will seem strange to start with that this means 'giving up' jacket potato and cheese (starch and protein) and apple pie (acid fruit and carbohydrate) – but there are many other things that can be eaten instead! The fun and challenge of rearranging meals, along with new-found vitality and digestive comfort, soon overcomes any sense of nostalgia for previous meal combinations.

You will still be eating the very same foods, but in a different combination.

How does this incorrect combining of food start?

The incorrect combining of foods starts soon after birth when it becomes customary for meals to be arranged in a particular way. The 'meat and two veg.' – or, for vegetarians, the 'jacket potato and cheese' – meal is thus established as 'normal'.

Instead of allowing our bodies to guide us in our selection of food we fall victim to the pressures of family, society and food manufacturers. Individual well-being and comfort are pushed to one side, and sacrificed to the processed convenience foods of our rapidly 'advancing' civilization. These, in many instances, are not easily or satisfactorily digested, and may lead to a 'clogged' body and subsequent depletion of energy and vitality. Nagging side-effects of indigestion, constipation, stiff joints and headaches may ensue but are invariably dismissed as 'oh, just a touch of . . .' – and then become accepted as part of everyday living.

Habits form, despite the consequential ill-health, and only when the 'touch of' manifests itself as something acute, or even chronic, do we awaken to the realization that the answer to our ills might actually lie in our own hands.

The importance of efficient digestion

According to Dr Hay 'It is not how much we eat, but how much we can fully digest, absorb, and metabolize, that counts.' Digestion of food is dependent on the alkalinity or acidity of the body's digestive system (not to be confused with the 'Alkali to Acid Ratio' discussed later and a completely different concept).

If alkalis and acids are mixed they neutralize each other. This fact strongly influences the efficiency, or otherwise, of carbohydrate and protein digestion.

Starchy Foods and Sugar (Carbohydrate) digestion

Carbohydrate foods require an *alkaline* medium for their complete digestion.

Unusual though it may sound, the most important part of the body for carbohydrate digestion is actually the mouth, where the food is mixed with saliva, an alkaline juice. The action of chewing breaks down the carbohydrate, preparing it for the next stage of digestion which takes place in the stomach. Without thorough chewing, the stomach cannot split the carbohydrate any further, food passes through the body largely undigested and the body is deprived of the natural goodness present. Thorough chewing of carbohydrate foods is therefore essential for good health. The more the better. This might seem strange to those who are so used to 'bolting' down their meals, but it helps to explain why so many of us suffer from digestive discomforts.

Protein digestion

Protein foods require an *acid* medium for their complete digestion.

Protein foods are digested after being acted upon in the stomach and thoroughly broken down by the release of acid gastric juices.

The results of mixed digestion

From the above we can see that when a mixture of starch and protein food is eaten together at one meal, we are asking our stomach to be both alkaline *and* acid at the same time – something it cannot by any known trick achieve. A wishy-washy medium of neither acid nor alkaline make-up ensues and the meal is plunged into digestive chaos.

It can be argued that as Nature combines carbohydrates and proteins in the same food, no harm should come to us from eating them together in different foods. On closer study, however, it is apparent that Nature does not (except in the case of the pulses, see page 55) combine in any one food a high concentration of both starches/sugars and protein. Where they do occur together it is in a ratio which ensures that either the digestion of one or the other predominates.

As the presence of both types of food in the stomach at the same time precludes the possibility of efficient digestion of either, then the only sensible plan is to separate them at source — the mouth!

The stomach acts as our 'food mixer' and it will only turn

out the perfect recipe if we supply it with the correct
ingredients combined in the correct manner.

'Balancing the alkali:acid ratio of the body'

Chemically-speaking, food is either alkali-forming or acid-
forming in its make-up, and for this reason has a direct
influence on the overall alkalinity or acidity of the body.

To establish the ratio present in the body, Dr Hay measured
the amount of alkaline and acid elements excreted through the
skin, lungs, bowel and kidneys and discovered that the alkaline
elements accounted for a loss four times greater than the acid.
To maintain this correct proportion of bodily elements he
concluded that it is necessary, therefore, to eat four times the
amount of alkaline as of acid foods. (i.e. to maintain the ideal
80:20 alkali to acid ratio.)

If the balance is 'upset', either by a deficiency of alkaline
foods or an excess of acid-forming ones, our body's delicate
equilibrium and efficient functioning suffer. Breakdown of
some form occurs, and the body is actively or potentially
susceptible to disease and germ invasion. The lower the alkaline
level, therefore, the further away we are from optimum health.

To counteract this the body, under normal conditions, has a
very large alkali reservoir which acts as a 'dam' or 'buffer'
against too much acid-forming food. Its job is to convert the
excess acid into alkaline or neutral elements, thus preventing
a breakdown in resistance. If this reservoir becomes depleted
due to an 'overdose' of acid foods without sufficient alkaline
foods to keep it 'topped up', the body is no longer able to
neutralize any excessive acid intake. As a result, an over-acid
state arises (most generally recognized as 'acid stomach'). This
destroys the alkali to acid proportions, interferes with bodily
function and, in many instances, may lead to illness.

Self-poisoning, auto-intoxication, toxaemia, etc, are terms
applied to an over-acid state. There are four main causes of
excess acid manufacture in the body:

* the use of too much concentrated protein food
* the use of too much concentrated starch and sugary food –
  especially refined and processed starches and sugars from

which the naturally occurring alkalis have been lost or destroyed
* wrong food combinations
* the retention of food waste in the body (constipation)

Careful adjustment of our diet, however, means that this need never occur. The alkaline elements occur abundantly in all fruit, vegetable and salad foods, and the acid elements chiefly in all concentrated starch and protein foods.

If you are already separating your food into compatible groups, acid production is automatically reduced, since starches/sugars and protein – the major acid-forming foods – are never taken together at one meal. Eating plenty of fresh fruit, vegetable and salad foods means that the 80 per cent alkalinity is easily and quickly achieved. This is especially so for the vegetarian whose diet is already largely made up of such foods. In order to ensure sufficient alkaline food is eaten, Dr Hay recommended that one meal a day be based solely on such foods.

For ease of reference the alkaline and acid foods are classified and tabulated (see page 66), allowing foods in the correct proportions to be selected.

Eating to conserve the alkali to acid ratio is straightforward and need not detract from the pleasures of dining – indeed because an abundance of fresh, unadulterated food, straight from Nature, is eaten, the palate is awakened and sensitized to a whole new world of exciting flavours.

'Ensure efficient elimination of food waste'

A question of elimination . . .

The subject of bowel movements and their frequency appears to be an acute cause for embarrassment, and a topic only discussed very self-consciously between doctor and patient, or whispered between sufferer and close confidant – and yet it is as natural as eating!

Dr Hay placed extreme emphasis on the question of efficient and regular bodily excretion and stressed the necessity of its regularity and efficiency before a healthy body could be attained.

The intestines, colon and bowel make up our 'drainage' or 'sewer' network, and just because they are hidden from sight does not mean we can 'turn a blind eye' to their operation. And yet this, for most people, is often the case.

We do not ignore blocked and odorous drains in our home; rather we are horrified to think that such uncleanliness exists in our otherwise spotless household, and rush to contact a plumber. It is a shame that such speedy treatment and elimination of the cause is not applied to our own 'choked drainage', for this would quickly improve the nation's and individual's state of physical and mental health. For just as a blocked drain harbours bacteria and toxins, so too does a blocked body, and just as the bacteria and toxins in the blocked drain multiply and feed off the waste collected there, then so too do those in our body.

So, if we do not activate some sort of internal plumbing mechanism what happens to all this decayed and decaying food waste? The idea really does not bear thinking about, for the obvious answer must be that we re-absorb it. It is allowed to infiltrate and swamp our body tissues, lower our body's reserves by the excessive accumulation of acid waste products, and, at the same time, provide the perfect conditions for disease to develop.

Thus, poor drainage – or 'constipation' – directly contributes to disease, just as incorrect food combining and an unbalanced alkali to acid state do, the one leading to the other and then each interacting to cause breakdown and subsequent illness.

What is constipation?: Constipation is the inability to remove regularly, efficiently and with ease the faecal debris resulting from the digestion and metabolism of food. It is greatly aggravated by Western diet with its refined, processed and denatured foods eaten in excessive amounts, and containing little or no fibre to encourage the lining of the digestive tract to push the food along and out.

Constipation will be greatly relieved by Dr Hay's diet. Its emphasis on attending to the whims of digestion – correct combination of foods, a predominance of bulky, fibrous ingredients in the form of fruit, vegetables and salad foods – creates vitality and optimum functioning to ensure that bowel movements and waste expulsion are regular and efficient.

The Hay System and You

Imagine an existence in which daily you wake up feeling buoyant and filled with the joys of life and living. Expectations and ambitions are high and a challenge to be met with keen vigour and excitement. No problem appears insurmountable and work and play are carried out with ease and to the full — physical discomfort replaced by glowing health, 'down' moments by optimism, and fatigue by renewed vitality.

Idealistic? No – attainable.

By following the natural principles of the Hay System it is possible to achieve a happy body, creating a happy mind, soul and spirit.

For as Dr Hay declared: 'The task of keeping yourself well is your own, no one else's, not even the physician's'.

How wonderful to know *why* you feel unwell, and also how to *stay* well in the future!

5
Disease and the Hay System

With the resurgence of interest in holistic and complementary medicine, we are becoming more and more aware of the importance of treating the causes of disease rather than its symptoms.

We are living in an age in which the standard of life and living is high. Many diseases previously afflicting man appear to have been eradicated. We have better sanitation, cleaner water and more appreciation of the need for fresh air, sunlight and exercise, than ever before. Yet in spite of these advances we are witnessing both an increase in degenerative diseases – those ailments regarded as the normal consequence of old age – and the frightening onset of new problems – such as AIDS and forms of cancer previously unknown. We are, in effect, either living longer to grow older quicker, or being attacked in our earlier years and dying before reaching full maturity.

Can you, then, think of any greater comfort which could possibly be brought to us than the confident belief that – excepting accidents – we need not be ill?

Dr Hay considered that 'food always and only' may be the culprit so far as many of our daily ills are concerned. How wonderful to think that we could avoid many of our current health problems.

How does illness begin?

Dr Hay decried the concept that illness suddenly strikes 'out of a clear sky', stating that it is our progressively worsening dietary habits which are responsible. Strokes, heart attacks, and similar crises, appear to come suddenly only because we are blind to the internal workings – or rather failings – of the body.

If this is the case, then **our bodies are the result of how we live from day to day, and only we are responsible for our health.**

This places an obligation on each of us to recognize that we cannot forever off-load our physical weaknesses on to external factors – germs, infections, viruses, heredity – but must realize that we expose ourselves to these conditions, and will be continually and progressively afflicted until we cease to do so.

After all, it was Seneca two thousand years ago who said: 'men do not die, they kill themselves'.

The relationship between disease and Dr Hay's concepts is apparent when we acknowledge that the majority of people start life near perfect. Provided we are educated in the correct manner of eating, and not encouraged to over-feed or develop bad habits, then this near-perfect health can be maintained – at least in theory.

We know this is seldom the case. A state of 'self-poisoning' soon occurs. This may not become apparent for many years, indeed perhaps for a life-time, but there will come a stage when maximum tolerance is reached. Symptoms and disease will ensue as Nature's reaction to an unnatural balance of the body's make-up.

Dr Hay, however, condemned medication – except as an emergency treatment. He saw it as adding to an already toxic state by its unnatural chemical composition, and concealing and 'squashing' symptoms, instead of treating the *cause*. Each symptom he said should be viewed as a signal of some form of internal suffering, attracting attention to the fact that 'something is up'. In the words of Voltaire: 'we put medicines of which we know little into bodies about which we know less to cure disease of which we know nothing at all'.

Dr Hay did, nevertheless, emphasize the need for physicians and medication for use in life-saving surgery and in the treatment of physical deformities and injuries, and held surgeons in the highest esteem for the excellent work done in these areas. It was only in the field of pathological diagnosis and prescription that he condemned the practice of many doctors of treating only the symptoms of disease rather than investigating the underlying causes.

The Hay System therefore views disease as a bodily 'cry for help' for detoxification and correction of dietary habits.

This is not being simplistic. Health need not be a complicated subject – it is only if we choose to ignore Nature's guidelines that overwhelming problems result.

It can be argued that many of us make dietary mistakes and continue to live and *appear* in good health. I stress 'appear' –

because appearances are deceptive. Although we might all build up and carry a tolerance for incompatible foods, the foregoing chapters indicate that this can be at some considerable sacrifice to our physical and mental performance.

Nature creates – in the majority of cases – a perfect body; why should we, therefore, accept anything less than perfect health in return?

I must emphasize that food is not a 'cure' for disease. This can be carried out only by our own regenerative processes. It is, however, a *cause* of disease and as such is instrumental in treatment – simply by ceasing to be that cause. For this reason, the Hay System pays minute attention to the relationship between food and disease. Hay's lifetime of observation and treatment of his patients, and the subsequent results, cannot be ignored. Although nowadays we tend to be 'baffled by science', we must take this opportunity to open our eyes and attribute our ills, partly or wholly, to: 'food always and only'.

Prior to reading this book you may have considered this an absurd statement to make and dismissed it as groundless. I trust this is no longer the case, and you now recognize that such claims can be substantiated. Following the Hay System not only improves digestion, but also helps to banish symptoms of disease and to cure disease itself.

I accept that the Hay System, not being founded on solely scientific findings, may still be regarded with some scepticism amongst the medically qualified today. It is, however, left for *you* to formulate your own opinions and conclusions on the subject, and to draw from the suggestions put forward the realization and encouragement that effective treatment of your own particular ill is possible.

Naturally the success of the Hay System is wholly dependent on the body being still able to regenerate itself. Unfortunately, in cases of long-standing deterioration complete recovery may be difficult or even impossible. Dr Hay was also careful to point out that improved health depends to a large extent on a strong desire to recover, along with an awareness of how and why recovery results, and the will-power and determination to see it through.

Mention should also be made that the Hay System is not a panacea for all ills. Dr Hay never claimed that it was. It is rather a means of achieving a healthy, trouble-free body and, hopefully, reducing and even eliminating susceptibility to disease.

The relationship between diseases and the Hay System

The following text on the Hay System and the treatment of disease has been drawn from research into Dr Hay's works and other more recent health publications. Comments made reflect Dr Hay's convictions and those of many present-day nutritionists – I, myself, make no claim to medical qualifications. Further reading for those who are interested is listed at the back of the book.

I feel sure, however, that many readers who are interested in the positive contribution which food can make to health will be able to satisfy themselves from their own observations that this system is well worth following.

Allergies/hay fever: These are caused by reactions to certain irritants – such as foods, pollens, foreign bodies – and, according to Dr Hay, are brought on by a specific lack of body resistance to these excitants. As body resistance is dependent on a predominance of alkaline-forming foods, a return to the correct alkali to acid balance should result in the distress caused by these allergies being relieved and, in some cases, cured completely. The former sufferer should then be able to eat the offending foods in comfort, or bury his nose in pollen without sneezing.

Arthritis and rheumatism: Arthritis and rheumatism are often caused by accumulated waste from the blood and body fluids being deposited where circulation is slowest, around the joints and muscles. This results in acute inflammation.

Infection is often cited as a cause for arthritic or rheumatic complaints.

As arthritis and rheumatism are not diseases of any particular organ, but represent a general saturation of the body with acid debris, they will attack those in apparently good health. Adherence to the Hay System, with specific attention to the alkali and acid ratio and strict internal hygiene, may aid a reversal of symptoms and allow Nature to heal the damage caused, provided, of course, that joints have not already become so attacked and congested as to be 'ankylosed' – fused.

Candida albicans: This condition is an invasion by a yeast living in all of us, which because of favourable conditions – unbalanced body chemistry and lowered immune system – grows and becomes uncontrollable. As yeast feeds on starches and sugars an acute sensitivity to food containing these develops, further aggravated by the yeast's natural presence in our intestines which gives it direct access to all that we eat. A weakened defence system and the use of too much refined carbohydrate – sugar and white flour products – have been cited as contributory factors to this condition. For these reasons the Hay System – which naturally eliminates such offending foods and restricts carbohydrate intake – should offer considerable benefit, detoxifying the body and strengthening its defence system at the same time.

Coronary heart disease: Coronary heart disease (CHD) is the one disease Dr Hay was never called upon to treat – and yet it is prevalent today. In fact it was only in the 1950s (approximately a decade following his death) that CHD became 'the single major cause of adult death' ('Diet, nutrition, and the prevention of chronic diseases: Report of a WHO study group', WHO, 1990). This study admits that the connection between a high-fat, low-fibre diet and its subsequent effect on health 'may be important in modifying the rate of progression of atherosclerosis' and that, 'On current projections, cardiovascular diseases will emerge or be established as a substantial health problem in virtually every country in the world by the year 2000.'

The diet of Western nations became more affluent during and after Dr Hay's lifetime (excluding, of course, the war years – during which time, incidentally, CHD was far less evident). This and the subsequent overwhelming reports of CHD indicate that diet over a period of time is directly contributory to this disease and, indeed, the similar development of other more recent diseases in our Western society.

Catarrh and catarrhal conditions: The formation of catarrh is a means by which the body rids itself of toxins. This and the related conditions of sinusitis, appendicitis, asthma, colitis, gall-bladder disease and gall-stones have all been found to improve by the application of a diet following Hay System guidelines.

Colds, influenza and pneumonia: Dr Hay stated that, as with so much disease, colds, influenza and pneumonia mark the end-point of the body's tolerance of accumulated internal toxic waste.

We cannot continue to blame the much maligned germ, for the germs often held to be responsible for such conditions reside permanently within everyone's nasal passages and throat. If they were solely responsible, life would be one long cold for us all! Mucus, phlegm, etc, are the body's means of eliminating unwanted waste.

It is interesting to note the increase of all these conditions following Christmas or a similar festive period, where much over-indulgence and excessive eating and drinking takes place. The abnormal intake of toxins tips the scales and adds the last straw to the body's resistance.

Constipation: See 'Ensure efficient elimination of food waste' (page 25).

Crime and disease: Dr Hay firmly believed that every criminal is a product of his own poor health.

Much research is being carried out today in detention centres, prisons and similar establishments on the relationship between crime and diet, and Alexander Schauss' book *Diet, Crime and Delinquency* (Parker House, 1980), is a worthwhile reference on this subject.

Diabetes mellitus (late onset/adult onset diabetes): Dr Hay believed that late onset diabetes occurs because of intoxication from incorrect feeding and a subsequent failing of the pancreas to produce insulin.

Indeed, the 1990 WHO report (*op. cit*) supports this view by stating, 'Diets high in plant foods are associated with a lower incidence of diabetes mellitus'.

Diet is widely acknowledged as being helpful to sufferers of diabetes with emphasis placed nowadays on reduced fat and unrefined carbohydrate consumption. The Hay System encompasses both these aspects and its use, with careful monitoring always of blood sugar levels, should benefit many sufferers.

Enervation – lack of energy – and food: The ingestion of habit-forming food or drink will always bring about a self-inflicted penalty. Stimulation requires re-stimulation to alleviate the depressing after-effects of the initial indulgence, until enervation – lack of vitality – results. Stimulating foods and drinks are acid-forming and therefore contribute further to the breakdown of the body's resistance. The Hay System automatically reduces or cuts out such food and drink, and this, together with its emphasis on increased alkaline intake, will reduce the dependency on (and physical and mental side-effects of) habit-forming foods.

Fatigue: Fatigue is either physiological – excessive mental or physical exercise – relieved by rest, or pathological – symptomatic of disease – for which some internal cause must be sought.

It was pathological fatigue which concerned Dr Hay, for as he declared, '. . . so many people, from all walks of life, seem to be tired, yawning, stretching, leaning, sprawling.' Indeed fatigue appears to have become a universal ill, as much a 'disease' as any other form of ill-health.

We need look no further than the dinner table to find an association between food and fatigue, with the heavy, distended feeling so often felt after a large meal. Food should fill us with 'pep' and vitality – not slumber! If it does not then we are obviously doing something wrong.

Fatigue must not be viewed lightly. Weariness leads to lost interest in life and living. We 'just cannot be bothered' and, as a result, miss opportunities. To experience a zest for life and a bounding vitality and enthusiasm is, surely, a wonderful release from its clutches.

Headaches and migraines: These must be one of the most common afflictions of mankind. They are caused, Dr Hay maintained, by faulty eating and digestive habits, except for those cases attributable to such causes as nerve pressure, the physical displacement of vertebrae or sunstroke.

He viewed migraine as a 'crisis' form of headache, the highest point of tolerance reached at which the body can still function. Forms of attack vary from blinding headaches through to violent sickness and total incapacity. A repugnance of, and inability to stomach, food is indication that diet, initially, may be causative. The relief following a migraine attack can be maintained only if the habits which brought it on are avoided. This and careful feeding along Hay guidelines should do much to relieve both headaches and migraines.

High blood pressure and its associated conditions of hardening of the arteries, degenerating kidneys and dilating heart: Dr Hay also experienced alleviation of the above conditions when treating his patients and again considered food as directly contributory to their improvement. Once again, the 1990 WHO report (*op. cit.*) also draws attention to the relationship between diet and high blood pressure, and states that. 'A recommendation to maintain normal weight with a diet low in fat and high in complex carbohydrates, and minimize the intake of alcohol, is relevant to the avoidance of both obesity and hypertensions; a low salt intake may also be beneficial in preventing the rise in blood pressure that is apparent in developed countries from early childhood'.

Hardening of the arteries, degenerating kidneys and dilating heart are often the consequences of high blood pressure and for these reasons, improvement may be possible through diet.

Indigestion: Indigestion literally means the absence of digestion. It results from the body's inability to cope with the type and amount of food taken at a meal. It includes the distressing symptoms of gas, bloatedness, and even pain, caused by the presence of putrefying and fermenting food anywhere along the digestive tract.

The relationship between food and indigestion, therefore, is obvious and it is safe to say that if each meal consisted of correctly combined foods, indigestion would be a very rare complaint.

Irritable bowel syndrome: This disease has become increasingly prevalent in recent years and is related to an increase in our consumption of refined, processed foods. The Hay System is designed primarily for digestive ease and should relieve this condition considerably.

Mental conditions, depression and stress: Just as the body depends on nourishment so too does the brain. Mental conditions, depression and stress can also be attributed to a toxic body. Dr Hay recognized man as a trinity – spiritual, mental and physical. The physical body acts as the instrument through which our spiritual and mental actions are expressed. So, if our physical body is 'out of sync' it will have a direct effect on our mental expression. A person suffering mentally will, in most cases, have little control over his eating habits and the subsequent side-effects of alkaline:acid imbalance and lethargic elimination. A refreshed healthy body leads to a more refreshed mind.

Multiple sclerosis: This condition is evidence of an acute disruption in the body's chemistry. There is wide documentation of the effects of diet on multiple sclerosis and the need to return the body to a correct chemical balance. This is a key objective of the Hay System and its principles should, for this reason, be a major consideration in the treatment of this condition.

Myalgic encephalomyelitis – M.E: The cause or causes of M.E are still not certain but, amongst many theories, a disordered immune system and poor nutrition are cited. It is medically upheld that a change in, and improvement of, diet are, for many sufferers, two of the simplest ways of effecting relief. The Hay System, which advocates both, should therefore be of benefit in the treatment of this condition.

Pre-menstrual syndrome – P.M.S.: Symptoms of pre-menstrual syndrome (PMS) are both physical and mental in nature, and nutrition is acknowledged as contributory to its cause. The Hay System instils improved eating habits and subsequently adjusts the body's 'upset' chemical balance. For these reasons it should offer relief to many women from the miseries of this condition.

Skin diseases: The skin acts as a 'viewing screen' for the internal condition of the body. Most skin eruptions, varying in severity from poor complexion, acne and eczema through to psoriasis, are evidence of a toxic state seeking elimination. Dr Hay's diet has been successful in easing these conditions.

Tooth decay and dental diseases: It is commonly believed that tooth decay is the result of mismanagement of the toothbrush and an over-indulgence in sugary foods. These are definitely contributory, but no amount of cleanliness or meticulous oral hygiene will prevent decay or disease unless the body is first corrected internally. Tooth decay and associated diseases often begin as a result of incorrect eating habits, poor digestion and a deficiency in the alkaline reserve – all of which can be corrected by following Dr Hay's principles.

Ulcers – gastric and duodenal: Eliminating acidic protein foods and, for a while, eating only alkaline foods in correct combination, as suggested in the Hay System has been found to be the kindest way to treat such conditions. It allows wounded areas to heal so that, with care and acknowledgement of the principles of digestion, the protein foods can once again be introduced.

Weight control: Weight control and its associated problems are often as much to do with an imbalance in the body's chemistry as any other form of illness and the relationship between weight control and eating is obvious.

Dr Hay believed that excessive weight, or obesity, may be evidence of an imbalance in the nutritional and chemical state of the body, rather than the result of mere greed, and is often a reflection of the types of food taken and their combination. Lack of care in this direction results in a less-than-efficient digestive system and the subsequent accumulation of fat deposits. Moreover, if our food is nutritionally depleted we may have to eat as much as three times the normal quantity merely to obtain a balance of vitamins and minerals, the remainder being stored as fat.

Just as an abnormal state of body chemistry may induce obesity it can, in some circumstances, lead to an underweight condition. We can eat and yet be seriously deficient in vital nutritional factors. This may result in a malnourished or even emaciated body. The dietary principles as laid down by Dr Hay will help to redress this imbalance. It should be noted, however, that there may be some further weight loss before weight adjustment and subsequent gain.

With the exception of candida albicans, coronary heart disease, irritable bowel syndrome, M.E, multiple sclerosis and pre-menstrual syndrome – those diseases more recently 'discovered' – the illnesses mentioned were treated successfully by Dr Hay – and this fifty or more years ago!

Research since that time has undoubtedly shown that many of the conditions treated have complexities of which he would never have dreamt. However, the case still stands that his methods of healing triumphed over the orthodox principles of his day – and, indeed, in many instances still do.

To support many of the above theories we need only look at those nations, tribes and races far removed from 'civilization' who have never seen an aspirin, stomach settler, pep pill, toothbrush, etc, but whose food and eating habits represent harmony with Nature. Study of their physical and mental characteristics will reveal little or no disease, and only when our 'Westernized' diets and habits have been introduced is evidences of disease and toxic build-up apparent.

I accept that claims of lack of 'positive proof' and substantiation for some of these opinions will be put forward by those who reject the idea of any relationship between food and disease – but not knowing how or why something happens does not invalidate its working – observation and practice are, in many instances, more effective than theorizing. For just as there was no simple explanation for the law of gravity or the world being round, both have since been proved beyond doubt and both are phenomena in harmony with Nature. Just so is food and its digestion.

Certainly Dr Hay speaks a somewhat different language from that of orthodox practitioners today, but no apology for this is required. His system sets out to deal with acute and chronic illness, and to improve the general health of those who follow the principles he recommended. Such improvement takes time – a greater or lesser amount depending on the constitution and state of health of those who undertake it. The system is not, and has never claimed to be, effective in cases of sudden emergency or surgical requirements.

Feeding is both an art and a science, and if correct nutritional and dietary principles are followed, life can improve enormously.

Recent medical research and its relationship to the Hay System

Throughout my studies of the Hay System and the ways it has been used in the treatment of disease, I have made a parallel investigation of modern-day findings on the relationship between diet/nutrition and the ever-increasing incidence of some diseases. Although the pattern may have changed over the past century with the near eradication of poliomyelitis, tuberculosis, typhoid fever, etc, we have witnessed instead the development of 'new' illnesses as mentioned above.

It was therefore with great interest that I came across the 1990 World Health Organization (WHO) report entitled 'Diet, nutrition, and the prevention of chronic diseases' – Report of a WHO study group' (WHO, 1990), which, in effect, supports and confirms the nutritional findings made sixty years earlier by Dr Hay!

Most important in the report is the statement that 'repeated and consistent findings of an association between specific dietary factors and disease suggest that such associations are real and indicative of a cause-and-effect relationship'.

The report finds that:
- sugar intake should be limited;
- cereal intake should be increased as this contributes to faecal bulking and the avoidance of constipation;
- vegetables and fruits are a rich source of a number of nutrients and contribute to the balance of the diet.

To see Dr Hay's work backed up by such reports and publications is indeed encouraging, and further substantiates the value of the Hay System as part of our daily routine.

6
Lifestyle on the Hay System

It is important that the Hay System is viewed as a *way of living* rather than a diet. It is easy to carry on with normal daily practices and routines without losing sight of its principles. There is no need to feel, as is often the case on 'diets', that you must turn down invitations or, in turn, not invite. Neither does it mean that you alone are subjected to any 'regime' – the whole family can join in, if they so wish. It does not focus on any one aspect of food and dietary control, but, most importantly, treats *you*, the whole person.

The Hay System and eating out

It is nearly always possible to sit at any restaurant/hotel table and eat compatibly simply by deciding beforehand the type of meal you wish to eat – starch, protein or alkaline – and then planning it accordingly from the menu offered. Salad bars are perfect for this. Chinese and Indian meals are also good options – especially as so many of their meals are vegetarian-based anyway. Sandwich bars, too, where you can select your own fillings, make an ideal lunch or after-work meeting place.

Personally, I find it easier, generally, to opt for a protein/alkaline meal, and have, say, plain avocado to begin the meal, followed perhaps by a vegetable stir-fry – requesting no rice and gently saying no to the offer of accompanying bread! – with a side-salad. This then allows me to have a dessert of fresh fruit. I tend to ask for say, fresh pineapple or strawberries in season, rather than fresh fruit salad which invariably contains sugar and banana!

Good first course choices are avocado, vegetable-based dishes such as asparagus or mushrooms, 'mini' salads or soups (starch-free if a protein or alkaline meal is to follow). Corn-on-the-cob makes a good starch starter, as does garlic/herb bread. Starch main courses can include pasta dishes – cheese and tomato-free though! – potato dishes and risottos/pilaus, etc. Protein main courses can be cheese, egg or tofu-based – so no indulging in your partner's left-over potato! Alkaline main courses can include vegetable and fruit dishes such as stir-fries, kebabs, stuffed vegetables (not tomatoes!) – provided rice, etc are omitted. Fresh fruit is the ideal dessert (see Desserts, pages 240-260) or select a compatible 'indulgence' – if the sweet trolley has something suitable to offer.

I am sure you will find, as I do, that most places are happy to fit in with Hay 'whims' when asked to do so.

It is always far easier to eat out in public than at a friend's house where a restricted or no-choice menu makes food combining very difficult. More diplomacy may be required here so as not to offend. You can either decide to 'indulge' and give your digestive system an easier time the next day, or graciously decline certain parts of the meal so that the principles of the Hay System can be accommodated

The Hay System and entertaining

Dinner parties/guests

These should present little bother as you are the host/hostess and the meal choice, after all, is yours! I have entertained both dinner party and staying guests on the Hay System – with no complaints so far. The fact that pizzas have no tomato and the sandwiches no cheese appears to go unnoticed! Occasionally, though, there are concessions; I usually, for example, supply bread with the soup, even if the meal is protein. I feel it is preferable not to inflict my own ideals too rigidly upon unsuspecting family/friends. Better that they go away intrigued by the idea of the Hay System, albeit that they have not absolutely conformed to its principles, rather than leave feeling dissatisfied and unwilling to eat at your table again.

Buffets/barbecues

These less formal occasions are also adaptable to eating on the Hay System. As for dinner parties/guests you may find it easier and more acceptable to your guests if you bend the 'rules' slightly! Eating in the Hay way will not restrict your choice of buffet/barbecue foods – buffet 'nibbles' can be prepared to cater for a starch, protein or alkaline meal-structure, as can the more spectacular displays of nut loaves, flans/pizzas, salads, etc; barbecued vegetables, burgers, kebabs can all take on a starch, protein or alkaline 'suit', and served with a selection of salads, provide a delicious array of foods. If desired, therefore, a totally compatible 'Hay' buffet/barbecue can be created.

The Hay System and pregnancy and baby/child-care

The value of the Hay System is as applicable to your baby or prospective baby as it is to yourself. There is never a more important time for optimum health than when a woman is carrying, or preparing to carry, a child. Pregnancy can be a difficult time physically and mentally, and the Hay System, embracing as it does the *whole* person, is particularly appropriate in its adoption here. It should help to relieve, or even to avoid, many of the discomforts – both physical and mental – experienced by the mother-to-be.

The health of an unborn child is determined largely by the health of both its parents – particularly that of its mother who is responsible for its feeding from conception through to birth. If the parents are in poor health it is likely that the child will be too. Future resistance to disease and any 'weak' spots are also dependent on the health of the parents. Moreover, it is not physical qualities only which are transmitted from parents to baby. Any toxic state, especially if it affects the mother-to-be, may also be passed on, and this can be nothing but a handicap to the child during its early years, even, possibly, for life. Therefore healthy 'Hay' eating before, during and after pregnancy can most definitely be recommended in the expectation that the vital and healthy condition of the mother will, naturally, be passed on to the child. As the Hay System represents food at its most nourishing, nothing could be better for the well-being of both.

With regard to baby-feeding, Dr Hay condemned the practice of introducing starch foods to an infant before all, or a sufficient number, of its teeth were in place to cope with this food type. He considered the incomplete digestion of starches and sugars one of the main causes of frequent illness and upset in children – bilious attacks, lack of appetite, sour vomiting, 'unhealthy' nappies, skin rashes, irritability and bedwetting.

As previously discussed, primary digestion of starch food begins in the mouth by complete and thorough chewing – how, then, can this ever be achieved if the baby has very few teeth? Moreover, the baby's saliva does not contain enough of the digestive enzyme responsible for splitting these starches and sugars until the teeth are well developed or, in some cases, all present.

If you plan to bring up a 'Hay baby', do discuss it with your doctor or health visitor first.

Dr Hay considered Nature never intended 'solids' to be given before teeth were formed but provided for the mother to feed the child herself during this interval between birth and teething. Should this not be possible, of course, arrangements are made to substitute cow's/goat's/sheep's/soya milk made up to the correct concentration, following medical advice, for an infant. It is unfair to impose on the undeveloped digestion of an infant a task that requires an adult's digestion to handle it properly.

A baby on the Hay System, therefore, can be fed on milk and a little orange juice until teeth development and general growth signals a readiness to take more solid food. Prior to this, at approximately six months old, puréed vegetable can be introduced in small amounts. If well tolerated it can be increased, and fruit such as puréed or grated apple added to the diet. This gentle, but nourishing, feeding can continue until the baby's development indicates a need for further nourishment in the form of starch and protein foods, and should, along with fresh air and sunshine, form the basis of a balanced and contented little body.

With further growth and development, any food which nourishes an adult will be equally nourishing for the baby of two years and older – or younger if growth and development are advanced – for a baby's nutritional needs are the same as an adult's, and only the quantities differ.

Babies and young children fed the Hay way are given the opportunity to develop a happy and healthy body, and at the same time establish a sound dietary basis for their future.

The Hay System and growing children

The Hay System is ideal for growing children. Its use in the early period of a child's growth will help to ensure good health later in life, for correct eating habits established before a child is seven are more likely to be continued throughout life than if introduced later, when the opportunity for sampling nutritionally inferior foods and forming unwise eating habits may have occurred. By school age, generally, the eating habits of children are fixed. The earlier this is done on the Hay System, the better, as the longer incorrect feeding persists the more difficult it is to make changes.

For this reason, the future efficiency and development of a child will depend on early parental guidance in nutrition and sensible eating.

It is vital that growing children receive daily the types of foods needed for their development. As children have high activity levels, emphasis should be placed on supplying them with extra 'fuel' – starch foods. Rapid growth rate, too, will demand an adequate supply of protein foods to keep up with the body's 'building' requirements. Children can, therefore, have extra starch and protein meals – although care must be taken not to overdo this and upset the delicate alkali to acid ratio. Naturally, strict control over their food intake in the school playground or with friends is not possible, but gentle teaching and guidance at an early age will instil in children an instinctive knowledge of what is 'good' and what is 'bad' from a nutritional angle.

Indeed, if all children were properly trained in correct eating as laid down in the principles of the Hay System, future generations, too, could benefit. The food demands of the child today become the feeding habits of the adult tomorrow, and this in its turn compels the suppliers of food in field, factory and restaurant, to alter their methods of food production and preparation to meet changing trends in eating.

The Hay System and the family

Eating in the Hay way will be as beneficial to your family as it is to you. If you are the 'meal provider' I would advise not even telling them of any change in the style of eating. Just go ahead and cook and feed to the Hay guidelines. I always find that making an announcement of change more often than not brings about its immediate condemnation. However if it is done quietly and with little fuss then it invariably goes unnoticed, but your partner may wonder why he or she no longer suffers from indigestion; your son may wonder why other children at school have colds and he does not; your daughter will be joyful that all her teenage 'spots' have gone . . . Best to let them think it is their natural good health and leave the rest to Dr Hay!

If you are not the food-shopper or cook in the house and wish 'to Hay' this need not present too much of a problem – provided you have an understanding partner/parent who accepts that suddenly you do not wish to eat his or her beautifully prepared (but incompatible) dishes. Incompatibilities can be avoided by careful explanation of the Hay concepts – alternatively, lend him/her the book to read – a 'converted' cook will make it much easier for you!

The Hay System and the older person

The Hay System is perfectly suited to the older person as it reduces the intake of concentrated foods, so often found difficult to digest in later years. Starch and protein foods can be reduced further in the case of the elderly as their 'body clocks' are, generally, a lot slower, and they require only small amounts of each. Of course for the more energetic older person reductions should be related to 'activity' level and the diet adjusted accordingly.

The Hay System and exercise

Dr Hay viewed exercise always as an off-shoot of sensible eating and living habits, not as a prerequisite. Without exercise we do become 'stagnant' and sensible exercise is necessary to assist the body in oxidizing and eliminating body waste – one of the vital concerns of the Hay System. Dr Hay's philosophy was basically to feel right inside and outside first, then let walking, running, swimming, etc, follow. Exercise should be done for pleasure and with a lightness of heart and mind – rather than as a means of 'burning' away any excess lumps and bumps; this only places natural, healthy pursuits under the heading of 'chore'. The Hay System, with its emphasis on vitality, means that healthy eating results in healthy living – and a desire to exercise walks hand-in-hand with these concepts.

The sports enthusiast too can benefit from the Hay System as it is now widely acknowledged that the high-protein diet once advocated for sports enthusiasts is not ideal for their particular bodily requirements, and that they are far better nourished for athletic pursuits on unrefined carbohydrate foods. The Hay System caters for this perfectly, where subtle adaptation only is needed to incorporate more of the starch foods in relation to the protein foods offering the perfect balance. In addition, as the Hay System leads to a detoxified body, the 'clean, new' physique should result in greater achievements in the sports arena.

It must be remembered, though, that exercise is only of value in restoring the body to a better condition if it is not an effort for that body to undertake it. Taken up to a point before fatigue is felt, it helps to develop the part of the body exercised; beyond fatigue and against the body's will, it is detrimental and can lead to deterioration. A healthy body is fit enough to take exercise – with no need for it to be prescribed. It will be taken naturally and as such will do no harm.

The 'less active' person on the Hay System will benefit from taking sensible, 'therapeutic' exercise daily – provided that the body is not put under stress. It will also offset the lack of oxidation which results from a 'sedentary' lifestyle, so long as it is not carried to the point of extreme fatigue.

The 'active' person on the Hay System may have to take care that more exercise does not lead to increased appetite!

The Hay System in relation to lifestyle

The Hay System accommodates different lifestyles very easily and naturally. Indeed, it's far-reaching application is contributory to its success. From youth to old age its principles of eating and living can be practised and found beneficial – what better recommendation could it have than that?

7

Putting the Hay System into practice

To 'Hay' and 'in the Hay way'

The verb 'to Hay' and the phrase 'in the Hay way' came about through conversations between myself and fellow Hay System followers. It feels natural for us to say that we are 'Haying' or doing something in the 'Hay way', rather than refer always to the rather laborious phrase: 'The Hay System of Eating'. This brings the System on to a more personal level, and also gives a sense of sharing in something rather than being – as can be the case when embarking on a new manner of living – the 'odd-man-out'. For as Dr Hay said: 'To adhere to a definite schedule that differs plainly from the usual is to be thought peculiar, even a little barmy'!

I therefore talk about 'Haying' or doing something 'the Hay way' in the text that follows, as well as referring to the Hay System, and I hope that you, too, will feel closer to Dr Hay's principles by this 'familiarization'.

Preparing to 'Hay'

Mini fasting

A little 'preparatory work' is recommended before starting to 'Hay'. Nothing too difficult – just a break from 'normal meals' for two to three days. I use the word 'break' in preference to 'fast', which so often conjures up an image of complete deprivation and ultimate starvation!

Refraining from set meals and living only on fruit juices, vegetable juices and fresh acid fruits (taken one variety at a time, preferably, to aid digestion even further), is all that is required. **This break from food is not essential.** I suggest it only because the average person will, by the very nature of his past and present eating habits, be in a rather 'clogged' state of health. It will give the whole digestive system a well-earned holiday and opportunity to 'spring clean'. Poor eating habits can then be replaced by new and better ones.

Even this 'mini-fasting' may be difficult for those used to plate-loads of food three times a day, but do persevere – and discover that when food is restricted, attention turns to other things in life and the events around you. Eating will become of secondary importance, and a feeling of 'pleasant indifference' to it may even be experienced! Life becomes more enjoyable and fulfilling when you realize that we eat to live – not live to eat!

Do not be put off by well-meaning family and friends having fits of various kinds and degrees, for fear that you are about to die of starvation. This will not be the case – I can assure you! After all, if the armies of Rome and Greece marched on empty stomachs – so too can we for a day or two!

This type of 'food break' is perfectly safe unless already ill or under medical supervision, in which case either seek the advice of a doctor, or wait until you feel well enough to undertake it. Any form of food-break for longer periods, however, should always be carried out with the supervision of someone trained and qualified in this field.

Your body and the Hay System

The basic rules and concepts of the Hay System have already been explained in Chapter 4; however, Dr Hay also advised us, in following the Five Basic Rules to have regard for four more general guidelines:

1   to recognize the difference between false appetite and true hunger
2   not to eat 'by the clock'
3   not to eat or drink in excess
4   not to eat when upset, stressed or tired

False appetite and true hunger

It is important to be able to differentiate between false appetite and true hunger, as far more nourishment will be gained from food eaten when genuinely hungry than if that same food is eaten under 'false pretences'.

False appetite is merely a result of habit, timing on the clock, and the smell, taste and sight of food.

True hunger, however, is an indication that the body *needs* food and that its 'fuel store' is depleted or empty.

The difference between false appetite and true hunger can only really be discovered by a break from food (see under 'Preparing to Hay', page 45). This has the added bonus of making us aware of the true flavour of foods, rather than what we normally taste with a 'tired' tongue. Know what the difference is by thinking of how you feel when, not having eaten for a few days because of illness, you have your first meal. A sense of eagerness and expectation is experienced and whatever is eaten tastes wonderful – even if it is only a peanut butter sandwich! These are all signs of true hunger for, and appreciation of, food – not merely the result of satisfying an habitual demand.

Eating by the clock

Not eating by the clock is an important consideration for us all. Quite simply, hunger is not subject to routine. We cannot, therefore, make ourselves hungry just because the clock says so! How often do we look at our watches and say, 'It's twelve o'clock! Time to eat!' – rather than forget our watches and say, 'I feel hungry! It is time to eat!' For this reason try, within reason, to adjust 'eating times' to fit in with 'hunger times', and as a result satisfy a physical need rather than a mental 'time-check'. If this means skipping a meal it will do no harm, far better to do so and eat the next one with relish and appreciation than to feel heavy and lacking in true hunger.

Avoid over-eating and over-drinking

How often do we sit at the table and eat because the food is there, not because we need it? We often eat to gratify our senses of sight, taste and smell – all to the detriment of our physical well-being. We need to learn to moderate our indulgence, so that the pleasure of eating and the task of digestion can work together. Over-eating can result in unnecessary physical and mental distress. Eating more than is required does not help sustain the body, but becomes a digestive burden.

After acquiring the habit of eating the right sorts of foods in the right combination at each meal it is unlikely that you will feel any inclination to over-eat.

Over-drinking refers to liquid intake in general, not just to alcoholic drinks. As true hunger indicates an actual need so too does a feeling of true thirst. Within reason, therefore, drink only when really thirsty or 'dry', rather than habitually 'gulp back cups of tea' just for the sake of drinking. Remember, too, that we do not obtain liquid solely from drinks but also from the food we eat. Liquid intake, therefore, when 'Haying' should not be a problem. Fruit, vegetable and salad foods are high in water content and the emphasis on the consumption of these means that our bodies will receive plenty, and there should be no need to over-drink.

It is best not to drink with meals or straight after. This only saturates the food eaten and interferes with efficient digestion, which can then lead to constipation. If you feel thirsty before a meal, drinking cool water in moderate amounts will not affect the digestion of the food that follows. Liquid on an empty stomach 'seeps' out in a short space of time, leaving the stomach free for the incoming meal. Try to remember, also, not to drink fluids too hot or too cold – both will irritate the stomach and hinder digestion.

In many cases over-eating and over-drinking are caused through boredom and lack of daily purpose. Try to fill your life with new and interesting activities – and divert the emphasis away from food and drink!

My best advice on the subject of over-eating and over-drinking is to: eat for need – not greed!

Do not eat when upset, stressed or tired

Our mental health and physical well-being are closely interrelated. Mental upset and stress hinder efficient digestion. A tense body draws on the energy required for the breakdown of food, using it instead to try and calm the nervous system. Similarly, if we are tired our energy reserves are depleted. A tremendous amount of energy is needed to digest food, and a weary body will be unable to offer the digestive system the vitality it requires to undertake food breakdown. Digestion will take longer, and, very often, be incomplete if you are in an upset, stressed or tired 'sluggish' state. This, as discussed previously, can then lead to illness.

Eating when upset, stressed or tired is therefore not advisable. Far better to miss a meal, or eat very lightly on fruit, vegetable and salad foods, than burden our bodies with unnecessary tasks which we cannot hope to carry out efficiently.

All the preceding principles and guidelines illustrate that eating in the Hay way has far more to offer than just advice about 'Diet, Drink and Digestion' – its greatest offering, without doubt, is its ability to show us how to *live*.

Meal structure and menu planning

If you are feeling rather overwhelmed by this new way of eating – don't worry! I did too! The best advice I can offer when starting to 'Hay' is:

Concentrate first on combining your food correctly

Once you have mastered this you can then move on to selecting those foods which provide nourishment and combine compatibly, at the same time as maintaining the correct alkali to acid ratio in the body. I remember it was many months before I really paid attention to correct alkali to acid balancing – all my efforts were taken up in avoiding the 'cheese sandwich' concept! Then, when I felt more able to concentrate on adjusting my alkali to acid intake, I found this had largely been achieved by correct food combining. This is one of the pleasures of following the Hay System – each principle interacts with, and supports, the others.

There is no reason to feel vexed or unable to manage – it truly is very straightforward, just remember, 'Mind your P's and S's' and the remainder will fall into place.

Dr Hay emphasized the need to maintain a balanced intake of starch, protein and alkaline foods when structuring meals and planning menus.

For most people, the easiest way to do this is to eat one starch, one protein and one alkaline meal each day. However, such a routine must *not* be considered rigid – the Hay System must be adapted to fit into your lifestyle and *never* viewed as a dictated set of rules. You may choose to eat two alkaline meals one day, and perhaps none the next, but you will find that over a week's programme of eating you will have achieved a balanced food intake.

Lists of foods for starch, protein and alkaline meals are given on pages 60-66 under the headings of 'Food and drink combination tables' and 'Alkali and acid food tables'.

Careful meal planning is essential to food combining, but is easy provided you start with meals that you are familiar with. Look at your eating patterns and meal arrangements to assess how food combining can be incorporated into your daily routine with least disruption. Cook meals which include favourite foods – this will help to reduce the 'transition period' between the old and the new way of eating.

As you become more familiar with the principles of food combining, you will find it easy to 'swap' ingredients and modify recipes according to your daily needs.

It is worth remembering that as starch takes longer to digest than protein it is better to eat this meal in the evening to allow it overnight digestion.

Bear in mind also that Dr Hay ranked foods in the order of their importance to the body as:

1 fruits
2 all salad and leafy green vegetable foods
3 all root vegetables
4 grains
5 proteins

This helps to show us where the emphasis on our daily meal ingredients should lie.

Always remember: structure your day's eating *to suit yourself*. You must feel happy and comfortable with the way you choose to adapt 'Haying' to suit your needs and lifestyle. Never feel 'pressurized' to do anything for which you do not feel ready. As the Hay System is a way of living and *not* a diet it will come, with time, to be just that – a way of living!

Checklist before commencing the Hay System

1 Concentrate first on food combining
2 The alkali to acid ratio and
3 the daily meal structure of:
 one starch meal,
 one protein meal,
 one alkaline meal each day
 may be left to follow later
4 Follow, where possible, the basic rules and guidelines. (See pages 18-27.)

Finally, from personal experience, the best piece of advice I can give is: **Avoid confusion, and do one thing at a time.**

Then, as Dr Hay said: 'After four weeks . . . I am willing to bet you even money that you will be sold for life to this plan and will not easily depart from it'.

The Hay Food List

The following food list is structured to help to answer some of the queries you might have about the way particular foods fit into the vegetarian Hay System of eating. Naturally there are many more ingredients which could be discussed, but the ones mentioned are the most important and represent a cross-section of different food types and the ways in which they are used in the light of Dr Hay's concepts.

Included as well as general ingredients, are foods which cause confusion in classification and warrant explanation, those which change classification when prepared in different ways, and those which should be eaten only in moderation, or eliminated altogether. (For an explanation of the **S/N/P** codes, see page 74.)

'**Manufactured foods**' — **tinned/packaged/processed/frozen foods**: Tinned, packaged or processed foods are useful standbys but do remember that if possible: 'fresh is best'. If buying 'manufactured' products examine labels carefully to ensure not only compatibility of ingredients but also that they are free of unnatural preservatives, colourings and flavourings, and any extra 'hidden' sugar, fat and salt.

Organic food: Wherever possible, and price, availability and quality allow, purchase organically grown foods.

Refined foods: Food today is so very often adulterated – stripped of all valuable nutrients, then, in many cases, further 'attacked' with sweeteners, spices and synthetic flavourings – that the average palate is easily taken in and becomes accustomed to such trickery, accepting it as normal. Highly refined food, used for long periods, robs the body of nutrients; deficiencies can then occur with the possibility of ensuing illness. These foods, therefore, should be avoided.

Chocolate and carob (S): The stimulating ingredients present in cocoa and chocolate powders (see under 'Drinks' below) are also in chocolate bars. This, combined with the 'addictive' qualities and high-fat, high-sugar and low-nutrient content of chocolate means that – chocoholics beware! – their consumption should be greatly reduced or, ideally, stopped altogether. Chocolate bars also often have a high milk content and this poor food combination (see 'Milk' below) makes them extremely difficult to digest.

An excellent alternative to chocolate is carob. This is far superior nutritionally and has no side-effects (you can therefore quite safely become a carobaholic if you so wish!), although care should be taken that the ingredients contained within a carob bar are compatible – like chocolate, it is a starch food and therefore not 'happy' with milk – and that they have a low-sugar or no-sugar content. Carob is also available in powder form.

Dairy products

Cream (N): Cream is classed as a fat and therefore compatible with all foods.

Cream cheeses (N): These are also classed as fats and likewise compatible with all foods – so, we can, after all, have our jacket potato and cheese! This applies only to *dairy* cream cheeses – soya cream cheeses are protein and therefore *not* compatible with starches. Do ensure that you buy cream cheese and not just a soft cheese – there is a difference!

Soft/hard cheeses (P): All soft/hard cheeses should be 'natural' varieties only. Processed cheeses, due to their highly adulterated methods of manufacture and chemical additives, should be avoided.

Eggs (P)/egg yolks (N)/egg whites (P): Eggs should always be bought 'free-range' from a reputable source. Egg yolks are compatible with all foods and extremely useful in this respect as a binding agent, for use in sauces, and in combination with starch ingredients in biscuits and cakes.

Egg whites are made up of a complex protein difficult to digest. It is therefore recommended that egg whites be used in moderation and only at protein meals.

Egg alternatives for vegans (P/S): There are now many commercially produced egg-replacing products on the market. They are generally suitable for use when 'Haying', although it is always wise to check the ingredients on the packet first. Should you not have access to any of these, soya flour mixed in the ratio of approximately one tablespoon to two tablespoons water is an excellent egg substitute in protein recipes. In starch recipes I have had a lot of success using chickpea flour as an egg replacer, mixed approximately one tablespoon to one of water.

Milk – cow's/goat's/sheep's/soya (P): Milk is not easily digested when mixed with starch and protein foods and should therefore be used only very sparingly in combination with these foods.

Milk should be treated as food and not drink. In bovine form it is intended for young cows and not for humans, and should be used only in small quantities. Goat's, sheep's and soya milk are more easily digested than cow's milk and are excellent alternatives. Sugar-free soya milks should always be bought in preference to the sweetened varieties available.

Milk should, ideally, be taken only with fruits (acid or sweet) and vegetables (but not starch vegetables).

Nut milks or diluted cream can be used as an alternative to milk in recipes, but in many instances, such as in soups and sauces, I find that milk can usually be omitted without any adverse effect on taste or consistency.

The soya bean and soya by-products (P): The soya bean is different from all other pulses/legumes (see below under Pulses/legumes) in being a protein, and not a starch, food. It should not, therefore, be eaten with starches or sugars. This applies also to its by-products – soya milk/flour, tofu, tempeh, etc.

The soya bean and its by-products are excellent sources of protein and other nutrients, particularly for vegans. Soya/soy 'cheeses' and 'milks', offer alternatives to the comparable dairy products. Tofu and tempeh are now also widely available and due to their low-fat and easily digestible protein content are ideal for the vegetarian diet.

Care should be exercised in the use of some soya products, notably the drinks and 'blancmange-type' desserts. Very often these are produced in banana or carob flavours (both starch foods) and as such are incompatible.

Drinks: Always buy drinks free from sugar and unnatural additives in the form of preservatives, flavourers or colourings.

Coffee/tea/cocoa/chocolate/alcohol: Coffee, tea, cocoa, chocolate and alcohol all contain stimulants and should be avoided or kept to a minimum. Herb teas and 'cereal coffees' make very good substitutes, but 'alcohol-free' varieties of normally alcoholic drinks are best avoided, as they are often chemically treated and liable to contain additives.

Fats/oils/margarine/butter (N)/fried foods (S/P/N): Fats and oils should be used in the diet in moderation only.

Used sparingly they do not interfere with the digestion of any other foods and so may be eaten at any meal.

Oils should be unrefined and, whenever possible, cold-pressed. I cannot recommend too highly the use of unrefined and cold-pressed virgin olive oil, not only for its excellent cooking and flavour-enhancing qualities, but also because its chemical make-up is such that it remains stable in all forms of cooking (with the exception of deep-fat frying, for which it should not be used). It is not, however, suitable in cake/biscuit/bread baking for which I always use a sunflower alternative.

Margarine/butter (N): Although margarine is still far from being a 'natural' product there have been considerable advances made in its manufacture.

Thought to contribute to the cause of heart attacks, strokes, angina and circulatory problems, newer methods of production are now being explored which do not alter the stability of the vegetable oils used. There are now a number of unhydrogenated margarines available with low saturated fat content. If these are always selected I believe that, as in most cases where good sense is used and moderation exercised, no harm will be done. If some form of 'spread' is required margarine (and butter too) can be replaced by nut and seed butters. All other fat requirements can be satisfied with olive or sunflower oil as mentioned above.

For the vegetarian who is happy to use butter, I agree that it is largely as Nature intended; it is, however, very high in saturated fats, and although this should always be borne in mind, provided care and moderation are exercised in its use on the Hay System the amount consumed can easily be dealt with by the body.

Fried foods: With regard to fried foods Dr Hay quoted the saying: 'Poison is quicker, of course, but she can give him fried food three times a day and avoid embarrassing publicity.'

I do not think I need to say more! Except that obviously fats and fatty food in excess are detrimental to health and where possible alternative means of cooking, such as baking, grilling, or shallow-frying rather than deep-frying, should be used. The occasional 'fry-up' as a treat, however, is permissible!

Fruit, vegetable and salad foods: These are the most valued of ingredients and represent Nature at her most 'vital' on the food scale. They contain the whole range of minerals and vitamins required by the body, and for this reason should form the backbone of meals when eating in the Hay way. They are, as previously discussed, of particular benefit in the Hay System in maintaining the alkali to acid ratio, and should therefore be used in abundance and in as natural a state as possible. They are also an excellent source of fibre and aid healthy digestion.

Some confusion lies in the classification of acid fruits such as oranges, lemons and grapefruits as 'alkaline-forming'. These fruits do contain acids in citric, malic or tartaric forms, but they easily and quickly evaporate, leaving the body within an hour or so of the fruit being eaten – chifly through breathing. This leaves the alkaline component of the fruit free of any acid association, and it can then go on to provide a highly valuable contribution to the body's alkaline reserve.

There are – as always – exceptions to this rule. They apply to rhubarb, plums and prunes, under-ripe black/red/white currants and gooseberries, which contain an acid less readily eliminated from the body. These, therefore, tend to draw on the alkaline reserve and should be eaten in moderation only.

Special mention should be made of the lemon, the most alkalizing of all fruits. A glass a day – especially first thing on rising – of the juice of half to one freshly-squeezed lemon diluted with mineral water, is extremely beneficial to the body.

The melon, too, deserves special mention. Due to the enzymes it contains, melon tends to cause digestive discomfort when eaten with other foods. It is therefore best eaten alone, say for breakfast or as a light lunch/supper, as a complete meal.

Fruit and vegetable juices: Fruit and vegetable juices are also strongly alkaline, excellent for neutralizing an acid state and extremely beneficial on the Hay System. Fruit and vegetable juices made from fresh ingredients are delicious and highly nutritious, but bottled, canned and vacuum packed fruit and vegetable juices are an excellent substitute; always ensure first, however, that they are sugar and additive free. Concentrated fruit juices, available in bottled form, are particularly useful, not only as drinks when diluted, but as natural sweeteners when added to dishes instead of sugar.

Nuts and seeds — excluding peanuts (S) (see under Pulses/legumes): Nuts are packed full of vitamins and minerals and as such form an important part of the vegetarian diet. With the exception of the chestnut – which is high in starch – they are also an excellent source of protein, and compatible at all protein meals. In addition, almonds, brazil nuts, coconut, hazelnuts and pine kernels are alkaline-forming and make a useful addition to the body's alkaline reserve at both protein and alkaline meals. Nuts, however, should be eaten in moderation to avoid consuming excessive amounts of concentrated protein: 2–3 oz (50–75g) a day is more than sufficient to provide the body with replacement building material.

Sesame, sunflower and pumpkin seeds also abound in vitamins and minerals and are an excellent nutritional addition to the Hay System.

Nut and seed butters/spreads are an excellent way of obtaining, in a more easily absorbed and assimilated form, the goodness present in nuts and seeds. This is especially so for those who have trouble digesting this group of foods. They should not, however, be eaten in excess because of their high fat content.

Pulses/legumes (S) – dried beans, peas and lentils, excluding the soya bean: This group of foods has a complex 'duality' of starch and protein composition and although their starch content is higher than their protein content there is still much confusion over their classification. Dr Hay listed them categorically as starch, and it is as such that I always treat them in cooking. This 'double-mixture' in one food, though, can cause uncomfortable digestive side-effects – often embarrassingly so! For this reason and also the fact that pulses/legumes are acid-forming, Dr Hay recommended eating them in moderation.

Peanuts (S): The peanut is also a legume and the same comments made above are applicable here.

For culinary purposes they are treated as a nut, but remember always that they are a starch, and not a protein, food. Although a nutritious and inexpensive food source, peanuts, like other legumes, are acid-forming and can be rather indigestible. They should, therefore, be eaten in moderation only. As in the case of nuts and seeds, they are easier to digest, and the nutrients present more readily assimilated, when in the form of peanut butter. The high starch/acid and fat content, though, means you should restrain yourself from spreading it too liberally on toast!

Sprouted pulses/legumes, nuts, seeds and grains (N): When sprouted, pulses/legumes, nuts, seeds and grains undergo a complete chemical change. Water content increases and starch content decreases, with the result that they can be classed as a salad or vegetable food. As well as now being more comfortably and easily digested they also abound in vitamins and minerals, making them a valuable addition when eating in the Hay way.

Sugars (S): Intake of refined sugars and all manufactured products containing these or their by-products, as found in confectionery, biscuits, cakes, puddings and similar foods, should really be avoided altogether or, if not, then strictly controlled when following the Hay System.

I cannot stress sufficiently how detrimental this group of food is to good health. White sugar is nothing but sweetness with all the nutritional goodness, from which we could gain benefit, removed. As such it is only 'low-grade fuel', offering brief stimulation and then a subsequent 'let-down' feeling. It is difficult to digest, containing little or no fibre, so the colon has nothing to act upon, and much of it is left to ferment instead of being eliminated. Sugar is, in effect, a 'dead' and 'empty' food. It is also acid-forming and draws on the body's precious alkaline reserve.

In cooking, sugar can be replaced by honey or maple syrup, or any of the other 'whole' and 'healthier' sugar substitutes given under Sugars and Sweeteners in the Food combination table on page 61. Avoid, also, any commercially produced low-calorie sugars and sweeteners – these, too, are empty of any nutritional value and can be largely chemical-based.

Grains/cereals, flours and breads (S): Bread can be the 'staff of life' only if wholegrain and free of additives. For these reasons only unrefined, wholefood varieties of grains/cereals/flours and breads should be used on the Hay System.

Tomatoes (N), fresh (N), cooked and purée (P): Raw tomatoes are alkaline-forming and combine with all meals. When cooked, however, the small amount of acid they contain greatly increases and draws on the body's alkaline reserve. This conversion into an acid state means that, when cooked, they should not be used at starch or alkaline meals. This applies also to the use of tomato purée, and tinned and vacuum-packed tomato juice, all of which have been heat-treated. For this reason tomato pasta products should also be avoided.

Vinegar and pickled foods (P): Acetic acid, present in all vinegars, is an extremely acid-forming compound which the body has difficulty in converting. For this reason, only cider and rice vinegars should be used when eating in the Hay way, as these are far less acidic than other commercially-produced vinegars. They should still, however, be used in small amounts only. Lemon juice provides an excellent vinegar substitute and can be more freely used. Remember never to use vinegar or lemon juice with starch foods.

As pickled foods rely on vinegar they should be eliminated when 'Haying', or taken only as an occasional treat. A pickling solution requires a large quantity of vinegar in relation to the food treated and for this reason even pickles made with cider or rice vinegar would be considered questionable.

Recipe and cooking advice

Set out below are hints and some general advice for preparing and cooking the recipes in this section. This should help to make your life in the kitchen easier.

I recommend that you read these directions closely. Not only do they offer you short-cuts with regard to food preparation, but they also expand on certain methods given in the recipes, so that the repetition of instructions can be avoided.

Breadcrumb substitutes in protein/alkaline recipes: A starch recipe containing breadcrumbs can be adapted to a protein or alkaline meal by replacing the breadcrumbs with wheatgerm or ground nuts.

Dairy products and their vegan equivalents: In the recipes vegans should always read milk as soya/soy milk, yoghurt as soya/soy yoghurt, cheese as soya/soy cheese and cream as nut or tofu cream.

Orange and lemon rind: These are excellent used as flavouring agents in cooking – especially when an orange or lemon flavour is desired in a starch-based recipe. However, I must emphasize that, wherever possible, rind from organically grown oranges/lemons only should be used. If these fruits are not available organically grown, then *scrub thoroughly* before grating.

Herbs: Herb measurements given are always for the fresh amounts – if using dried, halve the quantity given.

Always tear or split a bay leaf without breaking it (fresh or dried) before adding it to a recipe – this releases the flavour, allowing ît to be imparted to the dish prepared.

Measurements: Imperial, metric and American cup measurements have been given throughout this book. Do not mix sets of measurements – provided you follow only one set at a time in a recipe you should have no problems!

Spoon measurements: The British/American standard tablespoon and teaspoon measures of 15ml and 5ml respectively have been used throughout. These are all *level* unless otherwise indicated.

Mushrooms: If the recipe calls for 'very finely chopped' mushrooms this means they should be placed in a food processor or liquidizer/blender and blended until almost a pulp, or chopped very finely by hand.

Nuts/seeds and starch-free crackers: Reference is made throughout the recipe section to 'starch-free' crackers. There are numerous excellent savoury, starch-based crispbreads/crackers available. Starch-free crackers, however, do not appear to be available in the shops, and in order to have an alternative to bread/crispbreads/oatcakes, etc, with protein or alkaline meals, I have created some starch-free recipes. These are detailed in the section Crackers – savoury starch-free on pages 232 to 237).

Salt and pepper: Although salt and pepper have been included in recipes they are not essential and can be reduced or eliminated. If salt *must* be used, sea salt is most suitable, and chemically-based commercial alternatives should be avoided. Paprika is a useful alternative to pepper, it is less likely to irritate the mucous membranes at the back of the mouth.

Starch-free thickening agents for protein and alkaline dishes: Wheat flour, the thickening ingredient in every kitchen, is, due to its high starch content, unsuitable when preparing protein or alkaline dishes. An excellent alternative thickener, however, is potato flour which, because it contains so very little starch, will not disrupt protein or alkaline meal digestion. It is quick, easy and economical to use. Use up to one tablespoon of potato flour to 1 pt/570ml/2½ cups water/diluted milk/stock, depending on the desired consistency of the dish you are making.

I have also found that it is possible to thicken sauces and soups very satisfactorily with ground nuts (cashews and almonds are best for this purpose as they have little effect on the flavour). Add the ground nuts as you would flour and prepare the sauce using exactly the same method – although you will find that thickening is not as quick and you will have to continue stirring for quite a while.

Thickening sauces in this way will not produce as thick a sauce as when you use flour, but it is a marvellous and nutritious substitute. I find that 4 oz/100g/1 cup ground nuts to 1 pt/570ml/2½ cups water/milk/stock gives very good results, but I have indicated quantities throughout the recipes.

Soups and casseroles can be thickened by placing a little cooking liquid and some of the vegetables in a food processor or liquidizer/blender, and blending until smooth. Add this mixture to the soup or casserole and blend in to thicken.

Weighing fruits and vegetables: All quantities for fennel, leeks, peppers and pineapple are given as *cleaned* weight, that is, the outer leaves, stalks, seeds, skins and any damaged parts are removed before weighing. Any other fruit and vegetable foods such as apples and bananas, carrots and potatoes, are weighed with skins, etc, unless otherwise indicated.

Yoghurt: Use only natural/plain yoghurt, as opposed to the fruit-flavoured varieties which often contain sugar and other additives. Alternatively make your own and flavour with fruit of your choice.

Kitchen organization

The best piece of advice I can offer on cooking is to: 'be organized'! This will add to your enjoyment of food preparation and make cooking easier and less of the chore it can sometimes become. Before beginning to cook I always have all my ingredients washed and weighed and any pre-preparatory work done (such as ground nuts/breadcrumbs/soaked fruits, etc). I ensure that all necessary utensils are to hand and loaf tins/cake tins, etc are greased/lined. This saves much fumbling later – or trying to reach for that particular spoon/palette knife with the stickiest of fingers!

A well-prepared working area for foods and utensils will make for a refreshingly enjoyable time spent in the kitchen.

8

Food and drink combination tables

The starch and protein meals

The following food and drink combination tables have been drawn up to provide a quick and easy guide to food combining, and at the same time ease your task of meal structure and menu planning. Each food and drink group is clearly identified to show which foods can be 'crossed' with which – ensuring that only those foods 'happy' together are combined to make up each meal type.

They provide, as far as possible, exhaustive food lists of ingredients found in the vegetarian diet, and until food combining becomes second nature, continued reference should be made to them.

Starch foods *only* are listed under Starch meals

Protein foods *only* are listed under Protein meals

Foods listed under Neutral Foods can *all* be eaten with either Starch meals or Protein meals to produce a complete meal.

The Alkaline meal is covered in detail on pages 66-69, along with the Alkaline/alkali-forming tables.

Never

Mix the Starch meal column
with the Protein meal column

FOOD COMBINATION TABLE

STARCH MEALS	NEUTRAL FOODS	PROTEIN MEALS
Sugars and Sweeteners		
All the following in *moderation*: honey maple syrup dark *unrefined* sugars molasses – blackstrap malt extract date syrup carob spread/syrup concentrated pear juice/spread crystallized ginger★ mixed peel★ glacé cherries★ pear essence mirin chestnuts/chestnut purée fresh/dried fruits – see below	currants raisins sultanas coconut, desiccated/ creamed vanilla pod/essence almond essence rose essence orange essence peppermint essence	honey★ maple syrup★ concentrated fruit juices/spreads sugar-free fruit jams fresh/dried fruits — see below
Fruits — Dried and Fresh		
bananas – fresh/dried – if fresh should be well 'speckled' plantain figs – fresh/dried dates/USA Golden Dates – fresh/dried papaya – fresh/dried – if fresh should be very ripe and sweet pears – fresh/dried – if fresh should be sweet varieties only and very ripe grapes – sweet varieties only and very ripe	currants raisins sultanas olives – black only	All fresh fruits except those under 'Starch' all dried fruits except those under 'Starch' melon – best eaten alone as a fruit meal plums/prunes/ cranberries/rhubarb in moderation – not recommended gooseberries and currants – black/ red/white – only if ripe

★ use very sparingly

STARCH MEALS	NEUTRAL FOODS	PROTEIN MEALS
Cereals/Grains		
cereals/grains: barley buckwheat maize millet quinoa rice rye wild rice all cereal products except seitan	wheat bran/germ oat bran/germ	seitan
Pulses/Legumes – Dried Beans/Peas/Lentils		

Pulses/Legumes:
aduki beans
black-eyed beans
butter beans
canellini beans
chick peas
flageolet beans
haricot beans
lentils: brown
       green
       red
marrow fat peas
mung beans
peanuts
pinto beans
red kidney beans
split peas
		soya/soy beans

Nuts and Seeds		

chestnuts
tiger nuts
(peanuts – see
  pulses above)
	all nuts and seeds
	  except those under
	  'Starch'
	nut/seed butters/
	  spreads/tahini
		all nuts and seeds
		  except those under
		  'Starch'
		nut/seed butters/
		  spreads/tahini

Dairy Products/Fats and Oils		

milk – cow's*/goats/*
  sheep's*
ice-cream – if made
	butter/margarine
	buttermilk
	cream – all types
		milk cow's – in all
		  its forms but not
		  UHT or

* use very sparingly

STARCH MEALS	NEUTRAL FOODS	PROTEIN MEALS
Dairy Products/Fats and Oils		
with cream/egg yolks and other 'Starch' or Neutral ingredients	smetana crème fraîche cream cheese egg yolks ice-cream – if made from cream and flavoured with other ingredients from 'Neutral Meals' ingredients oils – olive/nut/seed – unrefined ghee – butter/ vegetable	homogenized – condensed milk unsweetened only milk – goat's/ sheep's yoghurt – cow's/ goat's/sheep's – natural and unsweetened ice-cream – made with cow's/goat's/ sheep's/milk or cream (if milk-based, in moderation only) and 'Protein' or 'Neutral' ingredients cheese – cow's/ goat's/sheep's – natural – not processed
Flavourings		
fresh vegetable stocks containing 'Starch' vegetables carob powder/flour	salt/pepper* gomasio all herbs and spices – fresh or dried herbs – 'hot' spices* fresh vegetable stocks – made without 'Starch' vegetables or tomatoes vegetable/bouillon stock cubes/pastes/ powders/liquids yeast extract tomato juice – fresh uncooked miso/tamari/shoyu lemon rind/orange rind coconut/vanilla pod/	tomato – cooked tomato purée/paste tomato juice – tinned/ vacuum packed umeboshi plums cider vinegar rice vinegar

* use very sparingly

STARCH MEALS	NEUTRAL FOODS	PROTEIN MEALS
Flavourings		
	various essences – see Sugars and Sweeteners Table	
Vegetables/Sea Vegetables		
potatoes sweet potatoes pumpkin winter squashes Jerusalem artichokes corn/sweetcorn Chinese water chestnuts yams kuzu	all vegetables except those under 'Starch' fresh corn – only if picked, cooked and eaten within 24 hours tomatoes – raw and dried sea vegetables	tomatoes – cooked
Salad Foods		
tomatoes – raw only	all salad foods including sprouted seeds/pulses/grains avocado	
Soya/Soy Products		
soya/soy milk*	soya/soy bran	soya/soy beans and all soya/soy products including TVP, tofu and tempeh – miso/tamari/shoyu see 'Flavourings Table'

* use very sparingly

DRINK COMBINATION TABLE

STARCH MEALS	NEUTRAL FOODS	PROTEIN MEALS
coffee/tea – strict moderation – sugar and milk* cereal coffee substitutes chocolate/cocoa* – made with water/ cream or very diluted milk carob drinks – sugar* made with water/ cream or very diluted milk grape juice – only if very sweet	water – tap/bottled dandelion coffee herb teas tomato juice – fresh vegetable juices – fresh/cooked/ vacuum packed/ bottled – non-starch only 'instant' vegetable/bouillon/ yeast extract drinks	coffee/tea – strict moderation – no sugar – milk* non-cereal coffee substitutes lemon tea fruit teas – unsweetened fruit juices – fresh/ bottled/vacuum packed – unsweetened grape juice – if not too sweet tomato juice cooked/ tinned/vacuum packed milk – cow's/goat's/ sheep's/soya* lassis – made with Protein fruits only – unsweetened
Alcoholic Drinks		
all in strict moderation: beer lager ale stout wine – sweet liqueurs – sweet sake	all in strict moderation: gin rum vodka whisky brandy	all in strict moderation: wines – dry cider – dry liqueurs – dry

* use very sparingly

9
Alkaline and acid food and drink tables

There can be confusion between the principles of food combining and eating to maintain the alkali to acid ratio. These are *two very different concepts* and should be regarded as such.

> **Food Combining** is the art of eating *at any one meal* only those foods which are 'happy' together – achieved by keeping starch separated from protein.

> **Eating to maintain the alkali to acid ratio** is taking in the course of each day, approximately four times as much alkaline as acid foods (as explained on page 24).

Alkaline foods: To maintain the alkali to acid ratio, alkaline foods should form the major part of our daily eating and are therefore an essential part of *every* meal in the form of fruit, vegetable and salad foods.

Acid foods: Acid foods should take 'back-stage' in our daily eating and appear mainly as the starch or protein component of these respective meals.

The alkaline meal

The Alkaline meal can be made up of *any* of those foods in the Alkali/Alkaline-forming and Neutral columns and should consist mainly of fruit, vegetable and salad foods. Many delightful dishes can be made from these: crisp fruity salads, vegetable stir-fries/bakes/soups, etc. This meal, along with those alkaline foods eaten at the starch and protein meals, will soon result in the correct bodily balance of alkali to acid ratio being achieved.

To avoid the risk of 'muddling' concepts when starting to 'Hay' I stress again – *concentrate first on food combining* – the alkali to acid ratio will then largely sort itself out.

ALKALINE AND ACID FOOD TABLE

Alkali/Alkaline-Forming Foods	Neutral Foods	Acid/Acid-Forming Foods
Dairy products/fats and oils		
milk yoghurt – unsweetened	cream cream cheese all fats and oils	milk – heated cheese – except cream cheese egg – white and yolk
Grains/cereals		
millet		all grains/cereals and by-products except millet
Pulses/legumes – dried beans/peas/lentils – soya beans and soya products		

	soya beans and all
	    soya products
		all pulses/legumes
		    includes peanuts
		    excludes soya
		    beans and all soya
		    products

Vegetable and salad foods/sea vegetables		

all vegetable and salad
    foods except
    spinach, cooked
    tomatoes and
    avocado
all sea vegetables
	avocado	spinach and cooked
		    tomatoes

Alkali/Alkaline-Forming Foods	Neutral Foods	Acid/Acid-Forming Foods
Fruits – fresh and dried		
all fruits – except olives and those under acid/acid-forming foods	olives	plums/prunes cranberries/rhubarb gooseberries/currants black/red/white – only if ripe
Nuts/seeds		
almonds brazil nuts chestnuts hazelnuts cobnuts pine kernels tiger nuts	pumpkin seeds sesame seeds sunflower seeds poppy seeds coconut	cashew nuts macadamias pecan nuts pistachios walnuts (peanuts: see under pulses/legumes, above)
Flavourings		
umeboshi plums miso tamari shoyu	all flavourings except those under 'acid' and 'alkaline'	salt/pepper vinegar 'hot' spices
Sugars/sweeteners		
jams – sugar-free pure fruit concentrates juices/spreads vanilla pod/esscence almond/rose/orange/ peppermint essences chestnuts/chestnut purée currants/raisins/ sultanas molasses – blackstrap fruit – fresh/dried – see Fruits above	coconut – desiccated/ creamed	all sugars/sweeteners and products made from these except those under 'alkaline'

ALKALINE AND ACID DRINK TABLE

Alkali/Alkaline-Forming Drinks	Neutral Drinks	Acid/Acid-Forming Drinks
all fruit juices – except prune juice all vegetable/bouillon drinks except cooked/tinned/vacuum-packed tomato juice yeast extract drinks tomato juice – fresh milk – cow's/goat's/sheep's/soya* lassis lemon tea fruit tea fruit teas dandelion coffee	water – tap/bottled herb teas	coffee** cereal/non-cereal coffee substitutes tea** cocoa chocolate carob tomato juice – cooked/tinned/vacuum packed prune juice all alcohol

*all milks should be regarded as 'food' and best taken with vegetables and fruit only

**although acid-forming, coffee and tea and permissible with an alkaline meal provided they are very weak and served without sugar

THE RECIPES

Introduction

It is now time to put your knowledge of the Hay System into practice.

I hope you gain much pleasure in preparing and sampling the following recipes, which have been compiled to offer as wide a choice of dishes and ingredients as possible. They have all been tested on 'personally-trained guinea-pigs' – family, friends and colleagues – who, with the exception of two persons very familiar with the Hay System, have all sampled without any knowledge of the Hay principles. This shows that cooking in the Hay way need not be any different from 'conventional' cooking – or 'brown, bland and boring' either!

All recipe and menu suggestions are just that – suggestions. Why not adapt mine or use your own favourites – bearing in mind always, of course, the compatibilities of the foods included. Serving suggestions have also been given for extra ideas. Vegetarian food is extremely versatile – so many dishes can double or even treble-up as other meal items.

Do not feel restricted in any way by the 'heading' of a recipe section – food and meal arrangements are flexible and often interchangeable and/or adaptable. For example, mushrooms on toast eaten for breakfast is more than adequate as a light lunch/evening meal!

Drinks with meals as previously discussed are not recommended but the Drink combination table on page 65 and the Alkaline and acid drink table on page 69 indicate a suitable accompaniment or before/after-meal beverage, should you still wish to do so.

All recipes can be frozen unless otherwise indicated.

Each recipe has been 'coded' to indicate whether it is starch, protein or alkaline, combines with all meals – is neutral – (salad and vegetable side-dishes especially), or is vegan.

For this purpose:

S =	starch dish only
P =	protein dish only
A =	alkaline dish only
N =	neutral, combines with all meals. The recipe/meal suggestion can be eaten as – or as part of – a starch, protein or alkaline meal
S or P =	recipe/meal suggestion can be eaten as – or as part of – a starch or protein meal
S or A =	recipe/meal suggestion can be eaten as – or as part of – a starch or alkaline meal
P or A =	recipe/meal suggestion can be eaten as – or as part of – a protein or alkaline meal
(S) or **(P)** or **(A)** =	the recipe can be adapted to this meal type – directions are given in the ingredients list and method
Ⓥ =	vegan dish or can be adapted to a vegan dish

Breakfast and Brunch

Breakfast
This may seem, at first, a hard meal to alter, as you begin to realize what food combining means . . . no toast and jam/marmalade, no bowls of cereal smothered in milk! Such 'delights' will become quite insignificant, however, when you try the alternatives.

Dr Hay considered breakfast a superfluous meal. He advised that, if eaten at all, it should be very light and easily digestible, consisting of fresh fruit (preferably of one kind only), with or without milk and/or fresh fruit juices.

Try also not to start the day on a cup of coffee – this is acid-forming and stimulating and will immediately put your body in the 'wrong gear' for the day. If you cannot do without this daily cup, try drinking it weak – freshly squeezed orange juice is far nicer though!

Breakfast, as the first meal of the day, leaves us with a wide-open choice of whether it is to be starch, protein or alkaline. This selection, then, will be instrumental in the choice of the remaining two meals of the day.

The emphasis on a fruit breakfast means that this meal most easily fits into the day's routine as 'alkaline', leaving the carbohydrate and protein meals for later, but suggestions are also given among the recipes for those wishing to have a starch or protein start to the day.

Breakfast need not be the monotonous 'cereal and toast' meal so often taken. There is a wonderful variety of ways to start the day – and if suggestions below are followed you could eat for a month before having the same dish twice!

Many dishes are substantial enough to be used for light lunches/evening meals, and some of the 'sweeter and fruitier' suggestions make delicious desserts – so adapt the ideas accordingly.

Wheatgerm can be added to starch, protein or alkaline breakfasts as a nutritional extra. Bran, too, can be taken if required.

S

Almond, banana and couscous balls

Definitely a favourite with children!

Imp/Metric	Makes 12/Serves 4	American
4oz/100g	couscous	⅔ cup
1oz/25g	currants	¼ cup
2	bananas	2
2oz/50g	ground almonds	½ cup
	extra ground almonds for coating	

1 Place the couscous and currants in a bowl, and add 10 fl oz/275ml/1⅓ cups boiling water.
2 Leave to stand until all the liquid is absorbed.
3 Mash the banana and mix in with the ground almonds to produce a sticky, but fairly firm mixture – add more ground almonds if necessary.
4 Shape into little balls.
5 Gently roll in the extra ground almonds then refrigerate for 2-3 hours to 'set'.

Serving Suggestion
These are moist enough to serve on their own or top with a little milk or cream. Delicious as a pudding, and an ideal lunch box/picnic addition.

S

Breakfast buns

A delicious way to start the day!

Imp/Metric	Makes 12/Serves 4	American
6oz/175g	plain whole wheat flour	1½ cups
1oz/25g	wheat bran	¼ cup
4 tsps	baking powder	4 tsps
1½oz/40g	walnuts/English walnuts – finely chopped	⅓ cup
1½oz/40g	sunflower seeds	⅓ cup
2½ tbsps	clear honey/maple syrup	2½ tbsps
6 tbsps	sunflower oil	6 tbsps
	3 fl oz/75ml/⅓ cup milk diluted with 5 fl oz/150ml/⅔ cup water	

1 Set the oven to 400°F/200°C (Gas 6).
2 Grease a bun tin/pan, then mix the dry ingredients together in a bowl.
3 Add the honey/maple syrup and oil and combine.
4 Pour in the diluted milk and, using a fork, mix to form a thick batter-like consistency.
5 Spoon into the prepared tin/pan, then bake for 12-15 minutes until the buns are risen and golden, and a knife, when inserted, comes out clean.

Serving Suggestion
Serve warm from the oven with butter/margarine or a sweet/savoury spread. They are also delicious cold, and can be served as an afternoon tea bun if wished.

Frozen Fruit Yoghurts
A frozen fruit and yoghurt mix is absolutely delicious, with the
natural sweetness of the fruit offset beautifully by the sharpness
of yoghurt. Make by simply blending fruit and yoghurt
together, and popping the mixture in the freezer to set. I have
given a recipe for frozen peach yoghurt below, but the principle
applies to other fruits, so do have fun experimenting with other
flavours!

P or A

Frozen peach yoghurt

Imp/Metric	Serves 3/4	American
12oz/350g	very ripe fresh peaches or 8oz/225g/ 1 cup unsweetened tinned/canned peaches	1½ cups
8oz/225g	plain yoghurt – thick-set (to convert to V, use plain soya yoghurt)	1 cup
2 tsps	honey/maple syrup	2 tsps

1 Place the peaches in a food processor or liquidizer/blender,
  and blend until smooth.
2 Add the yoghurt and honey/maple syrup, and blend again
  until well combined.
3 Pour into a plastic container and freeze for at least 4 hours.

Serving Suggestion
Serve as a breakfast dish or dessert. Perfect on its own, or
alternatively serve with chopped toasted nuts/seeds or a
sprinkling of desiccated/shredded coconut. Remove from the
freezer 30-45 minutes before serving to allow it to soften. Make
with other soft fruits such as strawberries, raspberries, etc –
orange and pineapple are also delicious.

Fruit and Nut 'Creams'
These are made by blending ground nuts with a fruit of your choice, along with enough fruit juice to achieve a creamy consistency.

| P or A |

Almond and apple cream

Imp/Metric	Serves 4	American
2lb/900g	cooking apples	2lb
1½ tbsps	concentrated apple juice	1½ tbsps
1½ tbsps	maple syrup	1½ tbsps
3oz/75g	ground almonds	¾ cup

1 Peel and core the apples, then roughly slice and cook covered in 2-3 tbsps water over a gentle heat until completely broken down and very light and fluffy. Stir occasionally.
2 Remove from the heat and leave to cool.
3 Stir in the concentrated apple juice, maple syrup and ground almonds, combine thoroughly, then chill before serving.

Serving Suggestion
Delicious as a breakfast dish or dessert, served on its own or with a little milk, yoghurt, cream or ice-cream.

Variations: Serve with a sprinkling of raisins/sultanas/golden seedless raisins and/or toasted seeds.

S or A

Banana, hazelnut and raisin cream

Imp/Metric	Serves 2	American
4oz/100g	lexia raisins – cooked in 2 fl oz/50ml/ ¼ cup water until soft and all the water is absorbed	¾ cup
2oz/50g	ground hazelnuts	½ cup
2-3	bananas – cut into slices	2-3
¼-½ tsp	vanilla essence	¼-½ tsp

1 Place the raisins in a food processor or liquidizer/blender, and blend until smooth.
2 Add the ground hazelnuts and banana, blend again until smooth and creamy, and flavour with vanilla essence to taste, then chill before serving.

Serving Suggestion
Serve as a breakfast dish or dessert. It is also delicious served with a sprinkling of toasted chopped hazelnuts. Banana does discolour on keeping, so do not prepare this dish too far in advance.

P or A

Citrus fruit and apple

A sharp but refreshing combination of flavours, complemented by the warm flavour of cinnamon.

Imp/Metric	Serves 2	American
12oz/350g	sweet red apple – peel and roughly chop	2 cups
4 tbsps	lemon juice	4 tbsps
4 tbsps	orange juice	4 tbsps
¼-½ tsp	cinnamon	¼-½ tsp
	optional	
	honey or maple syrup to taste	

1 Place the apple, lemon and orange juice in a food processor or liquidizer/blender, and blend to a smooth purée.
2 Stir in the cinnamon to taste, then chill for 2-3 hours before serving.

P   ⓥ

Apricot tofu 'fool'

A smooth, creamy 'fool', with a deliciously refreshing apricot flavour.

Imp/Metric	Serves 4	American
8oz/225g	dried apricots – soak overnight or 8-12 hours in 8 fl oz/225ml/ 1 cup water	1⅔ cups
10oz/275g	firm tofu	1¼ cups

1 Place the apricots and any remaining soaking juice in a food processor or liquidizer/blender, and blend until smooth.
2 Add the tofu, and blend again until very smooth and creamy, then chill.

Serving Suggestion
Serve sprinkled with toasted nibbed or flaked/slivered almonds, and a little light/pouring cream.

Variations: replace the apricots with dried peaches, pineapple, etc.

Fruit and Vegetable Drinks
These are an excellent and delicious way to gain the valuable nutrients present in fruits and vegetables. They are very simply and quickly made with the help of your food processor or liquidizer/blender – or you may have a fruit/vegetable juice extractor. There are many variations and combinations of fruits and vegetables which can be made so do have fun making your own, but I have given a few ideas below – also a recipe for mulled grape juice 'punch'!

Fruit and vegetable juices are especially good for serving at breakfasts, brunches, buffets and barbecues, or for taking as part of a packed lunch or picnic.

| P or A |

Apple and carrot

Imp/Metric	Makes 1pt/570ml/2½ cups	American
6oz/176g	apple – peel and roughly chop	1 cup
15 fl oz/425ml	carrot juice – fresh or vacuum-packed	2 cups
1 tsp	concentrated apple juice	1 tsp

1 Place the apple in a food processor or liquidizer/blender, and blend as smooth as possible.
2 Add the carrot juice and concentrated apple juice, and blend again until smooth, then chill.

Cannot be Frozen

| S or A |

Banana and papaya

Imp/Metric	Makes 1pt/570ml/2½ cups	American
1	papaya – 1lb/450g in weight, roughly chop	1
1-2	bananas	1-2

1 Place the papaya and banana in a food processor or liquidizer/blender, and blend until smooth.
2 Add 6 fl oz/175ml/¾ cup water and blend again – add more water to adjust the consistency if desired, then chill.

Cannot be Frozen

| N |

Carrot and beetroot/beet

Imp/Metric	Makes 1pt/570ml/2½ cups	American
6oz/175g	cooked beetroot/beet – roughly chop	1 cup
15 fl oz/425ml	carrot juice – fresh or vacuum-packed	2 cups

1 Place the beetroot/beet in a food processor or liquidizer/blender, and blend as smooth as possible.
2 Add the carrot juice, and blend again until smooth, then chill.

Cannot be Frozen

P or A
Melon

Imp/Metric	Makes 1pt/570ml/2½ cups	American
1	very ripe melon – 1½lb/675g in weight	1

1 Halve the melon and remove the seeds.
2 Scoop out the flesh, place in a food processor or liquidizer/blender, then blend until smooth and creamy, and chill – I drink the juice like this, but if you prefer a thinner drink, add a little water to adjust the consistency.

Cannot be Frozen

Variation: add a sprinkling of ground ginger for a 'sharper' flavour.

S or A
Mulled grape juice 'punch'

A deceivingly non-alcoholic punch!

Imp/Metric	Makes 1pt/570ml/2½ cups	American
2¾pt/1½l	red grape juice	7 cups
4	juniper berries	4
6	cloves	6
2	cardamom pods	2
1 tsp	nutmeg	1 tsp
1 dsp	grated/shredded fresh root ginger	2 tsps
1	rosehip teabag	1
	cinnamon stick	
	vanilla pod/bean	

1 Mix all the ingredients together in a large saucepan, bring to the boil then simmer gently for half-an-hour, or more, before serving.

Cannot be Frozen

| P or A | | |

Orange and pineapple

Imp/Metric	Makes 1pt/570ml/2½ cups	American
8oz/225g	pineapple – core and roughly chop	2 cups
10 fl oz	orange juice – fresh or unsweetened	1⅓ cups

1 Place the pineapple in a food processor or liquidizer/blender, and blend until smooth.
2 Add the orange juice and blend again until the ingredients are thoroughly combined, then chill.

Cannot be Frozen

| P or A | | |

Pineapple and kiwi fruit

Imp/Metric	Makes 1½pt/825ml/3¾ cups	American
8oz/225g	pineapple – core and roughly chop	2 cups
8oz/225g	kiwi fruit – roughly chop	1¼ cups
10 fl oz/275ml	pineapple juice – unsweetened	1⅓ cups

1 Place the pineapple and kiwi fruit in a food processor or liquidizer/blender, and blend until smooth.
2 Add the pineapple juice, and blend again until the ingredients are thoroughly combined, then chill.

Cannot be Frozen

Nut Milks
These are excellent and nutritious non-dairy substitutes.

| N | | |

Almond milk

Imp/Metric	Makes 1¾pt/1¼ cups	American
4oz/100g	ground almonds	1 cup
1½pt/825ml	water	3¾ cups

1 Place the ground almonds and water in a food processor or liquidizer/blender, and blend until smooth.
2 Leave the mixture to stand for at least 30 minutes, then pass through a sieve/strainer.
3 Return the ground almonds to the food processor or liquidizer/blender, add 12 fl oz/350ml/1⅓ cups water, prepare as above, and add to the milk from the first sieving/straining.

Cannot be Frozen
It will keep for 4-5 days in a refrigerator.

Serving Suggestion
Use as an alternative to dairy milk. Especially useful as a dairy substitute in starch meals or over cereals, etc – and it really does taste like milk! Ground cashews can be used instead of almonds, or pine kernels for an even richer alternative – or use a mixture of ground nuts.

Fruit and Nut 'Shakes'
Make these by blending fruit with yoghurt and/or milk until a creamy drink is achieved.

Fruit Compotes
Two truly delicious fruit mixtures; a perfect start to the day – or end to a meal!

P or A

Golden fruit compote

Imp/Metric	Serves 4	American
3oz/75g	dried apple rings – cut into large pieces	1½ cups
3oz/75g	dried peaches – cut into large pieces	½ cup
4oz/100g	dried apricots – cut into large pieces	⅔ cup
2oz/50g	lexia raisins	⅓ cup
2oz/50g	sultanas/golden seedless raisins	⅓ cup
1	rosehip tea bag	1
2	juniper berries	2
2	cloves	2
	vanilla pod/bean	
	cinnamon stick	

1 Place all the ingredients in a large saucepan and add 1½pts/800ml/3¾ cups boiling water.
2 Cover, bring to the boil, and simmer for 10 minutes.
3 Take the pan off the heat and leave covered overnight, or 8-12 hours, for all the flavours to mingle.
4 Remove the tea bag and spices.

Cannot be Frozen

Serving Suggestion
Serve hot or cold as a breakfast dish or dessert, with a little yoghurt or cream – delicious as a dessert with ice-cream.

| S or A | |

Orangey fruit compote

Imp/Metric	Serves 4	American
4oz/100g	dried pears – cut into large pieces	¾ cup
3oz/75g	dried figs – cut into large pieces	⅔ cup
3oz/75g	dried banana – cut into large pieces	½ cup
3oz/75g	dried dates	⅔ cup
3oz/75g	sultanas/golden seedless raisins	½ cup
1 tsp	finely grated/shredded orange rind	1 tsp
1	rosehip tea bag	1
2	juniper berries	2
2	cloves	2
1	cardamom pod	1
	cinnamon stick	

1 Prepare and serve as for Golden fruit compote above.

Mueslis
These are extremely nutritious, and an excellent way of gaining valuable minerals and vitamins. It is far better (and more fun!) to make your own than buy ready-made mueslis which often have a lot of added sugar, and are not always compatible. Below are some suggestions, but they can be easily adapted to fit in with the ingredients in your store cupboard. As the protein and alkaline mueslis are solely made up of dried fruits, nuts and seeds they are very 'chewy' – so do not try to eat in a hurry!
I recommend that muesli is soaked overnight in the

refrigerator in a liquid of your choice, depending on its starch, protein or alkaline base. This softens the nuts/grains/dried fruits and aids their digestibility and subsequent assimilation by the body. Alternatively, serve with boiling water. This is not as strange as it might sound and actually very palatable – and, as with overnight soaking, softens the nuts, grains and fruits.

Serving Suggestion
Muesli need not only be a breakfast dish – it is ideal for taking as part of a packed lunch, or with extra fruit and topped with cream it makes a delicious and unusual dessert!

Variations: starchy alkaline dried fruits can be used in alkaline mueslis, provided they are not mixed with the acid dried fruits. Fresh fruits in season can also be added to protein and alkaline mueslis – bearing in mind their compatibility with other dried fruits already in the mix. Fresh grated/shredded carrot makes a tasty addition to all mueslis, and for a 'savoury' protein muesli try grating/shredding in a little cheese as an unusual variation! A sprinkling of nutmeg and/or cinnamon is another delicious addition – or if you choose to soak your muesli overnight, add a small piece of vanilla pod/bean for a beautiful vanilla flavour.

Starch-based
Serve with boiling water, diluted cream, nut milks, vegetable juices (for example, carrot juice), sweet grape juice or very diluted milk (muesli – starch-based only – and breakfast cereal, ideally, should not be eaten with any type of milk). A little diluted milk can be taken by those who do not enjoy the suggested alternatives.

Pear and date

Imp/Metric	Makes 1lb/450g/3 cups	American
3oz/75g	dried pear – chop into small pieces	½ cup
2oz/50g	dried dates – chop into small pieces	⅓ cup
2oz/50g	rolled oats	½ cup
2oz/50g	barley flakes	½ cup
2oz/50g	wheat flakes	½ cup
2oz/50g	rice flakes	½ cup
1oz/25g	sultanas/golden seedless raisins	¼ cup
1oz/25g	flaked/slivered almonds	¼ cup
1oz/25g	sesame seeds	4 tbsps

1 Serve with boiling water, milk (any type), diluted cream, nut milks, nut creams, yoghurt, fruit or vegetable juices (not sweet/starch juices).

$\boxed{\text{P}}$ V

Peach, prune and coconut

Imp/Metric	Makes 1 lb/450g/3 cups	American
2oz/50g	dried peaches – cut into small pieces	⅔ cup
2oz/50g	prunes – cut into small pieces	⅓ cup
2oz/50g	desiccated/shredded coconut – toasted	⅔ cup
4oz/100g	flaked/slivered almonds – finely chop	1 cup
1oz/25g	pumpkin seeds – finely chop	¼ cup
2oz/50g	sultanas/golden seedless raisins	⅓ cup
2oz/50g	cashews – finely chop	½ cup
1oz/25g	sesame seeds	4 tbsps

1 Mix all the ingredients together and store in an airtight container.

Alkaline-based
Serve with boiling water, milk, yoghurt, diluted cream, alkaline nut milks, fruit or vegetable juices.

$\boxed{\text{P or A}}$
Hazelnut and apple

Imp/Metric	Makes 1 lb/450g/3 cups	American
2oz/50g	hazelnuts – roast and finely chop	⅓ cup
3oz/75g	dried apple – cut into small pieces	1½ cups
3oz/75g	flaked/slivered almonds – finely chop	¾ cup
3oz/75g	raisins	½ cup
2oz/50g	sesame seeds	½ cup
1oz/25g	sunflower seeds	¼ cup
1oz/25g	desiccated/shredded coconut	⅓ cup
1oz/25g	pumpkin seeds	¼ cup

1 Mix all the ingredients together and store in an airtight container.

Porridge
There is far more to porridge than just oats, and I hope you will enjoy the 'alternative' porridge recipes given below!

 S (V)

Oat and banana

Imp/Metric	Serves 2	American
4oz/100g	rolled or jumbo oats	1 cup
2	bananas – cut into thin slices	2
1pt/570ml	water	2½ cups
	optional	
	honey/maple syrup to taste	

1 Put the oats, banana and water into a saucepan.
2 Bring the mixture to the boil, then simmer gently until all the liquid is absorbed, stirring all the time. Sweeten to taste if desired.

Note: jumbo oats produce a chewier 'nuttier' flavoured porridge. It will need simmering for longer than the rolled oat porridge.

Cannot be Frozen

Serving Suggestion
Serve on its own or topped with a little cream. Stir in some carob powder for a 'chocolatey' banana porridge. A favourite with children (and adults, too!)

Rice and date

Imp/Metric	Serves 2	American
4oz/100g	rice flour	¾ cup
4oz/100g	dried dates – chop	¾ cup
	optional	
	honey/maple syrup to taste	

1 Place the rice flour and dates in a pan with 1pt/570ml/2½ cups water.
2 Bring to the boil, then simmer for 2-3 minutes, or until all the liquid is absorbed. Sweeten to taste if desired.

Cannot be Frozen

Serving Suggestion
Top with toasted chopped nuts/seeds for a more crunchy texture.

Spicy fruit loaf

A delicious, spicy loaf with a lovely moist texture.

Imp/Metric	Makes 1 × 1lb/450g loaf	American
10oz/275g	100% strong whole wheat flour	2½ cups
1½oz/40g	raisins	¼ cup
1½oz/40g	sultanas/golden seedless raisins	¼ cup
1oz/25g	nibbed almonds	¼ cup
1 tsp	mixed spice	1 tsp
½ tsp	nutmeg	½ tsp
1 tsp	orange rind	1 tsp
½ tsp	salt	½ tsp
½oz/15g	fresh yeast – or 2 tsps dried yeast/	1¼ tbsps
	½ sachet easy blend yeast – use	
	according to the instructions on the packet	
2 tbsps	malt extract	2 tbsps
	5 fl oz/150ml/⅔ cup warm water (3½ fl oz/	
	90ml/⅓ cup cold water mixed with	
	1½ fl oz/40ml/¼ cup boiling water)	
2 tsps	oil	2 tsps
	glaze:	
	2 tsps malt extract and 2 tsps water	

1 Grease a 1lb/450g/4 cup loaf tin/pan, then mix the dry ingredients together in a bowl.
2 Combine the yeast, malt extract and 2 fl oz/50ml/¼ cup of the warm water, and leave until the surface is frothy.
3 Pour into the dry ingredients, along with the oil and remaining water.
4 Mix thoroughly until a dough begins to form, then knead until smooth.
5 Cover, and leave to double in size in a warm draught-free place – approximately one hour.
6 Tip the dough out of the bowl, knock back/punch down by punching it in the centre, then knead again for a few minutes.
7 Shape, and place in the prepared tin/pan.
8 Cover, and leave to rise and double in size a second time – approximately 30-40 minutes.
9 Set the oven to 400°F/200°C (Gas 6).
10 Bake the loaf for 20-30 minutes – or until the base sounds hollow when tapped.
11 Towards the end of cooking time combine the malt extract and water in a small saucepan over a low heat, until gently heated through.
12 As soon as the loaf comes out of the oven turn out onto a wire rack, glaze the top using a pastry brush, then leave to cool completely.

Serving Suggestion
Serve warm or cold with butter/margarine or spread/topping of your choice – lovely served on its own though!

Tomatoes and mushrooms with cottage/pot cheese

The richness of mushrooms, tomatoes, and herbs is delicious with the contrasting cottage/pot cheese topping.

Imp/Metric	Serves 2	American
1 dsp	olive or sunflower oil	2 tsps
6oz/175g	mushrooms – thinly slice	2½ cups
1	8oz/225g tin/can chopped tomatoes	1
2 tsps	finely chopped fresh basil	2 tsps
	salt and freshly ground black pepper	
3 tbsps	cottage/pot cheese	3 tbsps

1 Heat the oil, and fry the mushroom slices until tender.
2 Add the tomatoes and basil, bring the mixture to the boil, and simmer uncovered until the mixture thickens.
3 Remove the pan from the heat, season, and either stir in the cottage/pot cheese, or use it as a topping.

Cannot be Frozen

Serving Suggestion
Serve on or with starch-free crackers, or slices of cucumber. Alternatively grill/broil or bake aubergine/eggplant slices until tender, pile the cheese and mushroom mix on top, and heat through. Excellent as a light lunch/evening meal dish – or quick and tasty main course!

Fruit Ices
A refreshing way to eat fruit – and the perfect way to ensure
that children receive their daily fruit quota without objecting!

| P or A | |

Orange and pineapple

Imp/Metric	Serves 4	American
8oz/225g	pineapple – core and roughly chop	2 cups
10 fl oz/275ml	orange juice	1⅓ cups
	Optional	
	honey/maple syrup to taste – use *sparingly*	

1 Place the pineapple and orange juice in a food processor or
   liquidizer/blender, and blend until smooth, sweeten to taste
   if desired.
2 Pour into a plastic container and freeze for at least 4 hours.

Serving Suggestion
Remove from the freezer 30-45 minutes before serving to soften;
delicious with sweet Almond and Poppy Seed or Hazelnut and
Almond crackers (pages 233 and 236).

Pineapple and kiwi fruit

Imp/Metric	Serves 4	American
8oz/225g	pineapple – core and roughly chop	2 cups
8oz/225g	kiwi fruit – roughly chop	1¼ cups
	Optional	
	honey/maple syrup to taste – use *sparingly*	

1 Place the fruit in a food processor or liquidizer/blender, and
   blend until smooth, sweeten to taste if desired.
2 Pour into a plastic container and freeze for at least 4 hours.

Serving Suggestion
As for Orange and Pineapple above.

P or A

Hazelnut stuffed grapefruit

The delicate sweetness of hazelnuts and the sharp flavour of grapefruit are a delicious combination in this dish.

Imp/Metric	Serves 2	American
2	large grapefruit (the 'pink' Florida grapefruit are delicious for this recipe)	2
1oz/25g	chopped roasted hazelnuts	4 tbsps
1½ tbsps	concentrated apple juice	1½ tbsps

1 Halve the grapefruits, scoop out the flesh and reserve two of the empty skins.
2 Drain away the juice (this makes a lovely sharp drink!), then roughly chop the grapefruit, at the same time removing the skin where possible.
3 Combine with the hazelnuts and concentrated apple juice.
4 Pile back into the two reserved skins then chill.

Cannot be Frozen

Serving Suggestion
This dish is also perfect as a starter/appetizer, and delicious topped with yoghurt.

Variation: serve hot – place under the grill/broiler for 2-3 minutes to heat through.

P

Tofu cube 'crunch'

The crispness of the nuts/seeds and the smooth texture of tofu are a lovely contrast in this dish.

Imp/Metric	Serves 2	American
5oz/150g	very firm tofu – cut into cubes	⅔ cup
1½ tbsps	lemon juice	1½ tbsps
2 tsps	tamari	2 tsps
pinch	paprika	pinch
1oz/25g	sesame seeds	4 tbsps
1oz/25g	ground almonds	¼ cup
1 tbsp	olive or sunflower oil	1 tbsp

1 Marinate the tofu in the lemon juice, tamari and paprika for an hour or more (can be left overnight or 8-12 hours if desired).
2 Mix the sesame seeds and ground almonds in a bowl, add the tofu cubes and lightly toss.
3 Heast the oil, and add the tofu along with any remaining seed and nut mix.
4 Fry until the tofu is browned, and the nut and seed mix crisp and golden – it tends to separate from the tofu, but this is what provides the lovely, crispy 'crunch'!

Cannot be Frozen

Serving Suggestion
Serve with grilled or fried mushrooms. Vary the ground nuts for different flavours. Also ideal as a light lunch/evening meal, or quick main course.

Brunch

Brunch invariably occurs close to midday and, as its name implies, is late breakfast or early lunch. Due to its timing, lunch (or an even later breakfast!) is eliminated and the next main meal will be in the evening.

If brunch is taken then the second meal of the day can be as follows:

Starch Brunch – Protein or Alkaline Evening Meal
Protein Brunch – Starch or Alkaline Evening Meal
Alkaline Brunch – Starch or Protein Evening Meal

On a 'two-meal day', eating brunch and evening meal, do not worry if only Starch and Protein meals are taken. Provided you eat plenty of fruit/vegetable/salad foods at these meals there is no fear of a deficiency in alkaline intake!

Conversely, if an Alkaline evening meal is taken do not worry about lack of starch or protein for one day – the body will actually benefit from this.

Light meals, packed lunches and sandwich fillings

Lunch

For most people this meal is eaten away from home as a packed lunch at work, or in the staff restaurant. If eaten in the staff restaurant careful choice must be made to ensure that compatibility of food is maintained.

A salad is a safe choice if available, as this can be starch, protein or alkaline-based depending on the ingredients. Remember if it is protein-based not to eat bread or any cereal/grain with it. As well as bread, or similar, with the starch or alkaline lunch you could have jacket potato, or potato cooked any other way (although the ubiquitous chips with everything should be avoided). You can then follow these suggestions with a piece of fresh fruit from the corresponding starch/protein/alkaline food lists, or some other compatible food that might be available. I recommend that you copy the food tables given and carry these around with you for reference!

For those persons dining out at a restaurant, or similar, read The Hay System and Eating Out (page 38).

If you have planned a packed lunch or are eating at home you obviously have total control over your selection. But to break away from the 'bread and cheese' lunch-box habit, I have made a few suggestions in the recipe section to help you vary this meal.

Selection of a starch, protein or alkaline lunch will be dependent on the type of breakfast already taken.

```
Reminder:
starch breakfast     = protein or alkaline lunch
protein breakfast    = starch or alkaline lunch
alkaline breakfast   = starch or protein lunch
```

I would recommend that you do not make lunch the heaviest

meal of the day. So much energy is required for digestion that if lunch is taken as the main meal much of the energy which could have been put to mental and physical use in the afternoon will be diverted, resulting in completion of digestion – but little else! Indeed, try eating nothing but salad and fresh fruit for lunch and see how much lighter and more comfortable the afternoon becomes – and how much more work is accomplished!

Evening meal

It is preferable to make the last meal of the day the largest and toughest and therefore starch-based. Starches and sugars (the carbohydrate group) require longer and more involved digestion which is most effectively achieved overnight, while we sleep, allowing our body to do justice to the ingredients.

An evening starch meal, however, is not always practical for those who, working all day, prefer to take a starch-based packed lunch, and if this is so then the protein or alkaline meal can be eaten in the evening.

Selection of a starch, protein or alkaline evening meal will be dependent on the type of breakfast and lunch already taken.

Reminder:
alkaline or protein breakfast or lunch = starch evening meal
alkaline or starch breakfast or lunch = protein evening meal
starch or protein breakfast or lunch = alkaline evening meal

A wide range of evening meal dishes are given in the recipes that follow.

Light lunches/evening meals/snacks

Light lunches/evening meals not only include the 'mushrooms on toast' type snacks but also scaled-down versions of the main meal of the day based on smaller portions, served with salad and/or vegetables. Small portions of pastas, topped with protein-free sauces, also make an ideal light lunch/evening meal, as do salads – you can also refer to the breakfast/brunch dishes for quick and simple light lunch/evening meal ideas!

Supper taken as a 'before-bedtime-snack' should, ideally, be eliminated or restricted to perhaps a drink and a piece of fruit, handful of nuts/seeds or very light sandwich. A heavy supper, taken before bed will just 'sit' in the body and its digestion will be poor.

On the other hand, supper taken in the form of a light evening meal, perhaps after having a 'cup of tea and a bite' late in the afternoon, is quite permissible and sensible.

Snacking between meals, unless in strict moderation, is best avoided. It results in unnecessary food being eaten, places an extra burden on our digestive system and robs us of energy. It also destroys the possibility of forming correct eating habits as it removes any sense of true hunger.

However, if you *do* feel peckish, a piece of fruit, handful of nuts, piece of raw carrot, etc, is far more suitable than a sticky cream bun or similar!

Drinks may be taken between meals provided this is not excessive.

Packed lunches

Eating in the Hay way means that packed lunches of peanut butter sandwiches can be a thing of the past as a whole new world is possible of exciting packed-lunch nibbles and surprises is opened. A vacuum flask can be used to take casseroles/soups/vegetable dishes, etc, – lovely for those cold winter days!

Starch packed lunch suggestions

1 **Starch Fruits** – fresh/dried
2 **Pitta breads** – stuff with a choice of S or N
   sandwich fillings/toppings, dips, pâtés, spreads,
   salads
3 **Potatoes — new** – serve cold
4 **Sproutings** – single variety, or mixture,
   combined with toasted seeds

Protein packed lunch suggestions

1 **Cheese cubes and an apple**
2 **Cottage cheese and orange segments**
3 **Crudités** – serve with starch-free sandwich fillings/toppings,
   dips, pâtés and spreads

4 **Egg** – hard-boiled/hard-cooked
5 **Protein Fruits** – fresh/dried
6 **Nuts, seeds and dried protein fruits** – 'bagged' or popped into a small plastic container
7 **Tomatoes and cheese**
8 **Yoghurt and fresh/dried fruits**

Alkaline packed lunch suggestions

Remember: if eating any starch-based foods with your alkaline packed lunch, do not eat any acid fruits or acid salad dressings!

1 **Artichoke bottoms** – serve with dressings of choice
2 **Avocado half** – serve with sproutings, A or N salad and dressing of choice
3 **Celery sticks/stalkes** – stuff with A or N sandwich spreads/toppings, dips, pâtés and spreads
4 **Fruits** – fresh/dried S *or* P fruits, do *not* mix S and P fruits!
5 **Palm hearts** – top with cream cheese, beaten until smooth and mixed with dried/freshly chopped herbs
6 **Papaya half** – serve with sproutings or A or N salad
7 **Tomatoes and fresh basil leaves**

Sandwich fillings/toppings

Sandwich fillings/toppings are not only excellent on breads, etc, but also delicious used as jacket potato and vegetable toppings, or pitta bread and pancake/crêpe fillings. They assist, too, in increasing the daily alkaline ratio of foods eaten. I have listed some of my favourites below, but I am sure you can think of many more! See also Dips, pâtés and spreads (pages 116-121 for further suggestions.

A dressing of your choice (see Dressings pages 132-138) can be added to the filling/topping suggestions – but ensure always that the ingredients are compatible.

Sandwich fillings/toppings suggestions

1 Avocado and sprouted alfalfa   N
2 Avocado and chopped watercress   N
3 Banana and carob spread   S
4 Bean sprouts and yeast extract   N
5 Beetroot/beet (raw) and carrot – grated   N
6 Carrot – grated – with desiccated/shredded
   coconut and raisins   N
7 Carrot – cooked and mashed – with toasted pine
   kernels and ground coriander and cumin   N
8 Celery – thinly sliced – with chopped walnuts/
   English walnuts   S or P
9 Cottage/pot cheese with toasted chopped walnuts/
   English walnuts and parsley   P
10 Cucumber and toasted flaked/slivered almonds   N
11 Cream cheese (*not* soya 'cream cheese') with miso
   and chives   N
12 Egg yolks – cooked and mashed – with cream
   cheese and Garlic   N
13 Fennel and carrot – grated   N
14 Mint and cucumber   N
15 Mushroom slices (raw) with red pepper and
   crushed fennel seeds   N
16 Nori flakes (toasted) with cheese   P
17 Papaya – mashed – with tomato slices   S
18 Peanut butter and miso with finely chopped onion   S
19 Pears – sweet and mashed – with toasted chopped
   hazelnuts   S
20 Pulses – cooked and mashed – with crispy
   lettuce/salad   S
21 Spinach leaves – shredded – with yeast extract   N
22 Tahini, miso, grated carrot and chopped
   chives/spring onion   N
23 Tomato with onion, chopped olives and basil   N

Starters/appetizers

Starters/appetizers play an important part in the meal as a whole. Their responsibility is to set the scene for what is to follow. As such they make or break a meal – the effects of a too large/too strongly flavoured/too rich starter will be felt right through to the pudding. This part of the meal should therefore be selected with care. Starters/appetizers include soups, dips, patés, spreads and salads. Some of the vegetable dishes can be converted into delicious beginnings to a meal, as can small portions of pasta shapes/spaghetti with a suitable sauce – you should also be able to glean some ideas from the breakfast, brunch and buffet sections.

Dr Hay would have advised a light salad or fruit starter/appetizer, but provided care is exercised in balancing the dishes throughout the meal, some indulgence can be permitted!

Cheese 'fries'

A very 'moreish' way to eat cheese – I vary the ground nuts used, or use a mixture, to achieve different flavoured 'nutty' coatings.

Imp/Metric	Serves 2	American
2 large	eggs – beaten	2 extra large
	(to convert to V, use 1½ tbsps soya/soy flour mixed with 2 tbsps water),	
	salt and freshly ground black pepper	
6oz/175g	Cheddar/New York Cheddar cheese/ soya/soy cheese – cut into 1in/2½cm cubes	6oz
4oz/100g	ground nuts of choice	1 cup
2-3 tbsps	olive or sunflower oil	2-3 tbsps

1 Season the beaten egg/soya/soy mix, then coat the cheese cubes.
2 Roll in the ground nuts until well covered.
3 Heat the oil until very hot, then carefully add the cheese cubes one at a time, until there are 5-6 in the pan.
4 Fry until crisp and lightly golden, then gently turn over and repeat – be careful not to fry them too long or they may suddenly melt and go flat!
5 Drain on a piece of kitchen paper before serving.

Cannot be Frozen

Serving Suggestion
Vary the cheese used according to taste. If using soft cheeses, such as a Brie or Camembert, ensure that they are thoroughly coated – in fact you can coat them twice for 'double insulation' to prevent them from melting away. Vary the nut coatings, or use ground seeds/soya/soy flour. A little shoyu/tamari added to the beaten egg/soya/soy mix is delicious too – or add finely chopped fresh/dried herbs. Use sesame oil for frying, for a rather special flavour. Although normally served hot, I actually also enjoy these served cold. Served hot they make a delicious starter/appetizer, light lunch/evening meal dish, or quick main course, with a salad accompaniment. Served cold they are ideal for packed lunches and picnics.

P

Coriander/cilantro and avocado bites

The sharpness of fresh coriander/cilantro combined with the subtle flavour of avocado and almonds produces a delightful flavour.

Imp/Metric	Serves 4 as a starter/appetizer/ 2 as a main course	American
10oz/275g	very firm tofu	1¼ cups
1	avocado	1
2 tbsps	lemon juice	2 tbsps
2 tbsps	finely chopped fresh coriander/cilantro	2 tbsps
3oz/75g	ground almonds	¾ cup
	salt and freshly ground black pepper	
	Coating	
2oz/50g	flaked/slivered almonds	½ cup
	– toast then chop into small pieces	

1 Place the tofu in a food processor or liquidizer/blender, and blend until smooth.
2 Add the avocado, lemon juice and coriander/cilantro, and blend until well combined.
3 Stir in the ground almonds and seasoning.
4 Use an ice-cream scoop or spoon to shape into 8 × 2oz/50g balls, and coat in the toasted almonds – this mixture will be very soft, so handle with care!
5 Place in the refrigerator to chill until firm.

Cannot be Frozen

Serving Suggestion
Serve as a starter/appetizer with salad garnish and Starch-free crackers. As a main course serve with salad or a stir-fry of vegetables. Also excellent served as a light lunch/evening meal.

S or P or A

Cheesy hazelnut croûtons

This simple dish is unfailingly popular whenever I serve it, and makes a useful standby for light lunches/evening meals.

Imp/Metric	Serves 8 as a starter/appetizer/ 4-6 as a lunch/supper dish	American
5oz/150g	cream cheese	⅔ cup
	(to convert to V, use 5oz/150g/⅔ cup soya/soy 'cream' cheese*)	
1½ tbsps	finely chopped fresh thyme	1½ tbsps
2	garlic cloves – crushed/minced	2
4oz/100g	hazelnuts – toast – remove the skins, then grind	¾ cup
6	thick slices whole wheat bread	6
	(to convert to P/A, use 24 nut/seed-based crackers of your choice)	
2-4	garlic cloves – whole	2-4
	extra freshly chopped/dried thyme	

1 Mix the cream cheese/soya/soy cheese with the thyme, the crushed/minced garlic, and half the toasted, ground hazelnuts.
2 Toast the bread (if using) – do not place the slices on top of each other until cold, as any warmth will produce steam and make them go soft – remove the crusts.
3 Rub both sides of the toast/crackers with the garlic cloves, then spread the cheese mix on top.
4 Sprinkle with the remaining ground hazelnuts and some extra fresh/dried thyme, and cut each slice of bread into 4 triangles.
5 Bake uncovered under a hot grill/broiler or in a hot oven – 375°F/190°C (Gas 5) – for 3-4 minutes until the cheese is heated through.

Cannot be Frozen

---

* using the vegan alternative of soya 'cream' cheese for this recipe means that the dish becomes protein only.

Serving Suggestion
Serve as a starter/appetizer with a salad garnish or as a light
lunch/evening meal dish with salad. Can also be served cold.
Vary the shape of these croûtons by cutting circles out of the
toast – you will need 8 slices of bread when presenting in this
way.

Egg and spinach 'nests'

Imp/Metric	Serves 4 as a starter/appetizer/ light lunch/evening meal	American
1¼lb/550g	frozen chopped spinach	2½ cups
2 tsps	nutmeg	2 tsps
½ tsp	vegetable stock paste/low-salt yeast extract	½ tsp
	salt and freshly ground black pepper	
	olive or sunflower oil for frying	
4	eggs	4

1 Cook the spinach according to the instructions on the
  packet.
2 Stir in the nutmeg and vegetable stock paste/low-salt yeast
  extract, season and put to one side.
3 Heat the oil and fry the eggs.
4 Reheat the spinach, divide between 4 small plates or dishes,
  forming a 'nest' in each – then fill each 'nest' with an egg!

Cannot be Frozen

Serving Suggestion
As a starter/appetizer serve with a salad garnish, or with a bowl
of salad as a light lunch/evening meal. This dish can also be
baked – to do this prepare to Stage 2 above, divide the spinach
between 4 ovenproof plates/dishes forming a 'nest' in each, then
carefully break an egg into each nest – try not to let the egg
spill out over the top. Cover and place in a pre-heated oven at
375°F/190°C (Gas 5) and bake for 20-25 minutes, or until the
egg is set – alternatively, poach the eggs. Also delicious topped
with a little grated/shredded cheese.

Egg 'asparagaise'

An alternative, delicious version of egg mayonnaise.

**Imp/Metric   Serves 4 as a starter/appetizer/   American
                 light lunch/evening meal**
            1 × quantity of Asparagus dip (page 116)
4   eggs – hard-boil/hard-cook and shell   4
                        Garnish
                 asparagus tips and paprika

1 Halve each egg, and place these, yolk side down, on 4 small
   plates.
2 Top with the asparagus dip mixture, then garnish with the
   reserved asparagus tips and a sprinkling of paprika.

Cannot be Frozen
But the dip can be frozen, and the dish made up as described
on thawing.

Serving Suggestion
As a starter/appetizer serve with a salad garnish; as a light
lunch/evening meal serve with a bowl of salad and Starch-free
crackers.

(S) or **P** or **A**	

Orange and sesame mushrooms

The lovely orange flavour with these mushrooms makes this dish a perfect light starter, or refreshing salad/side-vegetable.

Imp/Metric	Serves 4 as a starter/appetizer/ salad/side-vegetable	American
2 tbsps	sesame or olive oil	2 tbsps
1lb/450g	small button mushrooms	8 cups
3 tsps	ground coriander	3 tsps
2	fresh bay leaves	2
2	garlic cloves – crushed/minced	2
2 tbsps	fresh or unsweetened orange juice (to convert to S, omit)	2 tbsps
1 tsp	finely grated orange rind	1 tsp
1oz/25g	sesame seeds – toasted	4 tbsps
	salt and freshly ground black pepper	
3 tbsps	finely chopped fresh parsley	3 tbsps
	Garnish	
	orange twists	

1 Heat the oil and cook the mushrooms with the coriander, bay leaves and garlic for 4-5 minutes until tender, but not too soft, stirring all the time.
2 Tip them into a bowl, remove the bay leaves, then mix in the orange juice (if using), orange rind and sesame seeds and combine.
3 Season and leave to cool.
4 Refrigerate for 2-3 hours to allow the flavours to mingle.
5 Remove from the refrigerator 30 minutes before serving and mix in the parsley, then garnish with the orange twists.

Cannot be Frozen

Serving Suggestion
Serve on a bed of lettuce/parsley sprigs (flat-leafed Continental parsley is especially good for this) in glass dishes or on individual plates, and garnish with the twists of orange. It also makes a delicious pitta bread filling, and is ideal as a light lunch/evening meal dish with bread, crispbreads, oatcakes or Starch-free crackers, depending on the meal structure.

P

Pineapple stuffed avocado

A delicious combination of flavours – rather a special way to serve avocado.

Imp/Metric	Serves 4 as a starter/appetizer/ 2 as a main course	American
1 tbsp	olive or sunflower oil	1 tbsp
4oz/100g	onions – finely chop	⅔ cup
1	bouillon stock cube	1
½ tsp	turmeric	½ tsp
½ tsp	paprika	½ tsp
1½ tbsps	tomato purée/paste	1½ tbsps
4oz/100g	button mushrooms – thinly slice	2 cups
8oz/225g	fresh pineapple – cut into cubes	2 cups
1½ tbsps	lemon juice	1½ tbsps
2	avocados – halve, scoop out the flesh, saving the skins, and roughly chop	2
2oz/50g	pumpkin seeds – toasted	½ cup
	salt and freshly ground black pepper	

1 Set the oven to 375°F/190°C (Gas 5).
2 Heat the oil and fry the onion until soft.
3 Mix in the bouillon stock cube, then stir in the spices and tomato purée/paste.
4 Add the mushrooms, and cook for 1-2 minutes, then add the pineapple and cook a further minute.
5 Stir in the lemon juice and avocado to form a moist, soft mixture.
6 Add the seeds, combine and season, then pile into the reserved skins.
7 Place on a lightly greased ovenproof dish and bake covered for 30 minutes.

Cannot be Frozen

Serving Suggestion
Serve as a starter/appetizer with starch-free crackers, or as a main course with green beans/fine green beans and a large mixed salad.

N Ⓥ

Tricolour vegetable terrine

A quite spectacular terrine with its vivid, contrasting colours – a perfect dinner party/buffet dish.

Imp/Metric	Serves 8-10 as a starter/appetizer/ 6 as a main course	American
2 tbsps	olive or sunflower oil	2 tbsps
10oz/275g	carrots – cut into small pieces	1⅔ cups
1 tsp	each of ground cumin and coriander salt and freshly ground black pepper	1 tsp
4oz/100g	fennel – cut into small pieces	⅔ cup
4oz/100g	leeks – thinly slice	1 cup
2	fresh bay leaves	2
8oz/225g	frozen peas	1⅓ cups
2 tsps	finely chopped fresh mint	2 tsps
9 fl oz/250ml	water	1¼ cups
1½ tsps	agar agar powder	1½ tsps

1 Grease a 1lb/450g/4 cup loaf tin/pan and line the base with a strip of greased baking parchment, long enough to overhang at both ends.

2 Heat 1 tbsp of the oil in a saucepan and cook the carrots, cumin and coriander covered for ten minutes, or until tender, stirring occasionally; place the mixture in a food processor or liquidizer/blender, blend until very smooth, season and put to one side.

3 Heat the other tbsp oil in another saucepan and cook the fennel, leeks and bay leaves covered for 10 minutes, or until tender, stirring occasionally; remove the bay leaves, then place the mixture in a food processor or liquidizer/blender and blend until very smooth, season and put to one side.

4 Place the peas and mint in a saucepan without water, bring up to boiling point and cook covered for 5 minutes or until tender; place the mixture in a food processor or liquidizer/blender and blend until very smooth, season and put to one side.

5 Add 3 fl oz/75ml/⅓ cup of the water to the carrot purée, bring to the boil, stir in ½ tsp of the agar agar powder, mix well and boil for 1 minute.

6 Pour the purée into the prepared tin/pan and smooth.

7 Repeat steps 5 and 6 with the leek and fennel purée and finally the pea purée, then leave to cool.

8 Place in a refrigerator to set completely for at least 6 hours before serving.

Cannot be Frozen

Not suitable for freezing whole, but the three layers can be prepared in advance up to the water and agar agar stage, frozen separately, then the water and agar agar added and the terrine made as described once thawed.

Serving Suggestion

Garnish with carrot slices and fresh mint leaves and serve as a starter/appetizer with salad. As a main course serve:

as a starch meal – with a grain/pulse/legume-based salad or buttered new potatoes and green salad.

as a protein/alkaline meal – with steamed vegetables and salad.

Soups, Dips, Pâtés and Spreads

Soups

There is often nothing more pleasant than coming home to a bowl of delicious soup accompanied by fresh crispy bread, or Starch-free crackers, and a crisp salad. As such, soup is one of the most versatile of dishes; it can be served as a starter/appetizer, light lunch/evening meal or main course; it is also ideal for packed lunches or picnics taken along in vacuum flasks. Soup does not have to be hot to be soup – chilled soups, are delicious, and a refreshing change during the summer months.

I recommend, too, that you look at the Sauces section – when watered-down with diluted milk, water or stock, these become delectable soups!

| P or A | | (V) |

Apricot and apple soup

One of my favourite soups – light, refreshing and delicious hot or chilled – and very simple to make! An excellent dinner party starter/ appetizer.

Imp/Metric	Serves 4-6	American
2 tbsps	olive or sunflower oil	2 tbsps
6oz/175g	onion – finely chop	1 cup
6oz/175g	celery – cut into strips, then thinly slice	1½ cups
½	bouillon stock cube	½
6oz/175g	dried apricots – quarter	1⅓ cups
8oz/225g	cooking/tart apple – peel and roughly chop	1⅓ cups
1oz/25g	ground almonds	¼ cup
2½pts/1.4l	boiling water	6¼ cups
	salt and freshly ground black pepper	
	Garnish	
	toasted flaked/slivered almonds	

1 Heat the oil, and cook the onion and celery for 10 minutes covered, stirring occasionally.
2 Mix in the ½ bouillon stock cube.
3 Add the apricots and apple, and cook covered for a further 3 minutes.
4 Stir in the ground almonds, then remove the pan from the heat and add the water.
5 Season, bring to the boil, then simmer covered for 30 minutes.
6 Place the mixture in a food processor or liquidizer/blender, and blend until smooth.
7 Serve sprinkled with toasted flaked/slivered almonds.

Serving Suggestion
Serve sprinkled with toasted flaked/slivered almonds.

Ⓥ

Carrot and pea soup

A delicious sweet soup.

Imp/Metric	Serves 6	American
2 tbsps	olive or sunflower oil	2 tbsps
6oz/175g	onions – chop very finely	1 cup
1	clove garlic – crushed/minced	1
1	bouillon stock cube	1
1lb/450g	carrots – cut into small dice	2⅔ cups
1 tbsp	finely chopped fresh mint	1 tbsp
2 tsps	finely chopped fresh thyme	2 tsps
2oz/50g	ground almonds	½ cup
2pts/1l	boiling water	5 cups
	salt and freshly ground black pepper	
1lb/450g	frozen peas	2⅔ cups

1 Heat the oil, and fry the onion until soft.
2 Add the garlic, cook a further minute then mix in the stock cube.
3 Stir in the carrots and herbs, then cover and cook a further 5 minutes.
4 Add the ground almonds, remove the pan from the heat, and slowly stir in the water.
5 Return the pan to the heat, season and bring to the boil.
6 Add the peas, cover, bring back to the boil, and simmer for 3 minutes.

Serving Suggestion
Serve as prepared or place in a food processor or liquidizer/blender, and blend until smooth, adding a little extra water or stock to achieve the desired consistency – an excellent way of making children eat their peas and carrots without realizing it!

Parsley and tarragon soup

Parsley and tarragon combine beautifully in this lovely fresh, green soup.

Imp/Metric	Serves 4-6	American
2 tbsps	olive or sunflower oil	2 tbsps
8oz/225g	onion – chop very finely	1⅓ cups
8oz/225g	celery – cut into strips, then slice very thinly	2 cups
2	cloves garlic – crushed/minced	2
4	fresh bay leaves	4
1	bouillon stock cube	1
4oz/100g	finely chopped fresh parsley	4 cups
2 tbsps	finely chopped fresh tarragon	2 tbsps
2pts/1l 140ml	boiling water	5 cups
	salt and freshly ground black pepper	

1 Heat the oil, and cook the onion, celery and garlic covered along with the bay leaves for 15 minutes, stirring occasionally.
2 Mix in the bouillon stock cube, then add the parsley and tarragon, and combine.
3 Add the water, bring back to the boil, and simmer for 15 minutes, then season.

Serving Suggestion
Serve as prepared, or place in a food processor or liquidizer/blender, and blend until smooth. As a starter/appetizer serve with bread, crispbreads, oatcakes or Starch-free crackers, depending on the meal structure; likewise as a light lunch/evening meal, but with the addition of salad.

Vegetable soup

Packed full of flavour, this soup makes a tasty starter/appetizer or is substantial enough for a main course.

Imp/Metric	Serves 6	American
2 tbsps	olive or sunflower oil	2 tbsps
6oz/175g	leeks – thinly slice	1½ cups
6oz/175g	carrot – cut into small dice	1 cup
6oz/175g	celery – cut into strips, then thinly slice	1½ cups
6oz/175g	red pepper – cut as for carrots	1 cup
6oz/175g	courgette/zucchini – cut as for carrots	1½ cups
6oz/175g	button mushrooms – roughly chop	2¼ cups
2 tsps	low-salt yeast extract	2 tsps
1 tbsp	tamari	1 tbsp
3 tsps	finely chopped fresh thyme	3 tsps
3 tsps	finely chopped fresh marjoram	3 tsps
1 tbsp	light tahini	1 tbsp
2pts/1l 140ml	boiling water	5 cups
	salt and freshly ground black pepper	

1 Heat the oil, and cook the leeks, carrot and celery together covered for 5 minutes.
2 Add the pepper and courgettes/zucchini, cover and cook a further 10 minutes.
3 Finally add the mushrooms, cook another minute, then mix in the yeast extract, tamari and herbs.
4 Stir in the tahini, remove the pan from the heat, and slowly add the boiling water, stirring continuously.
5 Return the pan to the heat, bring back to the boil, simmer for 5 minutes, then simmer.

Serving Suggestion
Serve this soup as prepared or place in a food processor or liquidizer/blender and blend until smooth, adding a little extra water or stock to the achieve the desired consistency. As a starter/appetizer serve with bread, crispbread, oatcakes or Starch-free crackers, depending on the meal-structure; likewise as a light lunch/evening meal, but with the addition of salad.

Dips, pâtés and spreads

These, along with the sandwich fillings/toppings, can be used in a variety of ways other than as toast toppers or crudité accompaniments. They make ideal pancake/crêpe and pitta bread stuffings, and give jacket potatoes and vegetables a 'lift' when served as a topping.

Some of the nut/vegetable loaf recipes are moist enough to be served as a pâté.

S or P or (A)

Asparagus dip

This luxurious dip is very quick and easy to prepare, and always impresses my guests! It makes a rather special addition to any meal, and is ideal as a dinner party starter appetizer.

Imp/Metric	Serves 4 as a starter/appetizer/ 8 as a dip	American
2	12oz/350g tins/cans green asparagus spears – drain, saving the juice	2
4oz/100g	(S or P) use ground cashews – (to adapt to A) use ground almonds	1 cup
½	garlic clove – crushed/minced	½
¼ tsp	paprika	¼ tsp
	salt and freshly ground black pepper	

1 Cut 20×2½in/6cm lengths of asparagus tips off the asparagus spears, and put to one side.
2 Place the remaining asparagus in a food processor or liquidizer/blender, and blend along with the cashews/almonds, garlic and paprika until very smooth, adding 1-2 tbsps of the juice, if required, to achieve the desired consistency.
3 Season, then chill for 3-4 hours to allow the flavours to mingle.

Serving Suggestion
Place the dip in a bowl or individual ramekins and garnish with the asparagus tips, finely chopping some and arranging them on the surface, along with a sprinkling of paprika. Serve with crudités and/or toast, crispbreads, oatcakes or Starch-free crackers, depending on the meal-structure. It also makes an excellent sandwich/savoury pancake/crêpe filling, and as a topping puts vegetables and jacket potatoes in a class of their own! Will keep 4-5 days in a refrigerator.

S or A

Banana, miso and tahini spread

A lovely creamy mixture, and a favourite with children!

Imp/Metric	Serves 4	American
1	banana	1
1½ tbsps	light tahini	1½ tbsps
1 tsp	barley or rice miso	1 tsp

1 Mash the banana and combine thoroughly with the tahini and miso.

Cannot be Frozen

Serving Suggestion
Delicious on breads, crispbreads, oatcakes or Starch-free crackers (not cheese-based).

S or A ⓥ

Chestnut and olive pâté

The round, sweet flavour of chestnuts and the savoury sharpness of olives result in a delectable pâté – enjoyed even by those who do not normally like chestnuts or olives!

Imp/Metric	Serves 4 as a starter/appetizer/ 8 as a dip	American
8oz/225g	dried chestnuts – soak and cook, saving the cooking liquid – or 1 × 15oz/425g tin/can unsweetened chestnut purée	1½ cups
4oz/100g	black olives – stoned/pitted	1 cup
1½ tbsps	finely chopped fresh thyme	1½ tbsps
	freshly ground black pepper	
	Garnish	
	black olives and fresh/dried thyme	

1 Place all the ingredients in a food processor or liquidizer/blender, and blend until smooth – extra cooking juice may need to be added to achieve this if using the cooked dried chestnuts.

Can be Frozen
It will be slightly more moist on thawing, so do not add too much extra liquid during the processing stages if using the cooked dried chestnuts.

Serving Suggestion
Sprinkle the pâté with chopped thyme, and garnish with sprigs of thyme and extra olives. Serve with a salad garnish and crudités, toast, crispbreads, oatcakes or Starch-free crackers, depending on the meal structure. Scoop into balls using an ice-cream scoop, or present in a bowl, individual ramekins or turned out onto a serving plate. It also makes an excellent sandwich, pancake/crêpe or vegetable filling/topping, and will keep 4-5 days in a refrigerator.

S

Ⓥ

Hummus

You can make this dish as garlicky as you like!

Imp/Metric	Serves 6-8 as a starter/ appetizer/12-16 as a dip	American
8oz/225g	chick peas/garbanzos – soak then cook until *very* soft (this makes it easier to produce a smooth, creamy dip), save the cooking liquid – or 2 × 14oz/400g tins/cans chick peas/garbanzos – drain and save the tinned/canned stock	1 cup
3	garlic cloves – crushed/minced	3
3 tbsps	olive oil	3 tbsps
3 tbsps	light tahini	3 tbsps
¼ tsp	paprika	¼ tsp
3 tsps	finely grated lemon rind	3 tsps
8 fl oz/225ml	cooking liquid or tinned/canned stock	1⅓ cups
	salt and freshly ground black pepper	

1 Place the chick peas/garbanzos, garlic, oil, tahini and paprika in a food processor or liquidizer/blender.
2 Blend until thoroughly combined, add the lemon rind and cooking liquid and blend again to produce a very smooth, creamy consistency.
3 Season.

Can be Frozen
It is best used within 2 months as the garlic flavour will intensify with freezing.

Serving Suggestion
Present the hummus in a bowl or individual ramekins, sprinkle with paprika and/or parsley. Serve with crudités and/or warmed pitta bread and a salad garnish.

For a light lunch/evening meal serve with bread/pitta bread and salad, or use as a vegetable/jacket potato topping. It also makes an ideal sandwich filling. Will keep 4-5 days in a refrigerator.

| S or A | |

Papaya and avocado dip

The delicate flavour of papaya combined with the creamy richness of avocado makes a delicious dip.

Imp/Metric	Serves 4	American
1	papaya – 1lb/450g in weight	1
1	avocado – 8oz/225g in weight	1
	Optional	
	salt and freshly ground black pepper	

1 Place the papaya and avocado flesh in a food processor or liquidizer/blender, and blend until smooth.
2 Lightly season if desired – although I find this dip does not usually need seasoning.

Cannot be Frozen

Serving Suggestion
This is a 'thin' dip, so serve in a glass dish, and eat with crudités or toasted cubes of bread, depending on the meal structure.

| S | |

Savoury lentil and basil pâté

This pâté is unfailingly popular whenever I serve it.

Imp/Metric	Serves 4 as a starter/appetizer/ 8 as a dip	American
4oz/100g	brown lentils/split peas	½ cup
1 tbsp	olive or sunflower oil	1 tbsp
4oz/100g	onion – finely chop	⅔ cup
1	clove garlic – crushed/minced	1
½	vegetable bouillon stock cube	½
2 tsps	finely chopped fresh basil	2 tsps
1 tsp	rice or barley miso	1 tsp
	salt and freshly ground black pepper	

1 *Cover the lentils/split peas and leave to soak overnight – or 8-12 hours.

2 Discard the soaking liquid and place in a saucepan with 10 fl oz/275ml/1⅓ cups cold water.

3 Cover, bring to the boil and leave to simmer for approximately 30-45 minutes until soft and 'mushy' and all the water has evaporated – add more water during the simmering stage if necessary.

4 Stir towards the end of cooking time to help break the lentils/split peas down then put to one side.

5 Heat the oil, and fry the onion until soft.

6 Add the garlic, then blend in the ½ stock cube, combine and cook a further minute.

7 Add the basil and miso, mix thoroughly, remove from the heat and season.

8 Blend the cooked lentils/split peas and onion mix until smooth.

9 Leave to cool, then chill.

Serving Suggestion

Sprinkle the pâté with extra freshly chopped basil, garnish with basil leaves and serve with crudités, toast or oatcakes. It can be presented in a bowl, individual ramekins or turned out onto a serving plate. It also makes an excellent sandwich/savoury pancake/crêpe filling and vegetable and jacket potato topping. Will keep 4-5 days in a refrigerator.

---

* It is not essential to soak the lentils/split peas, but it will quicken the cooking time and make them more digestible. If, however, you do not have time to soak them then follow the above cooking instructions but simmer for approximately 1-1½ hours.

Salads and Dressings

I feel a meal is never quite complete without salad, and I always look forward to the fresh flavours and crisp textures alongside the other dishes – soup, sandwiches, vegetable bakes, nut loaves, etc. Salads can also be served as alternative starters/appetizers, or are delicious light lunches/evening meals when presented with breads and Starch-free crackers, etc. They can also be stuffed into pitta breads for a more substantial meal. Many vegetable side-dishes can be used as salads – either as warm or cold vegetable salads, lightly tossed in vinaigrette, or dressing of your choice.

Salads are so often regarded as labour intensive – all that peeling, chopping and grating/shredding! Personally I find all these actions have a wonderfully calming effect after a 'hard day at the office'! Their often vivid colours, and amazing array of textures and flavours, offer the opportunity for creativity. Salads form such an important part of the Hay System, and for this reason I feel that to view them as a form of 'art' will not only make their preparation more pleasurable, but their eating too – so enjoy your chopping and shredding and create some delicious bowls of food full of vitality and goodness!

Do experiment with making up your own salads. Remember that you can throw almost anything in – it need not just be raw salad and vegetable foods – use fruits, fresh or dried, nuts/seeds, cooked grains, diced/grated cheese, sliced/chopped/grated egg, etc.

See also the Extra salad suggestions on page 131 and the recipes that follow.

A dressing of your choice (see Dressings: pages 132-138) can be added to the salad suggestions – but once again ensure that the ingredients are compatible.

Salad suggestions and recipes are not suitable for freezing.

S   (V)

Walnut, raisin and banana couscous

An unusual and delicious combination of flavours – this salad makes an interesting side-dish, or is substantial enough for a meal on its own.

Imp/Metric	Serves 6 as a side-salad/ 4 as a main course	American
6oz/175g	couscous	1 cup
3oz/75g	raisins – preferably lexia raisins	½ cup
10 fl oz/275ml	boiling water	1⅓ cups
1½ tbsps	sunflower oil	1½ tbsps
3fl oz/75ml	cold water	⅓ cup
1 tsp	finely grated orange rind	1 tsp
1 tsp	finely grated lemon rind	1 tsp
1-2	bananas	1-2
3oz/75g	walnuts/English walnuts – roughly chop	⅔ cup

1 Place the couscous and raisins in a bowl, add the boiling water and leave to one side until all the water is absorbed.
2 Combine the sunflower oil, cold water and orange and lemon rind.
3 Pour over the couscous and raisin mix, combine thoroughly and leave to stand until cool and no liquid remains.
4 Chill in a refrigerator to allow the flavours to mingle.
5 Just before serving mix in the banana, cut into slices, and the chopped walnuts/English walnuts.

Serving Suggestion
Ideal as an accompaniment to main course vegetable dishes, or with light starch-based dishes. Alternatively serve as a light lunch/evening meal with steamed vegetables – courgettes/zucchini are particularly good. It also makes an unusual vegetable stuffing mixture.

S or (P)   (V)

Carrot, walnut/English walnut, pepper and corn salad with a creamy walnut and coconut dressing

The lovely 'sunshine' colours of this salad brighten any meal – and the delicious dressing will be hard to resist!

Imp/Metric	Serves 6 as a starter/appetizer/ salad/4 as a light lunch/evening meal	American
8oz/225g	iceberg lettuce – shred finely	4 cups
8oz/225g	carrot – grate/shred finely	1⅓ cups
24	(S) baby corn – cook (P, use orange segments)	24
3oz/75g	yellow pepper – cut into 24 strips select a 'long' pepper as opposed to a 'fat' one	3oz
2oz/50g	walnuts/English walnuts – finely chop	½ cup

Garnish
chopped parsley/walnut halves
Dressing
1 × quantity Creamy walnut and coconut dressing (page 133)

1 Spread the lettuce over a large serving plate, or divide between four side plates.
2 Arrange the carrot in the middle, then place the baby corn/orange segments and pepper in a 'flower' shape all round.
3 Sprinkle the chopped walnuts/English walnuts over the corn/orange segments and pepper, spoon the dressing over the carrot centre, or serve it separately, and garnish with the parsley/walnut/English walnut halves.

Serving Suggestion
Serve with bread, crispbreads, oatcakes or Starch-free crackers, depending on meal structure.

Ⓥ

S or P or (A)

Cashew and pistachio green salad

A fresh, crisp rather special version of a green salad.

Imp/Metric	Serves 4-6 as a starter/appetizer/ side-salad/4 as a light lunch/supper	American
4oz/100g	cucumber – thinly slice	1 cup
3oz/75g	green pepper – *very* finely dice	½ cup
2oz/50g	celery – cut into thin sticks	½ cup
3oz/75g	white cabbage – *very* finely chop or shred	¾ cup
½oz/15g	pistachio kernels – finely chop (to convert to A, use almonds)	1½ tbsps
½oz/15g	cashews – finely chop (to convert to A, use hazelnuts)	1½ tbsps
1½ tbsps	finely chopped chives	1½ tbsps

Garnish
8 slices of green apple
Dressing
1 × quantity Apple vinaigrette (page 136)

1 Arrange the cucumber slices around the edge of a dinner plate, or similar.
2 Arrange a ring of diced pepper within this circle, then place the celery sticks in a petal shape from the edge of this pepper ring, out towards the edge of the plate.
3 Fill the centre of the plate with the cabbage, then arrange the chopped pistachios/almonds and cashews/hazelnuts, one teaspoon at a time, alternately around the base of the cabbage to form a ring.
4 Sprinkle the chopped chives over the cabbage in the shape of a cross, then press two apple wedges, skin edge uppermost, into the cabbage between each 'arm' of this cross – pour the dressing on top, or serve separately.

Serving Suggestion
Serve with bread, crispbreads, oatcakes or Starch-free crackers, depending on the meal structure. This salad can also be prepared on four individual side plates following the above method.

S ⬛   Ⓥ

Corn, kidney bean and cucumber salad tossed in orange rind and herbs

A fresh tangy salad – bursting with colour and flavour.

Imp/Metric	Serves 8 as a side-salad/ 4 as a main course	American
6oz/175g	bulgar wheat	1 cup
6oz/175g	raisins – lexia raisins if available	1 cup
10 fl oz/275ml	boiling water	1⅓ cup
1 fl oz/25ml	sunflower oil	1 tbsp
3 fl oz/75ml	cold water	⅓ cup
2 tsps	finely grated orange rind	2 tsps
1½ tbsps	finely chopped fresh parsley	1½ tbsps
1½ tbsps	finely chopped fresh mint	1½ tbsps
1½ tbsps	finely chopped chives	1½ tbsps
7oz/200g	sweetcorn kernels	1¼ cups
4oz/100g	kidney beans – soak then cook – or 1 × 14oz/400g tin/can kidney beans – drained	⅔ cup
4oz/100g	cucumber – cut into 25 matchstick salt and freshly ground black pepper	1 cup

1 Place the bulgar wheat and raisins in a large bowl, add the boiling water and leave to one side until all the water is absorbed.
2 Combine the sunflower oil, cold water and orange rind, then stir in the parsley, mint and chives.
3 Pour over the bulgar and raisin mix, combine thoroughly using a fork to prevent the grains sticking together, and leave to stand until no liquid remains.
4 Finally fork in the sweetcorn, kidney beans and cucumber.
5 Season, then chill for 3-4 hours before serving to allow all the flavours to mingle.

Serving Suggestion
This salad makes a refreshing accompaniment to main course vegetable dishes, nut loaves, burgers, bakes, pies, etc. It also provides a substantial meal served with lightly steamed vegetables, or used as a pancake/crêpe, vegetable, pitta bread or jacket potato filling/topping.

ⓥ

Fennel coleslaw

One of my favourite salads.

Imp/Metric	Serves 4 as a salad/4-6 as a starter/appetizer	American
6oz/175g	finely grated/shredded fennel	1 cup
6oz/175g	finely grated/shredded carrot	1 cup
6oz/175g	finely grated/shredded white cabbage	1½ cups
2 tsps	fennel seeds – chop finely, or crush in a pestle and mortar	2 tsps
3 tbsps	mayonnaise	3 tbsps
	salt and freshly ground black pepper	

1 Mix the fennel, carrot and cabbage together in a bowl.
2 Combine the fennel seeds and mayonnaise, mix in with the other ingredients and lightly season.
3 Chill for 3-4 hours to allow the flavours to mingle.

Serving Suggestion
Especially good with cheese-based dishes, or strongly flavoured/rich main courses. Also a lovely fresh way to start a meal.

S   Ⓥ

Herb pasta with mint and garlic croûtons

A delicious garlicky salad – packed full of different flavours.

Imp/Metric	Serves 8 as a side-salad/ 4 as a main course	American
8oz/225g	whole wheat or corn pasta shapes or a mixture of the two	4 cups
2 tbsps	olive oil	2 tbsps
1 tsp	dried mint	1 tsp
2	slices whole wheat bread – toasted	2
2-3	garlic cloves – whole	2-3
4oz/100g	cucumber – cut into fine matchsticks	1 cup
2oz/50g	spring onions/scallions – finely chop	⅓ cup
	Optional	
24	black olives	24
	Dressing	
	1 × quantity Mint and parsley dressing (page 135)	
	salt and freshly ground black pepper	
	Garnish	
	lemon slices and mint leaves	

1 Cook the pasta according to the instructions on the packet.
2 Mix the olive oil with the dried mint and leave to stand for
   15-20 minutes.
3 Rub both sides of the slices of toast with the garlic cloves and
   remove the crusts, then brush both sides with the olive oil
   and mint mix, and cut into ½in/1¼cm cubes.
4 Combine the pasta, cucumber, spring onions/scallions,
   olives (if using) and diced toast in a serving bowl, add the
   dressing, mix thoroughly and season.
5 Chill for 3-4 hours before serving to allow all the flavours to
   mingle, then garnish with the lemon slices and mint leaves.

Serving Suggestion
Serve as a salad with light main course dishes. Alternatively
serve as a main course with or without the addition of a
pulse/legume or nuts/seeds of your choice.

P or A Ⓥ

Mushroom, avocado and orange salad

A lovely fresh-tasting salad – full of vitality.

Imp/Metric	Serves 4 as a light lunch/ evening meal/6 as a side-salad/ starter/appetizer	American
3 tbsps	orange juice – from the segmented oranges	3 tbsps
1½ tbsps	finely chopped fresh lemon balm – or 2 tsps lemon rind	1½ tbsps
	salt and freshly ground black pepper	
6oz/175g	button mushrooms – thinly slice	3 cups
2-3 tbsps	lemon juice	2-3 tbsps
1×10oz/225g	ripe avocados	1
12oz/350g	iceberg lettuce – finely shred	6 cups
3-4	large oranges – segmented – approximately 32 segments	3-4

Garnish

whole mushrooms, lemon balm leaves, and twists of orange and lemon

1 Mix together the orange juice, lemon balm/lemon rind, freshly ground black pepper and a pinch of salt in a bowl.
2 Add the mushrooms, toss in the marinade and leave to stand for at least 30 minutes.
3 Place the lemon juice in a shallow dish.
4 Halve the avocados, cut in thin slices lengthways, and coat in the lemon juice.
5 Spread the lettuce over a large serving plate, or divide between four side plates.
6 Arrange the mushrooms in the centre, and pour over any excess dressing.
7 Place a circle of avocado slices and orange segments, arranged alternatively, to form a 'flower' shape around the mushroom centre.
8 Garnish with whole mushrooms, lemon balm leaves and twists of lemon and orange.

Serving Suggestion
For a quicker version mix the ingredients together in a bowl;
in which case it is best to cut the avocado into large dice and
halve the orange segments, then toss together with the lettuce
and marinated mushrooms.

Tomato, cheese and olive salad with a basil dressing

*A very 'Mediterranean' salad, with an appealing array of colours
and flavours.*

Imp/Metric	Serves 4 as a side-salad/ 2 as a main course	American
12oz/350g	tomatoes – cut in thin slices	12oz
4-6oz/100-175g	Mozzarella or Cheddar/New York cheddar cheese – thinly slice (V – use 4-6oz/100-175g soya cheese or firm tofu)	4-6oz
2oz/50g	black olives	½ cup
	Garnish	
	fresh basil leaves	
	Dressing	
	1 × quantity of Basil, lemon and garlic dressing (page 132)	

1 Arrange the tomato and cheese slices alternately around the
  edge of a dinner plate, working inwards in circles.
2 Arrange the olives and basil on top.
3 Pour the dressing over the surface.

Serving Suggestion
For a quicker salad, cut the tomatoes into segments and dice
the cheese, then toss all the ingredients together, along with the
dressing, and serve in a bowl – substantial enough to be served
as a light lunch/evening meal with Starch-free crackers.

Extra salad suggestions

1 Apple – grated – with chopped celery and
   hazelnuts   P or A
2 Artichoke bottoms – chopped – with lemon
   rind and green pepper
3 Avocado, Tomato and toasted pine kernels   N
4 Bamboo shoots – chopped – with toasted
   peanuts and diced yellow pepper
5 Beetroot/beet and celeriac (raw) – grated   N
6 Beetroot/beet – cooked – with finely chopped
   spring onions/scallions   N
7 Broad/fava beans and diced potato with paprika   S
8 Cabbage (white and green) – grated/shredded
   – with chopped roasted cashews and tahini   S or P
9 Cabbage (white or red) – grated/shredded
   – with caraway seeds   N
10 Cheese – grated/shredded – with diced
   cucumber and chopped marjoram   P
11 Chinese leaves with toasted sunflower seeds   N
12 Courgette/Zucchini (raw) – grated/shredded
   – with sliced raw mushrooms and a sprinkling
   of tamari   N
13 Eggs (hard-boiled/hard-cooked) grated/shredded
   and served with cooked, mashed peas and
   chopped black olives   P
14 Green Beans/fine green beans – cooked –
   with finely chopped onion   N
15 Papaya, banana and pecan nuts on a bed
   of lettuce   S
16 Potato (baby new) diced with parsley and mint   S
17 Potato (sweet) diced with chestnut purée and
   toasted flaked/slivered almonds   S
18 Rice with peas, diced yellow pepper and
   fresh mint   S
19 Spinach – shredded – with grated/shredded
   celeriac   N
20 Sprouted pulses/legumes, grains, nuts/seeds
   with chopped dried dates and orange rind   S
21 Sweetcorn kernels with diced red and green
   pepper   S
22 Watercress and grated/shredded carrot   N

Dressings

These add zip to sandwich fillings/toppings, salads and vegetables. A simple lettuce salad will soon perk up if you simply toss it in lemon juice and olive oil. If you are a 'do not like salad' person on the Hay System I think the addition of some of the dressing suggestions and recipes might soon alter your view – and encourage you to eat salads more often and in greater quantity.

The variety of dressings is infinite – they can be creamy or thin, sweet or sharp, fruity or savoury; it is worthwhile experimenting with different flavouring agents, such as herbs and spices; and different bases such as mayonnaise, tofu, cream, cream cheese and yoghurt. The configurations really are endless – but I have given you a few suggestions to work on below.

Dressing suggestions and recipes are not suitable for freezing.

P or A

Basil, lemon and garlic dressing

A delicious tangy, garlicky dressing.

Imp/Metric	Serves 4	American
3 tbsps	olive oil	3 tbsps
1½ tbsps	finely chopped fresh basil	1½ tbsps
1 dsp	lemon juice	2 tsps
1	clove garlic – crushed/minced	1
pinch	paprika	pinch

1 Mix all the ingredients together, then refrigerate for one hour to allow the flavours to mingle.

Serving Suggestion
Delicious on grain, cheese and tomato-based salads or poured over vegetable dishes.

Ⓥ

S or **P**

Creamy walnut/English walnut and coconut dressing

An extremely 'moreish' dressing – rich and delectable!

Imp/Metric	Serves 4	American
1oz/25g	ground walnuts/English walnuts	¼ cup
1oz/25g	creamed coconut – roughly chop	½ cup
3 tbsps	walnut oil	3 tbsps
4 fl oz/100ml	water	½ cup
	freshly ground black pepper	

1 Place all the ingredients in a food processor or liquidizer/
   blender, and blend until smooth and creamy.
2 Put to one side in a cool place, but do not refrigerate as this
   will cause it to thicken and set.

Serving Suggestion
Very good on green and fruit-based salads, and with 'sharper'
tasting salad foods such as peppers, tomatoes, mooli, etc.

P or (A)

Mayonnaise

A rich, creamy mayonnaise.

Imp/Metric	Makes approximately 8 fl oz/225ml/1⅓ cups	American
2 large	egg yolks	2 extra large
2 tsps	cider or rice vinegar –	2 tsps
	(to convert to A, use 2 tsps lemon juice)	
	(making 4 with the 2 below)	
2 tsps	lemon juice	2 tsps
¼ tsp	mustard powder	¼ tsp
pinch	paprika	pinch
pinch	salt	pinch
8 fl oz/225ml	olive oil	1 cup

1 Place all the ingredients except the oil in a food processor
   or liquidizer/blender, and blend until combined.

2 With the machine on, add the oil *drop by drop* until approximately half the oil has been added and a thick, creamy mixture is developing. The remainder of the oil can then be added slightly more quickly in a *thin* stream.

3 If curdling occurs blend 1 tsp of very hot or very cold water into the mix; this should revert it back to smooth.

Serving Suggestion

Add freshly chopped herbs of your choice, curry powder, shoyu, etc, for 'alternative' mayonnaises. This mayonnaise will keep for 1-2 weeks in the refrigerator. A low-fat version may be prepared by adding an equal quantity of natural yoghurt to the mayonnaise.

P or A   Ⓥ

Egg-free mayonnaise

Although not a 'true' mayonnaise, this dressing makes a very good egg-free alternative.

Imp/Metric	Makes 6-8 fl oz/175-225ml/ ¾-1⅓ cups	American
1oz/25g	ground almonds	¼ cup
½ tsp	mustard powder	½ tsp
pinch	paprika	pinch
2 tbsps	lemon juice	2 tbsps
2 tbsps	milk	2 tbsps
pinch	salt	pinch
	freshly ground black pepper	
4-6 fl oz/100-175ml	olive oil	½-¾ cup

1 Place all the ingredients except the oil in a food processor or liquidizer/blender, and blend until well combined.

2 With the machine on, add the oil *drop by drop* until approximately half the oil has been added and a thick, creamy mixture is developing. The remainder of the oil can then be added slightly more quickly in a *thin* stream – the resulting mixture will not be as thick as an egg mayonnaise.

Serving Suggestion

Serve as for Mayonnaise above.

Mint and parsley dressing

A delicious, refreshing dressing.

Imp/Metric	Serves 4	American
2 tsps	lemon rind	2 tsps
3 tbsps	olive oil	3 tbsps
1½ tbsps	water	1½ tbsps
¼ tsp	paprika	¼ tsp
1 tsp	shoyu	1 tsp
2 tbsps	finely chopped fresh mint	2 tbsps
2 tbsps	finely chopped fresh parsley	2 tbsps

1 Mix all the ingredients together, then refrigerate for one hour to allow the flavours to mingle.

Serving Suggestion
Excellent served with grain-based or pasta salads, or spooned on top of vegetables and jacket potatoes.

Orange and herb dressing

A very herby dressing with a delicious orange flavour.

Imp/Metric	Serves 4	American
1½ tbsps	olive or sunflower oil	1½ tbsps
4 tbsps	water	4 tbsps
2 tsps	orange rind	2 tsps
1½ tbsps	finely chopped fresh parsley	1½ tbsps
1½ tbsps	finely chopped fresh mint	1½ tbsps
1½ tbsps	finely chopped fresh chives	1½ tbsps
	salt and freshly ground black pepper	

1 Mix all the ingredients together, then refrigerate for one hour to allow the flavours to mingle.

Serving Suggestion
Excellent on grain and pasta-based salads, and delicious on cooked vegetables and jacket potatoes.

P or (A)

Apple vinaigrette

A delightful fruity variation on vinaigrette.

Imp/Metric	Serves 4	American
4½ tbsps	olive oil	4½ tbsps
1½ tbsps	cider or rice vinegar –	1½ tbsps
	(to convert to A, use lemon juice)	
1 tsp	concentrated apple juice	1 tsp
¼ tsp	paprika	¼ tsp
pinch	salt	pinch

1 Mix all the ingredients together, then refrigerate for one hour
to allow the flavours to mingle.

Serving Suggestion
Very good on green and mixed salads and over leeks,
courgettes/zucchini, fennel and cauliflower.

P or (A)   (V)

Basic vinaigrette

A lovely tangy vinaigrette – quick and easy to make.

Imp/Metric	Makes approximately 4 fl oz/ 100ml/½ cup	American
3 fl oz/75ml	olive oil	⅓ cup
2 tbsps	cider or rice vinegar	2 tbsps
	(to convert to A, use lemon juice)	
pinch	salt	pinch
pinch	mustard powder	pinch
pinch	paprika	pinch
	freshly ground black pepper	

1 Mix all the ingredients together, then refrigerate for one hour
to allow the flavours to mingle.

Serving Suggestion
Delicious on green and mixed salads, or poured over vegetables.

Variations: use different oils, such as walnut, sesame, hazelnut, etc, for different flavours, and/or add chopped herbs of choice, crushed/minced garlic, etc.

N̄   Ⓥ

Tomato vinaigrette

A vinegar-free vinaigrette!

Imp/Metric	Makes approximately 6 fl oz/ 175ml/¾ cup	American
3oz/75g	very ripe tomatoes – peel and chop	½ cup
4 tbsps	olive oil	4 tbsps
pinch	paprika	pinch
½-1 tsp	tamari	½-1 tsp

1 Place the tomato in a food processor or liquidizer/blender, and blend until liquid.
2 Combine with the olive oil and paprika, then add tamari to taste.

Serving Suggestion
Delicious on salads or poured over cooked vegetables.

Extra dressing suggestions

1 **Almond and fennel dressing** – add crushed fennel seeds to mayonnaise and a few drops of almond essence to taste — P or A
2 **Avocado and mint** – mash or blend a ripe avocado until smooth then add mint to taste — N
3 **Banana and parsley** – blend 1-2 bananas until smooth and creamy, then add freshly chopped parsley — S
4 **Blue cheese dressing** – blend blue cheese with enough mayonnaise/cream to produce a smooth consistency; add a little lemon juice/cider or rice vinegar for extra flavour — P
5 **Carrot and pine kernel** – mix grated/shredded carrot and crushed toasted pine kernels with mayonnaise — P or A

 6 **Cream cheese and garlic** – blend cream cheese
    with mayonnaise and garlic   P or A
 7 **Lemon juice with paprika and crushed/
    minced garlic** – mix lemon juice with a good
    pinch of paprika and crushed garlic as desired   P or A
 8 **Olive oil or tamari** – mix olive oil and tamari
    together   N
 9 **Pineapple tofu dressing** – blend tofu with
    pineapple juice and a touch of lemon to
    produce a 'tangy' dressing   P
10 **Soured cream, lemon and paprika** – combine
    the cream with enough lemon rind to taste,
    then add a pinch of paprika   N
11 **Soya 'cream cheese' with tahini and chopped
    black olives** – blend soya 'cream cheese' with
    light tahini to produce a smooth creamy
    dressing then stir in the black olives   P
12 **Tomato, basil and onion** – blend ripe fresh
    tomatoes with dried/fresh basil and spring
    onion/scallions   N
13 **Tofu with lemon and parsley** – blend tofu
    until smooth then add lemon juice and freshly
    chopped parsley   P
14 **Yoghurt (any type) with chopped mint and
    chives** – mix yoghurt (Greek yoghurt is
    especially good) with chopped chives and mint
    to taste   P or A

Main courses

You will find that the whole of a recipe book from breakfast through to supper can be dipped into to provide main course recipes – excluding I hope, the sweet biscuits/cookies, cakes and desserts! So do look back to earlier sections – very often breakfast or brunch savoury dishes provide quick alternative main course meals which are especially useful when the family are all clamouring to be fed at once! A large portion of mushrooms on toast (often a breakfast dish) served with salad/vegetables is more then adequate as a main course item. Salads are often substantial enough as a main course; so too are the vegetable side-dishes, and soups, when served with bread, crispbreads, oatcakes or starch-free crackers, and salad.

S or (P)   Ⓥ

Almond loaf with lemon and thyme filling

A beautifully moist loaf – the delicate flavours of almond and lemon are a delightful combination – ideal for special occasions.

Imp/Metric	Serves 8-10	American
	lemon and thyme filling	
1 tbsp	olive or sunflower oil	1 tbsp
4oz/100g	onion – very finely chop	⅔ cup
1	garlic clove – crushed/minced	1
2 tsps	finely grated/shredded lemon rind	2 tsps
2oz/50g	(S) use whole wheat breadcrumbs	½ cup
	(to convert to P, use wheatgerm)	
2oz/50g	ground cashews	½ cup
1½ tbsps	finely chopped fresh thyme	1½ tbsps
1½ tbsps	finely chopped fresh parsley	1½ tbsps
	1½ tbsps milk diluted with 1½ tbsps water	
	salt and freshly ground black pepper	
	nut mixture	
2 tbsps	olive or sunflower oil	2 tbsps
8oz/225g	onions – very finely chop	1⅓ cups
2 tsps	low-salt yeast extract	2 tsps
1½oz/40g	whole wheat flour	⅓ cup
	(to convert to P, use 2oz/25g/½ cup ground nuts)	
	2½ fl oz/60ml/⅓ cup milk diluted	
	with 2½ fl oz/60ml/⅓ cup water	
	salt and freshly ground black pepper	
10oz/275g	ground almonds	2½ cups
4oz/100g	ground cashews	1 cup
4oz/100g	whole wheat breadcrumbs	2 cups
	(to convert to P, use 4oz/100g/1 cup wheatgerm)	
4oz/100g	mushrooms – chop *very* finely	1½ cups

1 Make the lemon and thyme filling first. Heat the oil, and fry the onion until soft, add the garlic and cook for a further minute.

2 Take the pan off the heat, add the remaining ingredients for the lemon and thyme filling, season, and combine thoroughly to produce a moist consistency.

3 Set the oven to 375°F/190°C (Gas 5).

4 Grease a 2lb/900g loaf tin/pan and line the base with a strip of greased baking parchment, long enough to overhang at both ends.

5 Now make the nut mixture. Heat the oil in a large saucepan, and fry the onion until soft.

6 Mix in the yeast extract, then the flour/ground nuts, remove the pan from the heat, stir in the diluted milk and season.

7 Mix together the ground almonds, cashews and bread-crumbs/wheatgerm, add to the onion mix and combine thoroughly.

8 Finally add the chopped mushrooms, and mix in well to form a moist but stiff consistency.

9 Press 14oz/400g of the nut mixture into the base of the prepared tin/pan, press the lemon and thyme filling on top, then cover with the remaining nut mixture.

10 Bake covered for 15 minutes, then uncovered for 10-15 minutes, or until firm to the touch and very lightly browned.

Serving Suggestion

For the starch version, serve hot with Chestnut or Mushroom sauce (pages 210 and 211), Almond potatoes (page 196), Cauliflower, broccoli and carrot with flaked/slivered almonds (page 194), and salad.

For the protein version, serve hot with Mushroom sauce (page 211), Cauliflower, broccoli and carrot with flaked/slivered almonds (page 194), steamed fennel and salad.

S or (P)		Ⓥ

Almond-stuffed courgettes/zucchini

Always a popular dish with my family and friends.

Imp/Metric	Serves 4 as a main course/ 8 as a starter/appetizer/ side-vegetable	American
4	courgettes/zucchini – select plump ones	4
1 tbsp	olive or sunflower oil	1 tbsp
4oz/100g	onions – very finely chop	⅔ cup
1	vegetable stock cube	1
1 tsp	finely chopped fresh marjoram	1 tsp
1 tsp	finely chopped fresh rosemary	1 tsp
4½ tbsps	finely chopped fresh parsley	4½ tbsps
	salt and freshly ground black pepper	
4oz/100g	whole wheat breadcrumbs (to convert to P, use wheatgerm)	1 cup
4oz/100g	ground cashews	1 cup
4oz/100g	flaked/slivered almonds – toasted	1 cup

Garnish
flaked/slivered almonds
Optional (P)
grated/shredded cheese to sprinkle on top

1 Set the oven to 375°F/190°C (Gas 5).
2 Top and tail the courgettes/zucchini, slice in half lengthways, then scoop out the flesh using a melon scoop or teaspoon.
3 Steam the skins until tender, and put to one side to cool.
4 Very finely chop the scooped out courgettes/zucchini.
5 Heat the oil and fry the onion until soft.
6 Mix in the stock cube, then add the chopped courgettes/zucchini and herbs, and cook a further 2-3 minutes.
7 Remove the pan from the heat, and season.
8 Add the breadcrumbs/wheatgerm, cashews and toasted almonds, and combine thoroughly.
9 If the mixture is a little dry add 1-2 tablespoons of water to achieve a moist but stiff filling.
10 Pile the mixture into the courgette/zucchini halves, place 5 extra flaked almonds at an angle diagonally along the length of each half, and bake covered for 25 minutes.

Freeze As Directed Below

This dish is best prepared fresh. The stuffing freezes very well, but frozen courgette/zucchini skins can become rather 'floppy' on thawing, and the dish needs greater care in serving; but freeze as follows for acceptable results. Steam the courgette/zucchini skins, and freeze; prepare the stuffing, omitting the toasted almonds, and freeze. On thawing, add the almonds to the stuffing and make up and cook as described above.

Serving Suggestion

Serve with Onion sauce (page 213). Alternatively, Cheese and cashew and Pine kernel sauces (pages 209 and 214) are also especially good with this dish when served as a protein meal.

These courgettes/zucchini are moist enough, however, to be served without a sauce for quicker and easier preparation! As a side-vegetable serve with or without a sauce to accompany vegetable-based dishes. Served singly with salad they make an ideal light lunch/evening meal. The stuffing is delicious in aubergines/eggplants, peppers, tomatoes, etc.

P or A   Ⓥ

Apple, kombu and onion bake

An unusual dish – the sweetness of the onion, combined with the sharpness of the apple and strong-flavoured kombu, is delicious.

Imp/Metric	Serves 4	American
2 tbsps	olive or sunflower oil	2 tbsps
1lb/450g	onion – slice in semi-circles	3 cups
4	garlic cloves – crushed/minced	4
1 dsp	tamari	2 tsps
1	bouillon stock cube	1
½oz/15g	kombu – soak in boiling water for 20 minutes	½oz
10fl oz/275ml	water	1⅓ cups
1½lb/550g	cooking apples	1½lb

1 Set the oven to 375°F/190°C (Gas 5).
2 Heat the oil, and cook the onion covered until tender.
3 Add the garlic and tamari, mix in the stock cube and cook for a further minute.
4 Cut the soaked kombu into *very* thin strips, then chop finely.
5 Add to the onion mix along with the water, bring to the boil, and simmer covered for 5 minutes.
6 Peel, core and finely dice the apple, add to the onion and kombu mix, and combine thoroughly.
7 Transfer to a greased 2pt/1 1/5 cup casserole dish.
8 Bake for 15 minutes covered, and 5 minutes uncovered, or until the apple is tender.

Serving Suggestion
Serve with a crisp green salad and steamed carrots – for a protein variation top with grated/shredded cheese.

S ⓥ

Artichoke and sunflower seed risotto

A beautiful nutty flavoured risotto, enhanced by the delicate flavour of artichokes.

Imp/Metric	Serves 4-6	American
8oz/225g	whole grain rice – dry weight	1⅓ cups
4oz/100g	sunflower seeds – toasted	¾ cup
2	bay leaves	2
1pt/570ml	water	2½ cups
2 tbsps	olive oil	2 tbsps
4oz/100g	onion – finely chop	⅔ cup
4oz/100g	green pepper – cut into small dice	⅔ cup
4oz/100g	red pepper – cut into small dice	⅔ cup
1	bouillon stock cube	1
1 tbsp	light tahini	1 tbsp
1 tbsp	tamari	1 tbsp

14oz/400g tin artichoke hearts –
drain, saving the tinned/canned juice,
and chop into small pieces
salt and freshly ground black pepper

1 Cook the rice with the toasted sunflower seeds and the bay leaves in the water until tender. Drain of any excess water and put the rice mixture to one side.
2 Heat the oil, and cook the onion and peppers covered for 10 minutes.
3 Mix in the stock cube, then add the tahini and tamari, and combine.
4 Stir in the artichoke juice, made up to 10 fl oz/275ml/1⅓ cups with water, then add the rice mix, and finally the chopped artichokes.
5 Heat through, adding more water if necessary, and serve.

Serving Suggestion
Serve with a green salad, and Gingered courgettes/zucchini, mushrooms and carrots (page 195). This mixture also makes a delicious pancake/crêpe or vegetable stuffing.

S

Beany vegetable crumble

Unfailingly popular with my family and friends – full of flavour, this is an excellent dish with which to tempt both your vegetarian and non-vegetarian friends!

Imp/Metric	Serves 4-6	American
	Crumble base	
2 tbsps	olive or sunflower oil	2 tbsps
3oz/75g	onion – finely chop	½ cup
3oz/75g	each of carrots and red pepper – cut into small dice	½ cup
3oz/75g	courgettes/zucchini – cut into small dice	¾ cup
3oz/75g	celery – cut into strips, then thinly slice	¾ cup
3oz/75g	mushrooms – thinly slice	1½ cups
1	garlic clove – crushed/minced	1
1	vegetable stock cube	1
2 tbsps	whole wheat flour	2 tbsps
10 fl oz/275ml	cooking liquid from the black-eyed beans plus 5 fl oz/ 150ml/⅔ cup water – or tinned/ canned stock made up to 15 fl oz/ 425ml/2 cups with water	1⅓ cups
1½ tbsps	light tahini	1½ tbsps
2 tsps	finely chopped fresh basil	2 tsps
2 tsps	finely chopped fresh marjoram	2 tsps
5oz/150g	black-eyed beans – soak then cook – or 1 × 14oz/400g tin/can beans	2½ cups
1½ tbsps	shoyu	1½ tbsps
	salt and freshly ground black pepper	
	Crumble topping	
3oz/75g	butter/margarine	⅓ cup
3oz/75g	plain whole wheat flour	¾ cup
3oz/75g	brown rice flour	½ cup
1½ tbsps	sunflower seeds	1½ tbsps
3 tbsps	sesame seeds	3 tbsps
4 tbsps	porridge oats	4 tbsps
1oz/25g	flaked/slivered almonds – toasted	¼ cup

1 Set the oven to 375°F/190°C (Gas 5).
2 Make the crumble base first. Heat the oil in a large saucepan
   and cook the onion, vegetables and garlic covered for 10
   minutes, stirring occasionally.
3 Blend in the stock cube, then add the flour and combine with
   the vegetables.
4 Take the pan off the heat, and gradually add the stock along
   with the tahini.
5 Return to the heat, bring to the boil and add the herbs.
6 Cover and simmer on a low heat for 15-20 minutes.
7 Meanwhile make the topping by rubbing the butter/
   margarine into the flours until the mixture resembles
   breadcrumbs. Add the seeds, oats and almonds and combine
   thoroughly.
8 Add the beans and shoyu to the vegetable mix and season.
9 Pour this mixture into a 3pt/1½ litre ovenproof dish, spread
   the crumble mix evenly on top, and bake for 25-30 minutes
   until crisp and golden.

Can be Frozen
For better results, though, I prefer to freeze the topping
separately and sprinkle on top once the dish has thawed, then
cook.

Serving Suggestion
Serve with a mixed salad, and steamed broccoli and leeks.

P   (V)

Cheese and fennel loaf with a pea and lemon stuffing

A very attractive 'stripy' loaf, with its green pea stuffing and creamy-coloured nut and vegetable mix – ideal for dinner parties, or buffets.

Imp/Metric	Serves 8-10	American
2 tbsps	olive or sunflower oil	2 tbsps
12oz/350g	fennel – very finely chop	2 cups
6oz/175g	leeks – very finely chop	1½ cups
4	fresh bay leaves	4
3oz/75g	finely grated/shredded Cheddar/	¾ cup
	New York Cheddar cheese/soya/soy cheese	
8oz/225g	ground cashews	2 cups
4oz/100g	ground almonds	1 cup
1 large	egg – beaten	1 extra large
	(to convert to V, use 1 tbsp soya/soy	
	flour mixed with 1½-2 tbsps water)	
	salt and freshly ground black pepper	
12oz/350g	frozen peas – cook	2 cups
1½ tbsps	lemon juice	1½ tbsps

1 Set the oven to 375°F/190°C (Gas 5).
2 Grease a 2lb/900g loaf tin/pan and line the base with a strip of greased baking parchment, long enough to overhang at both ends.
3 Heat the oil, and cook the fennel and leeks with the bay leaves covered for 10 minutes.
4 Take the pan off the heat, remove the bay leaves, then add the cheese and combine.
5 Mix in the nuts and egg/soya/soy flour mix, then season.
6 Place the cooked peas in a food processor or liquidizer/ blender, blend with the lemon juice until smooth, then season.
7 Place 12oz/350g of the cheese mixture in the base of the tin/pan and smooth over.
8 Place the pea mix on top, then add the remaining cheese mix.
9 Bake covered for 25 minutes, then uncovered for 5 minutes, or until lightly browned and firm to the touch – the vegan version may need slightly longer to 'set'.

Serving Suggestion
Serve hot with Onion sauce (page 213), Red pepper with courgettes/zucchini (page 197), and a mixed salad, or cold with salad – makes a stunning starter/appetizer, served hot or cold.

$\boxed{\text{P}}$

Cheese and parsley-stuffed mushrooms

A delicious way to serve mushrooms!

Imp/Metric	Serves 4 as a main course	American
1½lb/675g	medium-sized mushrooms – select 16 to make up this weight	1½lb
2 tbsps	olive or sunflower oil	2 tbsps
12oz/350g	onion – finely chop	2 cups
2	fresh bay leaves	2
2	garlic cloves – crushed/minced	2
½ tsp	paprika	½ tsp
1 dsp	tamari	2 tsps
4 tbsps	finely chopped fresh parsley	4 tbsps
4oz/100g	finely grated/shredded Cheddar/ New York Cheddar cheese/soya/soy cheese	1 cup

Garnish
sprigs of parsley

1 Set the oven to 400°F/200°C (Gas 6).
2 Wipe the mushrooms, then remove the stalks and any excess gills from the undersides to form a flat base.
3 Grease a large ovenproof dish, or baking tray/sheet, and place the mushrooms in it, bases upwards.
4 Finely chop the stalks and gills, and put to one side.
5 Heat the oil and fry the onion until soft, along with the bay leaves.
6 Add the garlic, paprika and chopped mushroom, cook a further minute, then stir in the tamari and parsley.
7 Remove the pan from the heat, add half the cheese, and combine thoroughly.
8 Spoon this mixture on top of the mushroom caps, then sprinkle the remaining cheese on top.
9 Cover and bake for 30-40 minutes until the mushroom bases are tender, then garnish with the sprigs of parsley.

Cannot be Frozen

Serving Suggestion
Garnish with sprigs of parsley and serve with Fennel and green pepper (page 196), and a tomato and onion salad.

P

Cheesy stuffed apples

An unusual, but delicious way, to eat a cooking apple!

Imp/Metric	Serves 4	American
2 tbsps	olive or sunflower oil	2 tbsps
8oz/225g	onion – very finely chop	1⅓ cups
10oz/275g	celery – very finely chop	2½ cups
4	fresh bay leaves	4
4	cooking apples	4
1	vegetable stock cube	1
1½ tbsps	finely chopped fresh thyme	1½ tbsps
4oz/100g	ground cashews	1 cup
4oz/100g	walnuts/English walnuts – chop very finely	1 cup
2oz/50g	finely grated/shredded Cheddar/ New York Cheddar cheese/soya/soy cheese	½ cup

salt and freshly ground black pepper

1 Set the oven to 375°F/190°C (Gas 5).
2 Heat the oil, and cook the onion, celery and bay leaves covered for 10 minutes.
3 Meanwhile remove the centre core from each apple, cut each in half widthways, then carefully scoop out the flesh so that the 'shells' remain intact.
4 Turn the skins upside down to lessen the chance of their discolouring, and put to one side.
5 Chop the flesh, add to the onion and celery mix, and cook covered for 5-10 minutes until broken down.
6 Mix in the stock cube and thyme, then remove the pan from the heat, add the nuts and cheese, and season.
7 Pile the mixture into the apple skins, and place on a lightly greased baking tray/pan.
8 Cover and bake for 30 minutes, or until the skins are tender.

Serving Suggestion
Serve with Spicy red cabbage (page 199), and a green salad.

Variation: omit the celery, and add 10oz/275g/1½ cups cooked frozen chopped spinach along with the cheese and nuts; replace the thyme with 1½ tbsps finely chopped fresh rosemary.

S

Coriander/cilantro and lemon rice balls

A delicious way to serve rice!

Imp/Metric	Makes 24 Serve 6 as a main course/ 12 as a starter/appetizer/ side-vegetable	American
8oz/225g	whole grain rice – dry weight – cook until tender and fluffy	2 cups
8oz/225g	finely grated/shredded carrot	1⅓ cups
2 tsps	finely grated/shredded lemon rind	2 tsps
3 tbsps	finely chopped fresh coriander/cilantro	3 tbsps
6oz/175g	ground hazelnuts	1½ cups
1½ tbsps	shoyu	1½ tbsps
1 tbsp	olive or sunflower oil	1 tbsp
8oz/225g	onion – chop very finely	1⅓ cups
2	garlic cloves – crushed/minced	2
1	bouillon stock cube	1
	salt and freshly ground black pepper	

1 Set the oven to 375°F/190°C (Gas 5).
2 Combine the rice, carrot, lemon rind, coriander/cilantro, nuts and shoyu in a large bowl.
3 Heat the oil, and fry the onion until soft.
4 Add the garlic and cook a further minute.
5 Mix in the stock cube, then take the pan off the heat, add to the rice mixture and season.
6 Using an ice-cream scoop or large spoon, scoop 2oz/50g quantities of the mixture and shape into balls.
7 Place on a lightly greased baking tray/sheet and bake for 20-30 minutes until golden.

Serving Suggestion
As a starter/appetizer serve hot or cold with salad garnish; as a main course serve with Mushroom sauce (see page 211), steamed courgettes/zucchini and baby sweetcorn. Alternatively, serve as a side-vegetable. Can also be served cold with salad or as part of a lunch box/picnic meal – excellent for buffets. The mixture can also be used as a vegetable or pancake/crêpe stuffing.

$\boxed{\text{S}}$

Dill and lentil oaten slice

Dill is a delicious herb, and especially good combined with lentils in this recipe.

Imp/Metric	Makes 12	American
	Filling	
1lb/450g	red lentils/split peas – cook (see step 3 below)	2⅔ cups
2 tbsps	olive or sunflower oil	2 tbsps
10oz/275g	onion – finely chop	1¾ cups
2	garlic cloves – crushed/minced	2
1	bouillon stock cube	1
1½ tbsps	shoyu	1½ tbsps
3 tbsps	finely chopped fresh dill	3 tbsps
	salt and freshly ground black pepper	
	Base and Topping	
12oz/350g	rolled oats	3 cups
6oz/175g	medium oatmeal	1½ cups
8oz/225g	ground peanuts	2 cups
2 tsps	baking powder	2 tsps
6oz/175g	butter/margarine – melted	¾ cup
	salt and freshly ground black pepper	
2oz/50g	pumpkin seeds	½ cup

1 Set the oven to 375°F/190°C (Gas 5).
2 Grease and line a 9in/22½cm × 12in/30cm (inside measurement) Swiss roll tin/jelly roll pan with a piece of greased baking parchment, large enough for the paper to come up above the sides.
3 Make the filling first. Place the lentils in a saucepan with 1¼pt/700ml/3 cups water. Bring to the boil and leave to

simmer gently for 20-30 minutes, or until soft and 'mushy' and all the water has evaporated. Add more water during the simmering stage if necessary. Stir occasionally to help break them down, then put to one side.

4 Heat the oil and fry the onion until soft.

5 Add the garlic, cook a further minute then blend in the stock cube, take the pan off the heat and add the shoyu and dill.

6 Add the onion mix to the cooked lentils/split peas, combine thoroughly and season.

7 Make the base by placing the rolled oats, oatmeal, peanuts and baking powder in a large bowl and stirring in the melted fat.

8 Lightly season, then pour in 4 fl oz/100ml/½ cup boiling water, and mix thoroughly to form a sticky consistency.

9 Put 12oz/350g of this mixture to one side, and press the remainder firmly into the base of the prepared tin/pan, using a potato masher, then spread the lentil/split peas mix on top.

10 To make the topping, add the pumpkin seeds to the reserved oat mix, and sprinkle this evenly over the surface of the lentil filling.

11 Press down by rolling over the surface with a rolling pin, then bake for 30-35 minutes until firm and golden-brown.

12 Leave to cool slightly in the tin, then cut into 3in/7½cm squares and serve; or cool completely, cut and serve cold, or reheat as required.

Serving Suggestion

Garnish with fresh dill and serve hot with Savoury brown or Onion sauce (pages 215 and 213), steamed carrots, courgettes/zucchini and salad, or cold with salad. These slices are ideal for family meals, lunch-boxes and picnics. The filling can also be made into burgers, coated with breadcrumbs/rolled oats/sesame seeds, then baked.

Flans and pizzas

Flan/pizza bases
Pastry/pie crust

These often make or break a dish – there is nothing worse than a 'cardboard' pastry/pie crust! Whole wheat pastry/pie crust can be difficult to handle, and I have therefore experimented with different flours, fats, etc, to try and produce a manageable dough, which, when cooked, has a light, crumbly texture.

An extremely light pastry can be obtained using self-raising/self-rising flour – the dough, however, does tend to be rather fragile on rolling out, and I would recommend starting with half self-raising/self-rising flour and half plain/all-purpose flour until you are proficient! I always place the required amount of water in the refrigerator for 1-2 hours before preparation to become really cold. I ensure, too, that the flour comes from a cool storage area – not a hot kitchen cupboard – and the fat straight from the refrigerator, using whenever possible half a soft and half a hard fat, but if you only have one or the other this will work perfectly well.

Shortcrust pastry

Basic quantity

Imp/Metric	Makes 8oz/225g – enough for 1 × 10in/25cm flan ring	American
4oz/100g	plain/all-purpose whole wheat flour	1 cup
4oz/100g	self-raising/self rising whole wheat flour	1 cup
pinch	salt	pinch
4oz/100g	butter/margarine – cut into small pieces	½ cup
3 fl oz/75ml	ice-cold water	⅓ cup

1 Sieve/sift the flours into a bowl, adding back any separated bran.

2 Mix in the salt, then gently rub/cut the butter/margarine into the flour, until the mixture resembles fine breadcrumbs.
3 Add the water, and combine to achieve a moist but not too sticky dough (if too moist add extra flour).
4 Cover, and place in the refrigerator to rest/stand for 30 minutes, then roll out as required.

Serving Suggestion
Use to make sweet/savoury flans, pies, croûtes, pastries, etc. Sweet pastry/pie crusts can be made with the addition of a little honey/maple syrup (reduce the water content accordingly), or almond/vanilla essence.

Note: a food processor makes excellent pastry, in a fraction of the time taken by hand!

Variations: replace 1oz/25g/¼ cup flour with 4 tbsps sesame seeds, or 1-2oz/25-50g/¼-½ cup flour with 1-2oz/25-50g/¼-½ cup ground nuts, for a 'nutty' pastry case/pie crust, or 1-2oz/25-50g/¼-½ cup or more of the flour, with buckwheat or cornmeal flour.

To prepare a pastry/pie crust flan base
1 Set the oven to 400°F/200°C (Gas 6).
2 Grease a flan ring/dish/pan, and place on a baking sheet.
3 Roll out the pastry, then gently and carefully ease into the prepared flan ring/dish/pan.
4 Prick the base, and bake 'blind' (line with greaseproof/waxed paper, fill with dried peas or ceramic baking beans and bake for 10–15 minutes, or until lightly browned and firm to the touch.

Pastry/pie crust quantities
The quantity of pastry/pie crust given in a recipe denotes the amount of flour used, that is, 8oz/225g/2 cups pastry/pie crust means pastry/pie crust made, as above, from 8oz/225g/2 cups flour.

Pastry/pie crust quantities for different-sized flan rings are as follows:

Pastry quantity	Flan size	Water*
6oz/175g/1½ cups	8in/20cm	2 fl oz/50ml/¼ cup
8oz/225g/2 cups	10in/25cm	3 fl oz/75ml/⅓ cup
10oz/300g/2½ cups	12in/30cm	4 fl oz/100ml/½ cup

The fat quantity is half the total weight of the flour/dry ingredients.

* water quantities can vary – you may need a little more/little less, alternatively adjust the flour quantities as appropriate to achieve a manageable dough.

Starch-free pastry/pie crust

As well as a flour-based pastry for flans, etc, I began, when commencing the Hay System of eating, to try to make an alternative pastry case/pie crust for protein or alkaline-based flans, and my 'nut/seed pastry/pie crust' recipes evolved. Do note, however, that nut/seed pastry/pie crusts are not suitable for use as pie 'lids', or croûte casings, etc, as they do not form a dough which holds together in one piece when rolled out.

P or A	Ⓥ

Nut/seed pastry/pie crust

Basic quantity

Imp/Metric	Makes 12oz/350g – enough for 1×10/25cm flan ring/pan	American
6oz/175g	ground sunflower seeds	1½ cups
6oz/175g	ground almonds	1½ cups
pinch	salt	pinch
1½ tsps	baking powder	1½ tsps
1½oz/40g	butter/margarine – melted	3 tbsps
	1½ tbsps milk diluted with 1½ tbsps water	

1 Set the oven to 375°F/190°C (Gas 5).
2 Combine the sunflower seeds, ground almonds, baking powder and salt in a bowl.
3 Mix in the butter/margarine, then add the diluted milk and stir in using a fork.
4 Bring the mixture together with your hand to achieve a firm but moist dough.

To Prepare a Nut/Seed 'Pastry/Pie Crust' Flan Base

1 Press the prepared nut/seed mixture into the base and up the sides of a greased flan ring/dish.

2 Bake 'blind' (line with greaseproof/waxed paper, fill with
   dried peas or ceramic baking beans) and bake for 15–20
   minutes until firm and browned.

Serving Suggestion
As for flour-based pastry/pie crusts.

Variations: use 6oz/175g/1½ cups ground walnuts/English
walnuts and 6oz/175g/1½ cups ground cashews – omit the fat,
as these nuts are already 'fatty', or use 6oz/175g/1½ cups
ground pecans and 6oz/175g/1½ cups ground cashews – omit
the fat, as these nuts are already 'fatty'.

   Alternatively, adapt the Starch-free cracker recipes (pages
232-237). All these make delicious pastry/pie crust cases.

Note: baking times will vary according to the nuts/seeds used
– bear this in mind and check your pastry/pie crust case at
regular intervals.

Starch-free pastry/pie crust quantities
The quantity of nut/seed pastry/pie crust given in a recipe
denotes the amount of nuts/seeds used, that is, 12oz/350g/3
cups pastry/pie crust means nut/seed pastry/pie crust made, as
above, from 12oz/350g/3 cups nuts/seeds.

   Nut/seed pastry/pie crust quantities for different sized flan
rings are as follows:

Pastry quantity	Flan size	Diluted milk*
8oz/225g/2 cups	8in/20cm	2 tbsps
12oz/350g/3 cups	10in/25cm	3 tbsps
16oz/450g/4 cups	12in/30cm	4 tbsps

Baking powder quantities are 1 tsp, 1½ tsps and 2 tsps
respectively.

   Fat quantities are 1oz/25g/2 tbsps, 1½oz/40g/3 tbsps and
2oz/50g/¼ cup respectively.

* diluted milk quantities can vary – you may need a little more/little less;
  alternatively, adjust the nut/seed quantities as appropriate to achieve a
  manageable dough.

'Scone'-based flans or pizzas
The following two 'scone' recipes, with their addition of rolled
oats, make delicious flan cases, and are ideal for pizza bases too:

S

Ⓥ

Oat and buckwheat flan/pizza base

Basic quantity

Imp/Metric	Makes 12oz/350g – enough for 1 × 10in/25cm flan/pizza base	American
4oz/100g	plain/all-purpose whole wheat flour	1 cup
4oz/100g	buckwheat flour	¾ cup
2oz/50g	rolled oats	½ cup
4 tsps	baking powder	4 tsps
pinch	salt	pinch
3oz/75g	butter/margarine – cut into small pieces	⅓ cup
	2 tbsps milk diluted with 2 tbsps water	

1 Sieve/sift the flours into a bowl, adding back any separated bran.
2 Mix in the oats, baking powder and salt, then gently rub/cut the butter/margarine into the dry ingredients, until the mixture resembles fine breadcrumbs.
3 Add the diluted milk, and combine to achieve a moist but not too sticky dough (if too moist add extra flour).
4 Roll out to fit the base of the ring, then cover with your chosen topping.

Variation: replace the buckwheat flour with corn flour.
  For an 8in/20cm ring use:
  3oz/75g/¾ cup whole wheat flour
  3oz/75g/⅔ cup buckwheat flour
  1½oz/40g/⅓ cup rolled oats
  3 tsps baking powder
  2oz/50g/¼ cup butter/margarine
  1½ tbsps milk diluted with 1½ tbsps water

Pizza bases

For quick and unusual pizzas use the 'Scone-based' recipe above. Protein or alkaline pizza bases can be made using the nut/seed pastry/pie crust recipes above, alternatively make the bread based pizza:

Imp/Metric	Makes 1 × 10in/25cm flan ring base	American
8oz/225g	strong whole wheat flour	2 cups
½oz/15g	fresh yeast – or ½ tbsp dried yeast/ ½ sachet easy blend yeast – use according to the instructions on the packet	1¼ tbsps
¼ tsp	salt	¼ tsp
	5 fl oz/150ml warm water (3½ fl oz/90ml/ ⅓ cup cold, 1½ fl oz/40ml/¼ cup boiling)	
1 tbsp	sunflower oil	1 tbsp

1 Thoroughly grease a baking sheet or 10in/25cm flan ring.
2 Place all the ingredients in a large bowl and combine to form a dough, adding more water/flour if necessary.
3 Knead the dough for approximately 5 minutes, or until it takes on a uniform smoothness.
4 Leave in a bowl covered with a damp cloth or cling film/plastic wrap in a warm, draught-free place to double in size, approximately 45-60 minutes – you can prepare your filling while waiting.
5 Set the oven to 400°F/200°C (Gas 6).
6 Knock back/punch down the risen dough, knead again for a few minutes, then roll out to fit the baking sheet or prepared tin.
7 Spread the prepared mixture on top, leave for 15-20 minutes to rise again, then bake for 15-20 minutes, or until the base is golden brown and puffy.

Serving Suggestion

Serve as a light lunch/evening meal with salad, or as a main course with steamed vegetables and salad. Cut in small portions for a starter/appetizer.

For a very quick and easy pizza base use French sticks cut in half lengthways, or pitta bread.

Hay flan/pizza topping suggestions

Vegetable purées (pages 200–202) are ideal Hay flan/pizza toppings, as are many of the vegetable side-dishes (pages 189–199). These can be mixed with a cream cheese/diluted single/light cream and egg yolk mix for a more classic quiche, suitable for all meal types. Diluted milk and whole egg mixes are compatible with the nut/seed bases, but should not be used on starch bases.

Several of the other recipes in the book also make delicious flan/pizza toppings. Also try the following:

| S or P or (A) | (V) |

Almond and leek flan

The delicious flavour of leeks, combined with the creaminess of ground nuts, makes this a very tasty, moist dish.

Imp/Metric	Serves 8	American
	Makes a 9-10in/22½-25cm flan	
	Base	
	1 × basic quantity Shortcrust pastry/Nut/	
	seed pastry/pie crust (pages 154-157)	
	depending on meal structure.	
	Filling	
3 tbsps	olive or sunflower oil	3 tbsps
1½lb/675g	leeks – thinly slice	8 cups
8oz/225g	almonds in their skins – very	2 cups
	finely shop, then toast	
2 tsps	finely chopped fresh marjoram	2 tsps
1½ tbsps	shoyu	1½ tbsps
15 fl oz/375ml	cold water	2 cups
4oz/100g	ground almonds	1 cup
4oz/100g	ground cashews	1 cup
	(to convert to A, use almonds)	
	salt and freshly ground black pepper	

1 Prepare the flan case as given in the pastry recipes. Set the oven to 375°F/190°C (Gas 5).
2 Heat the oil and cook the leeks (covered) until soft.

3 Add the toasted nuts and marjoram, and cook together for 2-3 minutes.
4 Take the pan off the heat and stir in the shoyu.
5 Place the water in a food processor or liquidizer/blender, add the ground almonds and cashews, and blend until smooth and creamy.
6 Add this nut cream to the leek mixture, combine thoroughly and season – add extra ground nuts if the mixture is too 'sloppy'.
7 Pile into the prepared pastry case, shape into a mound and bake 30-35 minutes until golden brown and set.

Serving Suggestion
Serve with steamed broccoli and carrots, and a mixed salad – it is also delicious served cold with salad.

Variation: the leek topping can be used as a protein main course. Place in a 2pt/1 l casserole dish, top with grated/shredded cheese, and bake until the cheese is melted, and golden and bubbly – it will serve 4 in this manner.

P

Asparagus flan

Asparagus is a lovely vegetable, and particularly good in this way – do use fresh lemon balm if available, as it has a beautiful, delicate flavour.

Imp/Metric	Serves 4-6	American
	Base	
	Hazelnut and almond crackers recipe	
	(page 236)	
	Topping	
1 tbsp	olive or sunflower oil	1 tbsp
8oz/225g	onion – very finely chop	1⅓ cups
1	garlic clove – crushed/minced	1
½	stock/bouillon cube	½
1 × 10oz/275g	tin/can green asparagus spears	1 × 10oz
	– drain, saving the juice	
	salt and freshly ground black pepper	
10oz/275g	very firm tofu	1¼ cups
4 tbsps	tinned asparagus juice	4 tbsps
3 tbsps	finely chopped fresh lemon balm	3 tbsps
	– or 2 tsps grated/shredded lemon rind	

1 Prepare the cracker dough, roll out, line an 8in/20cm loose-bottomed flan ring or flan dish and bake for 10-12 minutes at 375°F/190°C (Gas 5), then turn oven up to 400°F/200°C (Gas 6).
2 Heat the oil and fry the onion until soft.
3 Add the garlic and cook a further minute, then blend in the ½ stock cube.
4 Take the pan off the heat, roughly chop half of the asparagus spears and add to the onion mix and season.
5 Drain the tofu and place in a food processor or liquidizer/blender, and blend with the asparagus juice and the remaining half of the spears until smooth.
6 Stir in the lemon balm/lemon rind, season, then combine thoroughly with the onion mix.
7 Spread on top of the prepared case and smooth over.
8 Bake for 30 minutes or until firm and lightly browned.

Cannot be Frozen

Serving Suggestion
Serve with cooked baby beetroot/beet, strips of yellow pepper,
lightly steamed, and a salad.

[P]   (V)

Smoked tofu and mushroom flan

The rich, smoky flavour of the tofu makes this a delicious flan.

Imp/Metric	Serves 6-8	American
	Base	
	1 × quantity of cashew and walnut variation	
	of Nut/seed pastry/pie crust recipe (page 157)	
	Topping	
4 tbsps	milk	4 tbsps
10oz/275g	smoked tofu	1¼ cups
2 tbsps	olive or sunflower oil	2 tbsps
5oz/150g	mushrooms – thinly slice	2½ cups
4oz/100g	onions – chop very finely	⅔ cup
4	fresh bay leaves	4
2	garlic cloves – crushed/minced	2
3oz/75g	mushrooms – chop very finely	1½ cups
1	bouillon stock cube	1
1½ tbsps	finely chopped fresh rosemary	1½ tbsps
	salt and freshly ground black pepper	

1 Prepare the pastry as given in the recipe, roll out, line a
   10in/25cm loose-bottomed flan ring or flan dish and bake at
   375°F/190°C (Gas 5) for 15-20 minutes, then turn the oven
   up to 400°F/200°C (Gas 6).
2 Drain the tofu, then place in a food processor or
   liquidizer/blender with the milk, and blend until smooth.
3 Heat 1 of the tbsp oil and fry the sliced mushrooms until
   tender, remove from the pan and put to one side.
4 Add the remaining tbsp of oil to the pan and fry the onion
   until soft along with the bay leaves.
5 Add the garlic and chopped mushrooms and cook for a
   further minute.
6 Remove the bay leaves, and mix in the stock cube and
   rosemary.
7 Take the pan off the heat and stir in half the reserved sliced
   mushrooms.

8 Add this mixture to the blended tofu, combine thoroughly and season.
9 Spread the remaining reserved sliced mushrooms over the prepared base, top with the tofu mix and smooth the surface.
10 Bake for 25-30 minutes or until set and lightly browned.

Cannot be Frozen

Serving Suggestion
Serve with Aubergine/eggplant and cucumber tossed in lemon and garlic (page 190), steamed cauliflower and carrots.

Spinach and tomato flan

A very attractive dish – full of colour and flavour.

Imp/Metric	Serves 6	American
	Base	
	8oz/225g/2 cups of cashew and pecan variation of Nut/seed pastry/pie crust recipe (page 157)	
	Tomato Filling	
1 tbsp	olive or sunflower oil	1 tbsp
4oz/100g	onions – finely chop	⅔ cup
2	garlic cloves – crushed/minced	2
12oz/350g	very ripe tomatoes – skin and roughly chop – or 1 × 14oz/400g tin/can chopped tomatoes	2¼ cups
1½ tbsps	tomato purée/paste	1½ tbsps
3 tsps	finely chopped fresh basil	3 tsps
	salt and freshly ground black pepper	
	Spinach Filling	
10oz/275g	chopped frozen spinach	1¼ cups
1 tsp	nutmeg	1 tsp
1½ tbsps	lemon juice	1½ tbsps
	freshly ground black pepper	

1 Prepare the pastry as given in the recipe, roll out, line an 8in/20cm loose-bottomed flan ring or dish and bake at 375°F/190°C (Gas 5) for 15-20 minutes. Then make the tomato filling.
2. Heat the oil, and fry the onion until soft.

3 Add the garlic, cook a further 2 minutes, then add the tomatoes, tomato purée/paste and basil.

4 Bring to the boil, and simmer uncovered until the mixture reduces to a very thick sauce.

5 Season, and put to one side to cool.

6 Now make the spinach filling. Cook the spinach as directed on the packet, then stir in the nutmeg and lemon juice.

7 Cook a further minute uncovered to allow some of the liquid to evaporate.

8 Season with black pepper, and put to one side to cool.

9 Set the oven to 375°F/190°C (Gas 5).

10 Divide each mixture into three, and place alternately in triangles in the prepared pastry case.

11 Bake covered for 25 minutes, then uncovered for 5 minutes.

Serving Suggestion
Serve with Cheese and cashew sauce (page 209), Gingered courgettes/zucchini, mushrooms and carrots (page 195), steamed fennel and salad, or cold with salad.

Variation: vary the fillings using half the quantities given in the Vegetable purée recipes: (pages 200-202), selecting contrasting colours and flavours. If the tomato filling is omitted and an alkaline base prepared, the flan can be used as part of an alkaline meal.

| P or A | Ⓥ |

Courgette/zucchini and almond pizza

Using this recipe, you can eat pizza with cheese and tomato after all!

Imp/Metric	Serves 4-6	American
	Base	
	16oz/450g/4 cups Nut/seed pastry/pie crust	
	(page 156) for a thick pizza base; if you prefer	
	a thinner pizza, use a 12oz/350g/3 cup	
	pastry quantity	
	Filling	
1 tbsp	sunflower or olive oil	1 tbsp
8oz/225g	onion – finely chop	1⅓ cup
2	garlic cloves – crushed/minced	2
1 × 14oz/400g	tin/can chopped tomatoes	1 × 14oz
1 × 8oz/225g	tin/can chopped tomatoes	1 × 8oz
	salt and freshly ground black pepper	
1½ tbsps	finely chopped fresh marjoram	1½ tbsps
4oz/100g	finely grated/shredded Cheddar/	1 cup
	New York Cheddar cheese/soya/soy cheese	
8oz/225g	courgettes/zucchini – slim ones	2 cups
	– thinly slice and steam until tender	
1½oz/40g	flaked/slivered almonds	⅓ cup

1 Prepare the pastry as given in the recipe, roll out, line a 10in/30cm loose-bottomed flan ring or flan dish and bake at 375°F/190°C (Gas 5) for 15-20 minutes. Leave the oven on.
2 Now make the filling. Heat the oil and fry the onion until soft.
3 Add the garlic and tomatoes and combine, season then simmer the mixture uncovered until it reduces to a very thick tomato sauce.
4 Add the marjoram, cook a further minute, then leave the mixture to cool slightly.
5 Spread it on top of the prepared base, and top with the cheese.
6 Arrange the courgette/zucchini slices around the edge in a ring, then form a ring of almonds, and repeat until the surface is covered.
7 Bake for 20-25 minutes uncovered – cover the top with foil if the almonds start to burn.

Serving Suggestion
Serve with sautéed mushrooms, steamed broccoli, and Cashew
and pistachio green salad (page 125).

S or A

Golden sweetcorn and potato casserole

*A delicious casserole – the sweetness of corn combined with potato
produces a lovely warming flavour.*

Imp/Metric	Serves 6	American
2 tbsps	olive or sunflower oil	2 tbsps
10oz/275g	onion – cut in semi-circles	1⅔ cups
1	vegetable stock cube	1
2 tsps	turmeric	2 tsps
1¼lb/550g	potato – peel and cut into small dice	1¼lb
12oz/350g	sweetcorn kernels	2 cups
1½ tbsps	shoyu	1½ tbsps
1pt/½l	boiling water	2½ cups
	salt and freshly ground black pepper	

1 Heat the oil, and fry the onion until soft.
2 Mix in the stock cube and turmeric, and cook a further
  minute.
3 Add the potato, sweetcorn and shoyu, then stir in the boiling
  water.
4 Cover, bring to the boil, then simmer for 10-15 minutes or
  until the potato is tender, and season.

Serving Suggestion
Serve with mushrooms, spring greens/collards and a mixed
salad.

S

Leek, mushroom and pine kernel lasagne

One of my favourite dishes – the creamy pine kernel sauce provides a beautiful rich flavour – you do not even notice that the cheese is missing!

Imp/Metric	Serves 4-6	American
2 tbsps	olive or sunflower oil	2 tbsps
1lb/450g	leeks – very finely chop	4 cups
8oz/225g	mushrooms – finely slice	4 cups
8oz/225g	mushrooms – chop very finely	3 cups
1½oz/40g	pine kernels	⅓ cup
1½ tbsps	finely chopped fresh marjoram	1½ tbsps
1 tbsp	tamari	1 tbsp
	1 × quantity Pine kernel sauce (page 214) but add 5 fl oz/150ml/⅔ cup extra water to thin it down	
6oz/175g	pre-cooked lasagne sheets	6oz
	salt and freshly ground black pepper	
	Topping	
2 tbsps	pine kernels	2 tbsps

1 Set the oven to 400°F/200°C (Gas 6).
2 Heat the oil, and cook the leeks covered for 10 minutes.
3 Add the mushrooms, pine kernels, tamari and marjoram, cook a further 3 minutes, then remove the pan from the heat and season.
4 Place a layer of this mixture in the base of a 3pt/1.7l dish, (a deep square/rectangular dish is ideal), top with a layer of lasagne, and then add a little sauce.
5 Repeat the layers, leaving enough sauce to finish with a thick layer. Sprinkle the surface with the 2 tbsps pine kernels, then bake for 40 minutes, or until browned and the lasagne is tender.

Serving Suggestion
Serve with steamed courgettes/zucchini, and a tomato and basil salad.

P or A   (V)

Minted pea and apple courgettes/zucchini

A lovely way to prepare courgettes/zucchini. The fresh-tasting combination of apple and mint gives a special touch to this dish – it is excellent for dinner parties.

Imp/Metric	Serves 8 as a starter/appetizer/side-vegetable/4 as a main course	American
4	courgettes/zucchini – select plump ones	4
2 tbsps	olive or sunflower oil	2 tbsps
4oz/100g	onion – finely chop	⅔ cup
2	bouillon stock cube	2
4oz/100g	frozen peas	1 cup
1 tbsp	finely chopped fresh mint	1 tbsp
	salt and freshly ground black pepper	
12oz/350g	red apple	2 cups
3 tbsps	lemon juice	3 tbsps
6oz/175g	ground hazelnuts	1½ cups
	Garnish	
	thin slices/pieces of red apple and fresh mint leaves	

1 Set the oven to 375°F/190°C (Gas 5).
2 Top and tail the courgettes/zucchini, slice in half lengthways, and scoop out the centre using a melon scoop or teaspoon.
3 Steam the skins until tender and put to one side to cool.
4 Finely chop the scooped out courgettes/zucchini.
5 Heat the oil and fry the onion until soft.
6 Stir in the stock cubes, then add the peas, mint and chopped courgettes/zucchini, mix thoroughly and cook for a further minute.
7 Take the pan off the heat, and season.
8 Chop the apple into small dice, add with the lemon juice and nuts to the courgette/zucchini mixture, and combine thoroughly.
9 Pile into the courgette/zucchini skins, then place on a lightly greased baking tray/pan.
10 Cover with foil and bake for 30 minutes.
11 Garnish with the chopped/sliced apple and mint leaves.

Can be Frozen
This dish is best prepared fresh. If freezing, prepare the stuffing, omitting the apple and lemon juice, and freeze. On thawing add these to the stuffing and make up and cook as directed above.

Serving Suggestion
Serve hot or cold as a starter/appetizer accompanied with Minted pea and apple sauce (page 211) – likewise served hot or cold – and a salad garnish. As a main course, with sauce, serve hot with Cauliflower, broccoli and carrot with flaked/slivered almonds, sautéed mushrooms, and salad, or cold with salad. As a side-vegetable this dish makes a lovely fresh accompaniment to protein/alkaline-based nut loaves, burgers, vegetable casseroles, etc.

S

Mushroom and peanut loaf

A very savoury loaf – perfect for a family meal.

Imp/Metric	Serves 6 as a main course/ 10-12 as a starter/appetizer	American
2 tbsps	olive or sunflower oil	2 tbsps
6oz/175g	onion – very finely chop	1 cup
2	garlic cloves – crushed/minced	2
½	vegetable stock cube	½
1½ tbsps	tamari	1½ tbsps
2 tsps	finely chopped fresh sage	2 tsps
2 tsps	finely chopped fresh marjoram	2 tsps
	salt and freshly ground black pepper	
6oz/175g	whole wheat breadcrumbs	3 cups
8oz/225g	ground peanuts	2 cups
6oz/175g	mushrooms – chop *very* finely	3 cups
	Garnish	
	extra fresh sage/marjoram and mushroom slices	

1 Heat the oven to 375°F/190°C (Gas 5).
2 Grease and line the base of a 1lb/450g loaf tin/pan with a strip of greased baking parchment, long enough to overhang at both ends.

3 Heat the oil, and fry the onion until soft.

4 Add the garlic, ½ stock cube, tamari and herbs and cook a further minute.

5 Remove from the heat, season, add the breadcrumbs and peanuts and mix well.

6 Finally add the mushrooms, and combine very thoroughly to form a moist but stiff mixture.

7 Press into the prepared tin/pan, and bake uncovered for 25-30 minutes, or until browned and firm – cover if the top browns too quickly.

8 Turn out onto a serving plate, remove the baking parchment, and garnish.

Serving Suggestion
Serve hot with jacket or new potatoes, Celery and onion purée (page 200) and a green salad, or cold with salad.

Variation: use the mixture to make burgers, etc, or mash once cooked and cold and use as a sandwich/pitta bread filling.

Pancakes/crêpes
Pancakes/crêpes are always a popular dish – especially with children!

Egg-based mix

Imp/Metric	Makes up to 8 7in/18cm diameter pancakes/crêpes	American
3	egg yolks	3
	6 fl oz/175ml/¾ cup milk diluted with 6 fl oz/175ml/¾ cup water	
4oz/100g	whole wheat flour	1 cup
1 tsp	sunflower oil	1 tsp
pinch	salt	pinch
2-3 tbsps	oil for cooking	2-3 tbsps

1 Place the egg yolks and diluted milk in a food processor or liquidizer/blender, and blend until smooth.

2 Add the flour, blend again, repeat with the oil and salt, and leave to stand for 30 minutes.

3 Blend briefly again before required and pour into a jug.
4 Place the oil for cooking in a cup, then pour 1-2 tsps into a frying pan/skillet and heat until nearly smoking.
5 Pour any excess back into the cup, and heat the pan for a further few moments.
6 Pour approximately 3 tbsps of batter into the pan, tilt quickly to spread evenly over the base and cook until browned, turn the pancake/crêpe over, and repeat for the other side.
7 Follow the above method and make 8 pancakes/crêpes.
8 Lay each pancake/crêpe on a piece of kitchen paper/paper towel to cool. Do not place on top of each other until cold as any warmth will produce steam and they will go 'soggy'.

Egg-free mix

Imp/Metric	Makes up to 8 7in/18cm diameter pancakes/crêpes	American
	6 fl oz/175ml/¾ cup milk diluted with 6 fl oz/225ml/1 cup water	
4oz/100g	whole wheat flour	1 cup
4 tbsps	chick pea/garbanzo flour	4 tbsps
1 tbsp	sunflower oil	1 tbsp
1 tsp	baking powder	1 tsp
pinch	salt	pinch
2-3 tbsps	oil for cooking	2-3 tbsps

1 Place all the ingredients, except the last ingredient in a food processor or liquidizer/blender, and blend all until smooth.
2 Leave to stand for 30 minutes.
3 Follow the method above, from stage 3.

Can be Frozen
Place a piece of baking parchment between each pancake/crêpe, and place in a freezer bag/plastic container.

Serving Suggestion
See page 173 for pancake/crêpe filling ideas.
Serve singly with a filling topping of choice as a starter/appetizer or light lunch/evening meal, or likewise two as a main

course. Can also be served as a dessert with sweet fillings. Both batters can be prepared several hours in advance and used when required.

Variation: replace half the flour with either buckwheat, cornmeal flour/fine polenta, or rye flours for 'alternative' pancake/crêpe bases.

Fillings/toppings for pancakes/crêpes, vegetables and jacket potatoes

Pancakes/crêpes and vegetables such as aubergine/eggplant, courgette/zucchini, marrow/summer squash, tomato, mushroom, pepper and jacket potatoes are ideal receptacles for fillings and/or toppings. Prepared in this way they will make very tasty, quick and simple dishes, which all the family will enjoy.

Sauces/vegetable purées, dips, pâtés, spreads and dressings make excellent vegetable and jacket potato toppings.

Many of the recipes in this book can be used as, or adapted to, filling recipes.

S

(V)

Pine kernel croûte

An impressive dinner party/special occasion dish – very filling so serve a light starter/appetizer and dessert!

Imp/Metric	Serves 8	American
	2 × basic quantity Shortcrust pastry recipe (page 154)	
	Nut mixture	
3oz/75g	ground hazelnuts	¾ cup
3oz/75g	ground almonds	¾ cup
3oz/75g	ground cashews	¾ cup
3oz/75g	pine kernels	¾ cup
2oz/50g	long-grain brown rice – dry weight – cook in 6 fl oz/175ml/¾ cup water	½ cup
2 tbsps	olive or sunflower oil	2 tbsps
10oz/275g	onions – finely chop	1⅔ cups
1 tsp	low-salt yeast extract	1 tsp
1½ tbsps	finely chopped fresh oregano	1½ tbsps
5oz/150g	finely grated/shredded carrot	1 cup
	salt and freshly ground black pepper	
	Glaze	
	beaten egg yolk with diluted milk	

1 Prepare the pastry according to the recipe (there will be some pastry left over after lining the tin/pan, but it is easier to do this and any remaining can be used for pasties, tartlets, etc or frozen).

2 Set the oven to 375°F/190°C (Gas 5).

3 Grease a 2lb/1 kilo loaf tin/pan and line the base with a strip of greased baking parchment, long enough to overhang at both ends.

4 Mix the nuts and rice in a large bowl.

5 Heat the oil and fry the onion until soft, then mix in the yeast extract and oregano, and cook a further minute.

6 Remove the pan from the heat, stir in the carrots, season, then add this mixture to the nuts and rice, and combine thoroughly.

7 Roll out three-quarters of the pastry on a floured surface and carefully line the tin/pan leaving a ¼in/½cm height above the top of the tin/pan.

8 Press in the nut mixture.

9 Roll out the remaining quarter of pastry to make a 'lid', taking care to seal it all round by pressing the raised sides and lid edges together, then smoothing over.

10 Turn the tin/pan upside down onto a lightly greased baking tray and gently and carefully ease out the loaf.

11 Smooth over, sealing any rough/broken edges, then brush with the glaze, decorate with pastry leaves and berries, then bake for 25-30 minutes until golden brown.

Serving Suggestion

Serve with baby sweetcorn, mangetout/snowpeas and new potatoes or salad. Can also be served cold with salad. The nut mixture makes a delicious sandwich filling and vegetable or pancake/crêpe stuffing. This croûte is also a perfect Christmas dish, especially when a chestnut stuffing is incorporated.

Chestnut Stuffing

Soak and cook 4oz/100g/¾ cup dried chestnuts then blend with approximately 4 tbsps of the cooking liquid to produce a smooth, moist consistency, season with freshly ground black pepper, or use 8oz/225g/2⅓ cups tinned unsweetened chestnut purée, seasoned with freshly ground black pepper.

Follow the above Pine kernel croûte method until step 7, then place one third of the nut mixture into the base of the tin/pan, spread the chestnut purée on top, and top with mixture – there will be a little nut mixture left over but this can be made into rissoles or used as a sandwich filling.

Serve with a Chestnut or Mushroom sauce (pages 210 and 211), and the traditional Christmas vegetables – Brussels sprouts with Leeks, red pepper and dill (page 193), and/or Broccoli-stuffed tomatoes (page 192) are especially good.

Rice, pecan and mushroom bake

A creamy rice base, with a lovely, crunchy pecan topping.

Imp/Metric	Serves 4	American
8oz/225g	whole grain rice – dry weight – cook in 1pt/570ml/2½ cups water	1⅓ cups
1 tbsp	tamari	1 tbsp
4oz/100g	frozen peas	1 cup
	1 × quantity Mushroom sauce (page 211)	
3oz/75g	salt and freshly ground black pepper	¾ cup
	Optional	
½oz/15g	hijiki – soak in 5 fl oz/150ml/⅔ cup boiling water for 20 minutes, drain, saving the juice, and very finely chop	½ cup
	salt and freshly ground black pepper	
	pecan halves	

1 Set the oven to 375°F/190°C (Gas 5).
2 Combine the rice, tamari, peas, Mushroom sauce, and chopped hijiki and soaking liquid if using, in a large saucepan and gently heat through.
3 Season, then pour into a 2pt/1l ovenproof dish, and arrange the pecan halves on the surface in circles, working from the edge of the dish inwards.
4 Bake for 20 minutes covered, then 5 minutes uncovered.

Serving Suggestion
Serve with steamed courgettes/zucchini, leeks and a green salad. For a quicker version of this dish, heat through in a saucepan, then serve with a sprinkling of pecan halves.

Variation: replace 4oz/100g/⅔ cup of the whole grain rice with wild rice, or grain of choice.

P or (A)

Savoury nut rissoles

Moist rissoles – with a delicate flavour of herbs and hazelnuts.

Imp/Metric	Makes 8/Serves 4	American
2 tbsps	olive or sunflower oil	2 tbsps
6oz/175g	onion – very finely chop	1 cup
3oz/75g	celery – cut into strips, then very thinly slice	¾ cup
4	fresh bay leaves	4
1½ tsps	low-salt yeast extract	1½ tsps
2 tsps	finely chopped fresh thyme	2 tsps
2 tsps	finely chopped fresh marjoram	2 tsps
1 tsp	nutmeg	1 tsp
3oz/75g	finely grated/shredded carrot	½ cup
	salt and freshly ground black pepper	
4oz/100g	ground hazelnuts	1 cup
4oz/100g	ground cashews	1 cup
	(to convert to A, use ground almonds)	

Coating

1oz/25g/¼ cup each of very finely chopped cashews (to convert to A, use almonds) and very finely chopped hazelnuts

1 Set the oven to 375°F/190°C (Gas 5).
2 Heat the oil, and cook the onion and celery covered along with the bay leaves for 10 minutes, stirring occasionally.
3 Mix in the yeast extract, then add the herbs and nutmeg and cook a further minute.
4 Take the pan off the heat, remove the bay leaves, then stir in the carrot, and season.
5 Add the nuts and combine thoroughly.
6 If the mixture is a little dry, add 1-2 tbsps diluted milk to achieve a sticky consistency.
7 In a bowl mix together the very finely chopped nuts for coating.
8 Divide the rissole mixture into 8 portions.
9 Roll roughly into little balls, coat in the nut mix, then shape as desired.
10 Place on a non-stick or lightly greased baking tray/sheet, and bake for 20 minutes until browned.

Serving Suggestion

Serve hot with Tomato and oregano sauce (P only) (page 000), or Orange, apricot and pecan chutney (page 216), steamed green beans/fine green beans and cauliflower, or cold with chutney and salad. Made smaller, they are an ideal lunch box/ picnic snack.

P   Ⓥ

Spicy cashew nut casserole

You will find yourself cooking this dish time and time again – family and friends will love it. A good dish to try out on non-vegetarians.

Imp/Metric	Serves 4-6	American
2 tbsps	olive or sunflower oil	2 tbsps
8oz/225g	broken cashew nut pieces	1½ cups
8oz/225g	onion – finely chop	1⅓ cups
2	garlic cloves – crushed/minced	2
4oz/100g	courgette/zucchini – cut into small dice	1 cup
4oz/100g	carrot – cut into small dice	⅔ cup
4oz/100g	celery – cut into strips, then thinly slice	1 cup
¼-½ tsp	chilli powder	¼-½ tsp
1 tsp	ground cumin	1 tsp
1	vegetable stock cube	1
1 × 14oz/400g	tin/can of chopped tomatoes	1 × 14oz
1 dsp	tomato purée/paste	2 tsps
2 tsps	finely chopped fresh basil	2 tsps
1½ tbsps	tamari	1½ tbsps

5 fl oz/150ml/⅔ cup milk diluted
with 5 fl oz/150ml/⅔ cup water
salt and freshly ground black pepper

1 Heat 1 tbsp of the oil, and toast the cashew nuts until golden.
2 Remove from the pan and put to one side.
3 Heat the remaining oil, and fry the onion until soft.
4 Add the garlic, vegetables and cashew nuts, and cook covered for 10 minutes stirring occasionally.
5 Add the chilli and cumin, and cook a further 2 minutes.
6 Mix in the stock cube, then add the tomatoes, tomato purée/paste, basil and tamari, and combine thoroughly.
7 Stir in the diluted milk, then season and simmer gently for 15-20 minutes covered, stirring occasionally.

Serving Suggestion
Serve with Spinach and nutmeg purée (page 201), steamed cauliflower and salad. Also delicious topped with grated/shredded cheese.

S or (P)

Spinach and pistachio roulade with red pepper and chestnut filling

The unusual mixture of ingredients in this recipe results in a quite delicious combination of tastes and textures, and with its dramatic presentation it makes the perfect dish with which to impress your guests!

Imp/Metric	Serves 6	American
	Pistachio mixture	
4oz/100g	ground pistachios	1 cup
4oz/100g	ground walnuts/English walnuts	1 cup
4oz/100g	ground cashews	1 cup
2oz/50g	whole wheat breadcrumbs	½ cup
	(to convert to P, use wheatgerm)	
1 tbsp	olive or sunflower oil	1 tbsp
6oz/175g	onions – chop very finely	1 cup
1	garlic clove – crushed/minced	1
½	vegetable stock/bouillon cube	½
10oz/275g	frozen chopped spinach – cook and leave to cool	1¼ cups
2 tsps	finely chopped marjoram	2 tsps
2 tsps	finely chopped rosemary	2 tsps
	salt and freshly ground black pepper	
	Garnish	
4oz/100g	red pepper – cut into strips – steam for 3-4 minutes until tender	⅔ cup
	Filling	
1 tbsp	olive or sunflower oil	1 tbsp
4oz/100g	onions – chop very finely	⅔ cup
4oz/100g	red pepper – cut into small dice	⅔ cup
1	garlic clove – crushed/minced	1
2oz/50g	dried chestnuts – soak and cook then roughly chop – or 4oz/100g/⅔ cup	½ cup

tinned/canned whole chestnuts, roughly chop
(to convert to P, use 4oz/100g/1½ cups mushrooms, roughly chop)

1 Place the nuts and breadcrumbs/wheatgerm in a large bowl and combine.
2 Heat the oil and fry the onions until soft.

3 Add the garlic, cook for a further minute, then mix in the ½ vegetable stock cube.

4 Mix in the spinach and herbs then add to the nuts and breadcrumbs/wheatgerm.

5 Season, and combine thoroughly to form a moist but stiff mixture.

6 Now make the filling. Heat the oil and fry the onion until soft.

7 Add the pepper and garlic (and mushrooms if using) and cook a further 2-3 minutes.

8 Remove the pan from the heat, stir in the chestnuts, and season.

9 Now make up the roulade. Moisten two double thicknesses of muslin or similar cloth measuring 10in/25cm square.

10 Place half the steamed strips of pepper across one cloth 1in/2½cm in from all the edges, as shown in diagram 1.

11 Carefully press half the pistachio mixture on top of the pepper to cover the cloth, still leaving 1in/2½cm clear from each edge – diagram 2.

12 Place half the filling mixture widthways across the nut mixture 1in/2½cm from the bottom of the mixture – diagram 3.

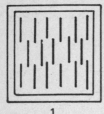
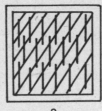
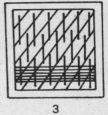

1   2   3

13 With the aid of the cloth, roll the nut mixture and stuffing to form a 'sausage', smooth the joining edges then wrap up firmly inside the cloth to seal.

14 Repeat with the remaining ingredients on the second cloth.

15 Place the roulades on a metal steamer in a large saucepan, cover, bring to the boil then simmer for 40 minutes.

16 Remove the roulades from the pan and place them with the cloth seam uppermost on a plate. Peel the cloth away from the sides then gently hold a serving plate on top and invert, so that the nut mixture 'seam' is on the base and the smooth surface is on the top, then lift away the cloth.

If following the roulade directions, freeze the nut mixture, filling and pepper strips separately, then make up and cook as directed once thawed; if preparing the recipe as a loaf make as directed and freeze whole, cooked or uncooked.

Serving Suggestion
For a starch meal, serve hot with Chestnut sauce (page 210), Rosemary and lemon roasted potatoes variation (page 197), steamed fennel and carrots, or cold with salad.

For a protein meal, serve as above but with Mushroom sauce (page 211), and omit the potatoes.

The nut mixture is delicious 'raw' as a pâté or spread, and ideal for making into burgers, or as a stuffing in vegetables.

Note: The roulades can be made several hours in advance or the night before, kept in a refrigerator and then steamed. Alternatively, make this recipe in a greased 2lb/900g loaf tin/pan lined with a strip of greased baking parchment, long enough to overhang at both ends. Arrange pepper strips widthways along the base of the tin (only 2oz/50g will be required), press a third of the nut mixture into the base, place the filling on top and then cover with the remaining nut mixture, bake covered for 15 minutes and uncovered for 15 minutes or until firm to the touch – this loaf will produce a layered effect on cutting.

Tomato, cheese and vegetable bake

This is a variation on the vegetable mix used for the Vegetable pasties/slices recipe, and makes a delicious bake.

Imp/Metric	Serves 4	American
3 tbsps	olive or sunflower oil	3 tbsps
6oz/175g	onion – finely chop	1 cup
6oz/175g	celery – cut into strips, then thinly slice	1½ cups
6oz/175g	red pepper – cut into small dice	1 cup
6oz/175g	carrots – cut into small dice	1 cup
2	garlic cloves – crushed/minced	2
½	vegetable stock cube	½
1 × 8oz/225g	tin/can of chopped tomatoes	1 × 8oz
1 tsp	finely grated/shredded lemon rind	1 tsp
2 tsps	finely chopped fresh marjoram	2 tsps
1½ tbsps	finely chopped fresh parsley	1½ tbsps
1½ tbsps	shoyu	1½ tbsps
1 dsp	light tahini	2 tsps
3oz/75g	flaked/slivered almonds	¾ cup
4oz/100g	grated/shredded Cheddar/	1 cup

New York Cheddar cheese/soya/soy cheese
salt and freshly ground black pepper

1 Set the oven to 375°F/190°C (Gas 5).
2 Heat the oil, and fry the vegetables and garlic covered for 10 minutes or until soft, then mix in the ½ stock/bouillon cube.
3 Stir in the tomatoes, and cook for 5 minutes uncovered.
4 Add the lemon rind, herbs and shoyu, and cook uncovered a further 3 minutes.
5 Stir in the tahini, almonds, and half the cheese, then season.
6 Place the mixture in a 2pt/1l casserole dish, and top with the remaining cheese.
7 Bake for 20-30 minutes until the topping is melted and browned.

Serving Suggestion
Serve with cauliflower, spring greens/collards and a green salad.

| S | |

Tricolour buckwheat galette

A visually appealing dish (tastes delicious too!) – excellent for dinner parties, and well worth the intricate preparation involved.

Imp/Metric	Serves 4-6	American
	Pancake/crêpe recipe (page 171) replacing	
	half the whole wheat flour with buckwheat flour	
	Red pepper layer	
1 tbsp	olive or sunflower oil	1 tbsp
8oz/225g	red pepper – finely dice	1⅓ cup
4oz/100g	onion – finely chop	⅔ cup
1	garlic clove – crushed/minced	1
2 tsps	finely chopped fresh basil	2 tsps
	salt and freshly ground black pepper	
	Leek and fennel layer	
2 tbsps	olive or sunflower oil	2 tbsps
6oz/175g	leeks – finely chop	1½ cups
6oz/175g	fennel – finely chop	1 cup
4	fresh bay leaves	4
	Spinach and nutmeg layer	
10oz/275g	frozen chopped spinach	1¼ cups
1 tsp	nutmeg	1 tsp
¼ tsp	vegetable stock paste yeast extract	¼ tsp

1 Make 7 pancakes/crêpes as given in the recipe.
2 Make the red pepper layer. Heat the oil and cook the pepper, onion and garlic covered for 10 minutes, stirring occasionally, add the basil and cook a further minute.
3 Place all the ingredients in a food processor or liquidizer/blender, and blend until almost smooth – retain a little texture – then season and leave to cool.
4 Now make the leek and fennel layer. Heat the oil and cook the leeks, fennel and bay leaves (covered) for 10 minutes.
5 Remove the bay leaves, then place in a food processor or liquidizer/blender, and blend to a thick purée, season and leave to cool.
6 Cook the spinach according to the instructions on the packet.
7 Stir in the nutmeg and vegetable stock paste/yeast extract, season and leave to cool.

8 Set the oven to 375°F/190°C (Gas 5).
9 Grease a 7in/17½cm spring-release or loose-bottomed tin/ springform pan.
10 To make up the galette, place a pancake/crêpe in the base of the tin/pan, and spread half the red pepper mixture on top.
11 Cover with another pancake/crêpe, and repeat with half the leek and fennel mixture.
12 Do once again using half the spinach and nutmeg mixture.
13 Repeat the sequence and top with the last pancake/crêpe.
14 Cover with foil, and bake for 45 minutes.
15 Leave to rest in the tin/pan for a couple of minutes, then remove carefully. Do not attempt to remove the galette from the base of the tin/pan, it can be cut and served from this.

Can be Frozen
For best results, freeze the pancakes/crêpes and red pepper and leek and fennel mixtures separately, then make up as directed once thawed; the spinach filling can be made when required.

Serving Suggestion
Serve with a Pine kernel or Mushroom sauce (pages 214 and 211), mangetout snowpeas, Almond potatoes (page 196) and mixed salad.

Vegetable pasties/slices

These are delicious, and will be a firm favourite with family and friends. For variation, make vegetable-filled pastry slices – the methods for both are given below.

Imp/Metric	Makes 8 pasties/12 slices	American

2 × basic quantity of shortcrust pastry recipe (page 154), substituting 2oz/50g of the flour with 2oz/50g/½ cup sesame seeds – keep in the refrigerator or a cool place until required

Filling

3 tbsps	olive or sunflower oil	3 tbsps
6oz/175g	onion – finely chop	1 cup
6oz/175g	celery – cut into strips, then thinly slice	1½ cups
6oz/175g	red pepper – cut into small dice	1 cup
6oz/175g	carrots – cut into small dice	1 cup
2	garlic cloves – crushed/minced	2
½	vegetable stock cube	½
1 tsp	finely grated/shredded lemon rind	1 tsp
2 tsps	finely chopped fresh marjoram	2 tsps
1½ tbsps	finely chopped fresh parsley	1½ tbsps
1 tbsp	shoyu	1 tbsp
1 dsp	light tahini	2 tsps
3oz/75g	flaked/slivered almonds – toasted	¾ cup
	salt and freshly ground black pepper	

Glaze

beaten egg yolk or diluted milk

1 Set the oven to 400°F/200°C (Gas 6).
2 If making pasties, lightly grease a baking sheet. For the slices grease a 9in/22½cm × 12in/30cm (inside measurement) Swiss roll tin/jelly roll pan, and line with greased baking parchment.
3 Heat the oil, and fry the vegetables and garlic (covered) for 10 minutes, or until soft, then blend in the ½ stock cube.
4 Add the lemon rind, herbs and shoyu and cook uncovered for 3 minutes.
5 Stir in the tahini and almonds, then season and put to one side to cool.
6 To make the pasties divide the pastry into 8, and roll out each piece on a floured surface into a circle approximately 6-7in/15-18cm in diameter. Place ⅛ of the vegetable mixture down the middle of each circle, then bring up the pastry sides and press together. Brush with the glaze, and prick once or twice with a fork to make steam-holes.

To make the slices, roll out half the pastry on a floured surface to fit the base of the tin/pan. Spread the vegetable mixture on top and smooth over. Roll out the other half of the pastry and place on top. Gently mark the pastry top into 12 squares; this will make it easier for cutting into slices once cooked. Prick the surface with a fork and brush with the glaze.

7 Bake the pasties/slices for 25 minutes, or until firm and golden brown.

Serving Suggestion
Serve hot with new potatoes and a green vegetable, or cold with salad. Both the pasties and slices are ideal as picnic or lunch box items. If serving cold, the squares can be left in the tin/pan until completely cool and then removed.

P

Walnut, orange and mushroom loaf

The richness of the walnuts/English walnuts and mushrooms are beautifully offset by the addition of orange rind in this loaf.

Imp/Metric	Serves 6-8 as a main course/ 10-12 as a starter/appetizer	American
2 tbsps	olive or sunflower oil	2 tbsps
6oz/150g	onions – finely chop	1 cup
6oz/150g	mushrooms – finely chop	2¼ cups
2	garlic cloves – crushed/minced	2
½	vegetable stock cube	½
6oz/150g	ground walnuts/English walnuts	1½ cups
6oz/150g	ground cashews	1½ cups
6oz/150g	finely grated/shredded carrots	1 cup
1 tsp	finely grated/shredded orange rind	1 tsp
1½ tbsps	finely chopped fresh parsley	1½ tbsps
1 large	egg, beaten	1 extra large
	(to convert to V, use 1 tbsp soya/soy flour mixed with 2 tbsps water)	
	salt and freshly ground black pepper	

1 Set the oven to 375°F/190°C (Gas 5).
2 Grease and line a 1lb/450g loaf tin/pan with a strip of greased baking parchment, long enough to overhang at both ends.
3 Heat the oil and fry the onion until soft.
4 Add the mushrooms, garlic and ½ stock cube, combine and cook a further 1-2 minutes.
5 Take the pan off the heat, and add the nuts, carrot, orange rind, parsley and beaten egg/soya/soy flour to the onion mix.

6 Season, then press into the prepared tin/pan – add extra ground nuts or wheatgerm if the mixture is too moist.

7 Bake for 30-45 minutes until browned and firm to the touch.

Serving Suggestion

Serve with Celery and onion purée (page 200), steamed courgettes/zucchini and broccoli. Also lovely served cold with salad or as a 'pâté'.

Kebabs

These are a visually appealing and fun way of eating vegetables, fruits, cheese and tofu, and ideal for using up oddments of vegetables in your refrigerator. Their attractive presentation is the perfect way, I find, of encouraging children to eat vegetables – they love the novelty!

Kebabs can be prepared and eaten as a starter, main course or side-vegetable; as a salad using salad and/or raw vegetable foods; or as a dessert using fruits. They do not have to be cooked – fresh/dried fruit, raw vegetable/salad foods and cheese variations are also especially delicious.

Vary the length of kebabs according to which part of the meal it serves – and the appetite of the diners – and make as colourful a selection of ingredients, and contrast of flavours and textures, as possible.

Thread your selected ingredients on to skewers, and very quickly and simply you will have an unusual and tasty dish or meal. Always bear in mind, though, the compatibility of ingredients when preparing kebabs.

Kebabs can be eaten with a sauce, dressing, or marinade (see Sauces and Dressings). A marinade can be prepared by mixing together olive or sunflower oil with fresh/dried herbs (rosemary and basil are particularly good), then adding various flavouring agents such as shoyu, tamari, tomato purée/paste (depending on meal structure), grated/shredded orange/lemon rind, garlic, etc. The prepared kebabs should then be left to marinate for 3-4 hours, or overnight.

To cook kebabs, place on a baking tray/pan and bake at 375°F/190°C (Gas 5), turning occasionally. Baste at regular intervals with any left-over marinade, if using, until the vegetables are tender. If not using a marinade, dribble a little olive oil over the kebabs, or top with a knob of butter/margarine to keep them moist. 'Tough' vegetables, for example carrots and potatoes, are best partly cooked before placing onto a skewer.

Some kebab ingredient suggestions

1 **Croûtons** – toasted cubes of bread flavoured with herb butter, garlic, etc
2 **Cheese** – cut into cubes
3 **Fruits** – fresh and/or dried
4 **Herbs** – fresh 'leafy' ones, placed between ingredients on the skewer
5 **Salad foods** – served raw or cooked
6 **Tofu** – very firm, cut into cubes
7 **Vegetable foods** – served raw or cooked

Vegetable stir-fries

Vegetable stir-fries are a delicious way of serving vegetables – and excellent for using up all the odd vegetables in your refrigerator! The best results are achieved in a wok, but a large frying pan/skillet is suitable.

I have not given specific recipes for stir-fries – the mixtures are endless, and it is fun to make up your own combinations with favourite and seasonal vegetables. Cooked grains of your choice are also a good addition for a more substantial starch-based meal. Try using different oils to enhance flavours – sesame oil, both toasted and untoasted, is excellent for this. Freshly chopped herbs can be added, and other ingredients such as shoyu/tamari, lemon juice, beansprouts, toasted nuts/seeds, dried fruits, coconut, etc, all add colour and variety of flavour and texture. Allow 3½lb/1.65kg ingredients to serve 4 people as a main course, 6-8 as a side-vegetable.

Vegetable side-dishes

These, along with salads, are one of the most important foods in the Hay System. They help to provide the required alkaline back-up needed to combat over-acidity. You will find that many vegetable dishes are equally good served either hot or cold, and topped with, or tossed in, a compatible dressing or sauce brighten up any meal! There are many wonderful flavour, appearance and texture combinations of vegetables, so do experiment and discover that there is more to them than just boiled cabbage!

All vegetable side-dishes are excellent served as main course alkaline dishes and, accompanied by a compatible sauce and salad, make a substantial and highly nutritious meal. Vegetable portions will serve half the number of people indicated when presented as main meals. Small portions of some of these vegetable dishes make perfect starters/appetizers. They can also be used to stuff pasties, fill pies and, topped with cheese, make a quick, simple and nutritious protein meal. Vegetable purées are excellent as jacket potato toppings/stuffings and as pancake/crêpe fillings.

Aubergine/eggplant and cucumber tossed in lemon and garlic

A delicious and unusual array of flavours.

Imp/Metric	Serves 4	American
2 tbsps	olive or sunflower oil	2 tbsps
4	garlic cloves – crushed/minced	4
1lb/450g	cucumber – score the skin with a fork then cut into ¾in/2cm cubes	4½ cups
1lb/450g	aubergine/eggplant – cut into cubes	
4 tsps	finely grated lemon rind	4 tsps
	salt and freshly ground black pepper	

1 Heat the oil, and gently fry the garlic for 1 minute.
2 Add the cucumber, and cook covered for 5 minutes.
3 Add the aubergine/eggplant and lemon rind, cover and cook a further 5-8 minutes or until tender, adding water to the saucepan if necessary.
4 Season.

Serving Suggestion
This dish is also very tasty cold as a salad with a few drops of olive oil – very garlicky so beware!

Beans and carrots encircled in cucumber

Another favourite of mine, with a lovely combination of flavours and colours. The unusual presentation makes it ideal for special occasions – and certainly rules out any suggestion that 'vegetables are boring'!

Imp/Metric	Serves 4 as a starter/ appetizer/side-vegetable	American
8	¾in/2cm wide cucumber slices – remove the centres and reserve for the dressing	8
32	fine green beans – top and tail into equal lengths	32
10oz/275g	carrots – trim and cut into 32 sticks, the same size and length as the beans	10oz
	Dressing	
1½ tbsps	sunflower oil	1½ tbsps
1½ tbsps	finely chopped fresh dill	1½ tbsps
2 tsps	lemon rind	2 tsps
1	garlic clove – crushed/minced	1
¼ tsp	paprika	¼ tsp
	cucumber centres (see above)	
	salt and freshly ground black pepper	

1 Steam the cucumber rings for 8-12 minutes, then place in a large bowl.
2 Steam the beans and carrots for 12-15 minutes until tender, but still slightly crunchy.
3 Meanwhile prepare the dressing by placing all the ingredients in a food processor or liquidizer/blender, and blending briefly (do not over blend as this will release the bitterness from the cucumber seeds and lemon rind).
4 Add the cooked beans and carrots to the bowl, along with the cucumber rings, and while still hot pour the dressing over, combine and cover.
5 Leave to cool, drain off the dressing and reserve.
6 Arrange four beans and four sticks of carrot through the centre of each ring.

Cannot be Frozen

Serving Suggestion
Garnish with fresh dill, and serve chilled as a starter/appetizer or side-vegetable with the dressing (do not drain it off); or place on a baking tray/pan, cover with foil, and warm through at 375°F/190°C (Gas 5) for 5-10 minutes and serve hot with the dressing (do not drain it off).

| Served Cold – N; Served Hot – P | |

Broccoli-stuffed tomatoes

An impressive way to serve tomatoes with a most appealing combination of flavours and colours – perfect for Christmas dinner!

Imp/Metric	Serves 4 as a starter/appetizer/ side-vegetable/2 as a main course	American
1 tbsp	olive or sunflower oil	1 tbsp
4oz/100g	onion – finely chop	⅔ cup
12oz/350g	broccoli – finely chop	4 cups
1½ tbsps	finely chopped fresh basil	1½ tbsps
1 dsp	tamari	1 tsp
	salt and freshly ground black pepper	
2	large tomatoes – approximately 8oz/ 225g each in weight, halve and scoop out the centres, reserving them	2

Garnish

12 fresh basil leaves/4 cherry tomatoes

Dressing

1½ tbsps	olive oil	1½ tbsps
1½ tbsps	finely chopped fresh basil	1½ tbsps
	tomato centres (see above)	
	salt and freshly ground black pepper	

1 Heat the oil, and fry the onion until soft.
2 Add the broccoli and cook covered for 10 minutes, or until tender.
3 Add the basil and tamari and combine.
4 Season, and blend in a food processor or liquidizer/blender until smooth.
5 Use an ice-cream scoop to form four broccoli balls.
6 Divide the remaining broccoli mixture between the four tomato shells, and press into each base.
7 Place three basil leaves around the edge to form 'petals'.
8 Place the broccoli ball on top, then garnish with a cherry tomato.
9 Place all the dressing ingredients in a food processor or liquidizer/blender, and blend until combined.
10 Pour the dressing over each tomato half or serve separately.

Cannot be Frozen

Serving Suggestion
This dish is delicious served hot or cold – to serve hot, place covered on a lightly greased baking tray/pan, without the basil leaves or cherry tomatoes, and bake in an oven set at 375°F/190°C (Gas 5) for 10-15 minutes, or until heated through, then garnish as described above.

Brussels sprouts with leeks, red pepper and dill

An interesting array of tastes and colours: another perfect Christmas dinner accompaniment!

Imp/Metric	Serves 4	American
1 tbsp	olive or sunflower oil	1 tbsp
8oz/225g	leeks – cut into strips or thinly slice	2 cups
4oz/100g	red pepper – cut into small dice	⅔ cup
2 tbsps	finely chopped fresh dill	2 tbsps
8fl oz/225ml	boiling water	1 cup
1lb/450g	Brussels sprouts – halve or quarter depending on their size	1lb
	salt and freshly ground black pepper	

1 Heat the oil, and cook the leeks and red pepper covered for 10 minutes.
2 Stir in the dill, add the boiling water, then add the sprouts.
3 Bring back up to the boil, then simmer covered a further 5 minutes or until the sprouts are tender, and season.

Cannot be Frozen

Serving Suggestion
Serve as a side-vegetable, or topped with cheese as a delicious main course.

N

Cauliflower, broccoli and carrot with toasted flaked/slivered almonds

A delightful mixture of flavours, colours and textures.

Imp/Metric	Serves 4	American
6oz/175g	broccoli florets	1½ cups
6oz/175g	cauliflower florets	1½ cups
4oz/100g	carrot – slice, then cut in semi-circles	⅔ cup
	salt and freshly ground black pepper	
2oz/50g	flaked/slivered almonds – toasted	½ cup

1 Steam the vegetables together until tender, but still slightly crunchy.
2 Season, then stir in the flaked/slivered almonds and serve.

Serving Suggestion
Serve as a side-vegetable, or sprinkle with cheese for a light lunch/evening meal or main course dish.

N

Celery and garden peas cooked with cinnamon and cloves

A warming, spicy vegetable mixture.

Imp/Metric	Serves 3-4	American
2 tbsps	olive or sunflower oil	2 tbsps
4oz/100g	onions – cut in semi-circles	⅔ cup
12oz/350g	celery – cut into sticks	3½ cups
2 tsps	ground cinnamon	2 tsps
4	cloves	4
8oz/225g	frozen peas	1⅓ cups
	salt and freshly ground black pepper	

1 Heat the oil, and cook the onion and celery covered together with the spices for 25 minutes.
2 Add the peas, cook a further 5 minutes, then season.

Serving Suggestion
Use to accompany delicate-flavoured main courses, or serve on
its own as a main course dish.

N

Gingered courgettes/zucchini, mushrooms and carrots

The rich flavour of fresh root ginger beautifully complements these vegetables.

Imp/Metric	Serves 4 as a main course/ 6-8 as a side-vegetable	American
2 tbsps	olive or sunflower oil	2 tbsps
1lb/450g	carrots – cut into strips	3 cups
4	fresh bay leaves	4
½	bouillon stock cube	½
1lb/450g	courgettes/zucchini – cut on a slant	5 cups
1oz/25g	fresh root ginger – peel and grate/shred	1oz
1½ tbsps	finely chopped fresh rosemary	1½ tbsps
1lb/450g	button mushrooms	8 cups
1½ tbsps	light tahini	1½ tbsps
1½ tbsps	tamari	1½ tbsps
1½oz/40g	sunflower seeds – ground	6 tbsps
4 fl oz/100ml	water	½ cup
	salt and freshly ground black pepper	

1 Heat the oil, and cook the carrots along with the bay leaves covered for 5 minutes.
2 Mix in the stock cube, then add the courgettes/zucchini.
3 Squeeze the grated ginger, and add the juice only to the pan, along with the rosemary, cover and cook a further 5 minutes.
4 Add the mushrooms, then stir in the tahini, tamari, ground sunflower seeds and water.
5 Cover, cook a further 5 minutes, then season.

Serving Suggestion
Use to accompany delicate-flavoured main courses, or serve as a main course with rice or grain of choice, or a cheese topping, depending on meal structure, steamed vegetables and a green salad.

Fennel with green pepper

A light, refreshing combination of vegetables.

Imp/Metric	Serves 4	American
12oz/350g	fennel – cut in slices lengthways	2 cups
6oz/175g	green pepper – cut into thin strips	1 cup
	salt and freshly ground black pepper	

1 Steam the fennel for 10-15 minutes until tender, but still slightly crunchy.
2 Add the green pepper, and cook a further 3-5 minutes until tender, then season.

Serving Suggestion
Also delicious topped with cheese or toasted flaked/slivered almonds, and served as a protein main course.

Almond potatoes

A lovely nutty combination.

Imp/Metric	Serves 4	American
1½-2lb/675-900g	potatoes – scrub or peel, then cut into large dice	1½-2lb
2oz/50g	flaked almonds – toast, then roughly chop	½ cup
	salt and freshly ground black pepper	

1 Boil the potatoes until tender, drain away any excess water, add the flaked almonds, and season.

Cannot be Frozen

Serving Suggestion
Alternatively mash the potatoes, season, form into 'croquettes', roll these in the flaked almonds, then heat through in a hot oven.

S　　　　　　　　　　　　　　　　　　　　Ⓥ

Lemon potatoes

Lemon gives potatoes a lovely tangy, refreshing flavour.

Imp/Metric	Serves 4	American
1½-2lb/675-900g	potatoes – scrub or peel, then cut into large dice	1½-2lb
1oz/25g	butter/margarine	2 tbsps
1-2 tsps	finely grated lemon rind	1-2 tsps
	salt and freshly ground black pepper	

1 Boil the potatoes until tender, drain away any excess water, then toss in the butter/margarine, add the lemon rind to taste and season.

Cannot be Frozen

Serving Suggestion
Lemon roasted potatoes is a variation of this recipe. Roast the potatoes in a sunflower oil and finely grated lemon rind mixture, basting at regular intervals. Alternatively, prepare Rosemary lemon roasted potatoes by adding some finely chopped fresh rosemary (or dried if unavailable) to the oil and lemon rind mixture.

N　　　　　　　　　　　　　　　　　　　　Ⓥ

Red pepper with courgettes/zucchini

A colourful and tasty vegetable mix.

Imp/Metric	Serves 4	American
1lb/450g	courgettes/zucchini – cut in thin slices	4½ cups
6oz/175g	red pepper – cut into thin strips	1 cup
	salt and freshly ground black pepper	

1 Steam the courgettes/zucchini for 3-4 minutes.
2 Add the red pepper, combine and steam a further 5 minutes, or until both are tender, then season.

Serving Suggestion
Provides a delicious accompaniment to grain or pulse/legume-based dishes.

S or A Ⓥ

Savoury parsley potatoes

A delicious mashed potato variation.

Imp/Metric	Serves 4-6	American
1 tbsp	olive or sunflower oil	1 tbsp
8oz/225g	onion – finely chop	1⅓ cups
1 dsp	rice or barley miso	2 tsps
1½lb/675g	potatoes – scrub or peel and cut into large dice	1½lb
12fl oz/350ml	water	1½ cups
6 tbsps	finely chopped fresh parsley	6 tbsps
1 tsp	nutmeg	1 tsp
	salt and freshly ground black pepper	

1. Set the oven to 400°F/200°C (Gas 6).
2. Heat the oil, and fry the onion until soft.
3. Take the pan off the heat and blend in the miso, remove the mixture from the saucepan and put to one side.
4. Add the potato to the saucepan, along with the water, bring to the boil, then simmer until soft, adding more water if necessary.
5. Once cooked mash to a purée, draining away any excess water first, or adding more if required.
6. Stir in the onion mix, then add the parsley and nutmeg, and season.
7. Use an ice-cream scoop or spoon and shape into balls, or spoon into a greased ovenproof dish and smooth over.
8. Bake uncovered for 25 minutes, or until the top is crisp and browned.

Cannot be Frozen

Serving Suggestion
Serve as a vegetable accompaniment, or with Mushroom or Onion sauce (pages 211 and 213), and mixed salad as a main course.

N

Spicy red cabbage

A lovely warming vegetable dish – ideal for cold winters!

Imp/Metric	Serves 4	American
1 tbsp	olive or sunflower oil	1 tbsp
8oz/225g	onion – cut in semi-circles	1⅓ cups
1 tsp	nutmeg	1 tsp
½ tsp	mixed spice	½ tsp
¼ tsp	ground cloves	¼ tsp
1lb/450g	red cabbage – chop or shred very thinly	4 cups
2oz/50g	sunflower seeds – toasted	½ cup
	salt and freshly ground black pepper	

1 Heat the oil, and fry the onion until soft.
2 Blend in the spices, and cook a further minute.
3 Add the cabbage and sunflower seeds, season, then cover and simmer very gently for 1½ hours; alternatively bake covered for 2 hours at 325°F/170°C (Gas 3).

Serving Suggestion
Serve with nut loaves, burgers, bakes, pies, pancakes/crêpes, etc, or serve as a main course with rice, or topped with mashed potato, chopped nuts or grated cheese, depending on the meal structure.

Variation: omit the spices, and add 1½ tbsps finely chopped fresh dill and 2 crushed/minced cloves of garlic instead.

Vegetable purées

Vegetable purées make a pleasant change in texture and appearance from whole vegetables. They can also be served as a thick sauce, or pancake/crêpe or jacket potato filling/topping.

Celery and onion purée

Imp/Metric	Serves 4	American
2 tbsps	olive or sunflower oil	2 tbsps
12oz/350g	celery – finely chop	3 cups
12oz/350g	onion – finely chop	2 cups
4	fresh bay leaves	4
	salt and freshly ground black pepper	

1 Heat the oil, and cook the celery, onion and bay leaves covered for 10 minutes or until tender.
2 Remove the bay leaves, then place the mixture in a food processor or liquidizer/blender, blend until smooth, then season.

Leek and fennel purée

Imp/Metric	Serves 4	American
3 tbsps	olive or sunflower oil	3 tbsps
12oz/350g	leeks – finely chop	3 cups
12oz/350g	fennel – finely chop	2 cups
6	fresh bay leaves	6
	salt and freshly ground black pepper	

1 Heat the oil, and cook the leeks, fennel and bay leaves covered for 10 minutes or until tender.
2 Place in a food processor or liquidizer/blender, blend to a thick purée, then season.

Red pepper purée

Imp/Metric	Serves 4	American
2 tbsps	olive or sunflower oil	2 tbsps
1lb/450g	red pepper – finely chop	2⅔ cups
8oz/225g	onion – finely chop	1⅓ cups
2	garlic cloves – crushed/minced	2
1½ tbsps	finely chopped fresh basil	1½ tbsps
	salt and freshly ground black pepper	

1 Heat the oil, and cook the pepper, onion and garlic covered for 10 minutes, or until tender, add the basil and cook a further minute.
2 Place in a food processor or liquidizer/blender, blend until smooth, then season.

Spinach and nutmeg purée

Imp/Metric	Serves 4	American
1¼lb/550g	frozen chopped spinach	2½ cups
2 tsps	nutmeg	2 tsps
½ tsp	vegetable stock paste/yeast extract	½ tsp
	salt and freshly ground black pepper	

1 Cook the spinach according to the instructions on the packet.
2 Stir in the nutmeg and vegetable stock paste/yeast extract, and season.

Variation: omit the vegetable stock paste/yeast extract and flavour with 2 tbsps lemon juice – suitable at P and A meals only.

Tomato and basil purée

Imp/Metric	Serves 4	American
2 tbsps	olive or sunflower oil	2 tbsps
8oz/225g	onion – finely chop	1⅓ cup
2	garlic cloves – crushed/minced	2
1½lb/675g	very ripe tomatoes – skin and roughly chop – or 2 × 14oz/400g tin/can chopped tomatoes	4 cups
3 tbsps	tomato purée/paste	3 tbsps
1½ tbsps	finely chopped fresh basil	1½ tbsps
	salt and freshly ground black pepper	

1 Heat the oil, and fry the onion until soft.
2 Add the garlic, tomatoes, tomato purée/paste and basil, and mix well.
3 Cook uncovered until the tomatoes are soft and the mixture reduced to a thick purée, then season.

Variation: delicious served topped with cheese.

N

Winter vegetables flavoured with oregano

A rather special way to serve winter vegetables.

Imp/Metric	Serves 4	American
1 tbsp	olive or sunflower oil	1 tbsp
3oz/75g	onion – cut in semi-circles	½ cup
3oz/75g	celery – cut into strips, then thinly slice	¾ cup
4	fresh bay leaves	4
6oz/175g	parsnips – quarter, then slice	1 cup
6oz/175g	turnip – cut into ¾in/2¼cm cubes	1 cup
6oz/175g	swede/rutabaga – cut into ¾in/2¼cm cubes	1 cup
6oz/175g	carrot – cut into ¾in/2¼cm cubes	1 cup
1½ tbsps	finely chopped fresh oregano	1½ tbsps
10fl oz/275ml	boiling water	1⅓ cup
	salt and freshly ground black pepper	

1 Heat the oil, and cook the onion and celery covered along with the bay leaves for 10 minutes.
2 Add all the remaining ingredients except the seasoning.
3 Bring back to the boil, then simmer covered for 15-20 minutes until the vegetables are tender.
4 Cook uncovered for a further 2 minutes to reduce some of the remaining liquid, leaving sufficient to form a nice moist dish, remove the bay leaves, then season.

Serving Suggestion
This dish makes an ideal base for a casserole – simply add chopped nuts or pulses/legumes of your choice, and some extra stock – or top with mashed potato or cheese, depending on meal structure, for a 'pie' dish.

Buffets and barbecues

These are becoming increasingly popular ways of eating and entertaining and are easily adapted to the Hay System. You will find some buffet and barbecue menu ideas throughout the recipe section – but for good measure, I have given a few extra suggestions!

Buffet suggestions

To be served on cocktail sticks/toothpicks:

Apple Cubes in Lemon Juice with Pecan Halves	P
Baby New Potatoes and Parsley Sprigs	S
Baby Tomatoes and Basil Leaves	N
Button Mushrooms and Carrot Cubes	N
Cucumber and Mint Leaves	N
Pasta Shells and Baby Radishes	S
Papaya and Celery	S
Pineapple and Cheese	P
Pineapple and Olives	P
Bowls of Assorted Nuts and Seeds mixed with Raisins	S or P or A
Cheesy Hazelnut Croûtons	S or P or A
Cucumber/Firm Tomato Slices – serve with a choice of sandwich spreads/toppings, dips, pâtés and spreads	S or P or A
Dried Apricots/Prunes – stuff with cream cheese/soya/soy 'cream cheese', nuts or P, A or N dips, pâtés and spreads	P or A
Dried Dates/Figs – stuffed with cream cheese, nuts or S or N dips, pâtés and spreads	S or A
'Miniature' P and A Crackers Starch-free* served with a choice of P, A or N sandwich fillings/toppings, dips, pâtés and spreads	P or A

'Miniature' S Crackers, Crispbreads, Oatcakes –
served with a choicee of S or N sandwich spreads/
toppings, dips, pâtés and spreads   S

'Miniature' Triangular Sandwiches – with S and N
sandwich fillings/toppings, dips, pâtés and spreads   S

Vol-au-Vents – Nut/Seed 'Pastry' – served with
P, A or N sandwich fillings/toppings, dips, pâtés
and spreads – use Starch-free cracker/pastry recipes,
cut small circles of biscuit mix to form a vol-au-vent
base and then a smaller ring to form a top, bake
as directed*   P or A

Vol-au-Vents – Pastry – with choice of S or N
sandwich fillings/toppings, dips, pâtés and spreads   S

Walnut/Pecan Halves – sandwich together with
cream cheese soya/soy 'cream cheese' or P
sandwich spread/toppings, dips, pâtés and spreads   P

* these nut/seed 'pastry/pie crust' vol-au-vents are also ideal for starch
spreads/toppings, etc, and can be used at a starch buffet if an alternative
to bread/pastry/pie crust, etc, is desired.

Barbecue suggestions

Artichoke Hearts – brush with olive oil and lemon
juice then wrap in foil, place on the barbecue and
heat through, turn occasionally**   N

Bean Sprouts – wrap in 'bundles' in foil with a knob
of butter/margarine and a sprinkling of shoyu,
crushed/minced garlic and herbs, place on the
barbecue and heat through, turning occasionally   N

**Bread – Garlic/Herb/Herb and Cream Cheese/Nut
Butters** – prepare the bread with a spread of your
choice, wrap in foil, place on the barbecue and heat
through   S

Celery Hearts – wrap in foil with a knob of
butter/margarine, sprinkle with toasted seeds and
crushed/minced garlic, place on the barbecue and
heat through**   N

Corn-on-the-Cob – pre-cook then wrap in foil with a
knob of butter/margarine and sprinkling of
dried/chopped fresh marjoram, place on the
barbecue and heat through, turn occasionally   S

** use tinned artichoke, celery and palm hearts for quicker and easier
barbecuing.

Flat-Cap Mushrooms – select large mushrooms, remove the stalks, brush with olive oil and crushed fennel seeds, place on the barbecue and cook through, turning occasionally · N

Kebabs – marinate overnight or 6-8 hours, remove from the marinade, place on the barbecue and cook through, brush with any left-over marinade and turn occasionally · S or P or A

Nut Loaves – cut in slices, lightly brush with olive oil, place on the barbecue and cook through, turning occasionally · S or P or A

Onions – select onions weighing approximately 4oz/100g each, bake in the oven until tender, then wrap in foil with a knob of butter/margarine and a sprinkling of tamari and dried/freshly chopped rosemary, place on the barbecue and heat through, turn occasionally · N

Palm Hearts – brush with olive oil and dried/chopped fresh basil, place on the barbecue and heat through, turn occasionally** · N

Polenta Burgers – make polenta, adding some chopped fried onions and shoyu and herbs to taste, spread in a baking tin/pan, leave to cool and set then cut into shapes, lightly brush with olive oil, place on the barbecue and cook through, turning occasionally · S

Potatoes – Jacket Potatoes/New Potatoes/Sweet Potatoes – pre-bake, then brush lightly with olive oil, place on the barbecue and cook through, turning occasionally, and serve with butter/margarine, or S or N sandwich spreads/toppings, dips, pâtés and spreads · S

'Sausages'/Burgers – use nut loaf/rissole recipes of choice and shape into 'sausages'/burgers, lightly brush with olive oil, place on the barbecue and cook through, turn occasionally · S or P or A

Vegetable Sticks – marinate carrot, celery and courgette/ zucchini sticks – approximately 3in/7.5cm long, ¾in/1.5cm wide – in olive oil, lemon rind and dried/chopped fresh mixed herbs overnight, place on the barbecue and cook through, turning occasionally · N

** use tinned artichoke, celery and palm hearts for quicker and easier barbecuing.

Sauces and chutneys

Sauces and chutneys not only give extra flavour to meals, but act as a moist accompaniment to otherwise 'dry' ingredients. They add visual appeal and interest to complement the overall finish of a dish. Although this is not their original purpose, they can also act as excellent 'concealers for what lies underneath – particularly useful when feeding children who may be unaware that their most-hated food is hidden, and will munch away quite merrily! On the Hay System they are an excellent way of increasing the daily alkaline intake.

As already mentioned under Soups, sauces can also make delicious soups – simply by adding extra water, milk or stock!

Vegetable purées can also be used as thick sauces, or be thinned down further to the desired consistency.

S or P or (A)

Asparagus sauce

A variation on the Asparagus dip recipe earlier – also very quick and easy to make!

Imp/Metric	Serves 4 as a sauce/ 2 as a soup	American
1	12oz/350g tin/can green asparagus spears	1
3oz/75g	ground cashews	¾ cup
	(to convert to A, use ground almonds)	
½	garlic clove – crushed/minced	½
pinch	paprika	pinch
5 fl oz/150ml	juice from the tinned/ canned asparagus	⅔ cup
	salt and freshly ground black pepper	

1 Place the asparagus spears with the cashews, garlic and paprika in a food processor or liquidizer/blender, and blend until combined.
2 Add the asparagus juice, blend again until very smooth, then season.

Serving Suggestion
Serve as prepared, cold, or heat through and serve hot. Use as a pasta or vegetable topping, or as an accompaniment to nut loaves, bakes, burgers, pancakes/crêpes, etc – also delicious thinned down and served as a soup.

S or (P) or (A)

Carrot and lemon sauce

The sharp lemony flavour in this sauce contrasts beautifully with the sweetness of carrot.

Imp/Metric	Serves 6	American
1 tbsp	olive or sunflower oil	1 tbsp
4oz/100g	onion – finely chop	⅔ cup
4	fresh bay leaves	4
1	garlic clove – crushed/minced	1
½	stock/bouillon cube	½
4oz/100g	very finely grated/shredded carrot	⅔ cup
2 tsps	finely chopped fresh thyme	2 tsps
1 tsp	finely grated/shredded lemon rind	1 tsp
1½oz/40g	whole wheat flour	½ cup
	(to convert to P or A, use 4oz/100g	
	ground cashews/ground almonds	
10 fl oz/275ml	carrot juice	1⅓ cups
10 fl oz/275ml	water	1⅓ cups
	salt and freshly ground black pepper	

1 Heat the oil, and fry the onion until soft along with the bay leaves.
2 Add the garlic and cook a further minute.
3 Mix in the stock/bouillon cube, and add the carrot, thyme and lemon rind.
4 Stir in the flour/ground nuts, then remove the pan from the heat.

5 Slowly add the carrot juice and water, stirring all the time to avoid any lumps.
6 Return the pan to the heat, bring gently to the boil, stirring continuously until the sauce thickens, then season.
7 Remove the bay leaves.

Serving Suggestion
Serve as prepared, or place in a food processor or liquidizer/blender, and blend until smooth. The flavour of this sauce is enhanced when used to accompany mildly-flavoured main course dishes, and it is delicious served with vegetables.

P

Cheese and cashew sauce

A rich, creamy cheese sauce.

Imp/Metric	Serves 6	American
1oz/25g	butter/margarine	2 tbsps
4	fresh bay leaves	4
4oz/100g	ground cashews	1 cup
½ tsp	paprika	½ tsp
	10 fl oz/275ml/1⅓ cups milk, diluted with	
	10 fl oz/275ml/1⅓ cups water	
3oz/75g	finely grated/shredded Cheddar/	¾ cup
	New York Cheddar cheese/soya/soy cheese	
	salt and freshly ground black pepper	

1 Melt the butter/margarine, then add the bay leaves.
2 Stir in the ground cashews to form a 'roux', add the paprika, then remove the pan from the heat.
3 Slowly add the diluted milk, stirring all the time to avoid any lumps forming.
4 Return the pan to the heat and bring to the boil, stirring continuously until the sauce thickens.
5 Remove the pan from the heat, season, then stir in the cheese until thoroughly combined.
6 Heat through gently to prevent the sauce becoming 'stringy'.

Serving Suggestion
Serve with protein-based nut loaves, burgers, bakes, etc. Delicious as a vegetable topping.

S or (A)   (V)

Chestnut sauce

A beautiful sauce – the sweet chestnut flavour is delicately offset by the addition of herbs.

Imp/Metric	Serves 6	American
1 tbsp	olive or sunflower oil	1 tbsp
6oz/175g	onion – chop very finely	1 cup
1	garlic clove – crushed/minced	1
1 tsp	finely chopped marjoram	1 tsp
1 tsp	finely chopped rosemary	1 tsp
1 dsp	tamari	2 tsps
2oz/50g	dried chestnuts – soak and cook –	½ cup

saving the cooking liquid for stock –
then finely chop – or 4oz/100g/⅔ cup
tinned/canned whole chestnuts – saving
the tinned liquid for stock – then finely chop

1oz/40g	whole wheat flour	¼ cup

(to convert to A, use
3oz/75g/¾ cup ground almonds)

1pt/570ml	chestnut stock – or tinned stock	2½ cups

and water
salt and freshly ground black pepper

1 Heat the oil and fry the onion until soft.
2 Add the garlic, herbs, tamari and chestnuts and cook a further minute.
3 Mix in the flour/ground nuts then remove the pan from the heat.
4 Slowly stir in the chestnut stock/stock and water.
5 Season, return the pan to the heat and bring to the boil, stirring continuously until the sauce thickens.

Serving Suggestion
Serve as prepared, or place in a food processor or liquidizer/blender and blend until smooth. Use as a accompaniment to burgers/bakes/pies/roulades, nut loaves, pancakes/crêpes, etc.

| P or A | |

Minted pea and apple sauce

A light, fruity sauce – also makes an excellent hot or chilled soup.

Imp/Metric	Serves 4 as a sauce/ 2 as a soup	American
10oz/275g	red apple – peel and thinly slice	1⅔ cups
4oz/100g	frozen peas	⅔ cup
1 tsp	finely chopped fresh mint	1 tsp

1 Place the apple in a saucepan with 1 tbsp water and cook gently, covered, for 5-10 minutes or until soft.
2 Add the peas and mint and cook a further 5 minutes.
3 Blend the mixture until smooth.

Serving Suggestion
Serve hot or cold with Minted pea and apple courgettes/zucchini (page 169), or as an accompaniment to other vegetable and main course dishes.

| S or (P) or (A) | |

Mushroom sauce

A rather special mushroom sauce, well worth preparing and a favourite with children.

Imp/Metric	Serves 6	American
2 tbsps	olive or sunflower oil	2 tbsps
4oz/100g	mushrooms – thinly slice	2 cups
4oz/100g	onion – finely chop	⅔ cup
½	vegetable stock cube	½
2	garlic cloves – crushed/minced	2
4oz/100g	mushrooms – chop *very* finely	1½ cups
1 dsp	tamari	2 tsps
1½oz/40g	whole wheat flour	½ cup
	(to convert to P or A, use 4oz/100g/ 4oz/100g/⅔ cup ground cashews/almonds)	
15 fl oz/425ml	boiling water	2 cups
5 fl oz/150ml	milk	⅔ cup
	salt and freshly ground black pepper	

1 Heat 1 tbsp of the oil and fry the sliced mushrooms for 3-4 minutes until tender.
2 Remove from the pan and put to one side.
3 Add the remaining 1 tbsp oil to the pan, heat and then fry the onion until soft.
4 Blend in the ½ stock cube, then add the garlic, chopped mushrooms and tamari, and cook a further 2-3 minutes or until the mushrooms are tender.
5 Mix in the flour/ground nuts and combine thoroughly.
6 Take the pan off the heat and slowly stir in the water.
7 Return the pan to the heat, bring to the boil, stirring continuously, and simmer gently uncovered for 3-4 minutes until the mixture thickens.
8 Blend until smooth in a food processor or liquidizer/blender, then add the reserved mushrooms and milk and season.
9 Bring back to the boil, stirring continuously, then simmer for 3-4 minutes.

Serving Suggestion
Serve this sauce with nut loaves, roulades, burgers, bakes, pies, pancakes/crêpes, vegetables, jacket potatoes, etc – it also makes a tasty and useful alternative to a cheese or white sauce in lasagnes and other pasta dishes.

Ⓥ

| S or (P) or (A) |

Onion sauce

A popular sauce – lovely as a vegetable/potato topping.

Imp/Metric	Serves 6	American
2 tbsps	olive or sunflower oil	2 tbsps
12oz/350g	onion – very finely chop	2 cups
4	fresh bay leaves	4
1	garlic clove – crushed/minced	1
1 tsp	low-salt yeast extract	1 tsp
2 tsps	finely chopped fresh oregano	2 tsps
1½oz/40g	whole wheat flour	½ cup

(to convert to P or A, use 4oz/100g/1
cup ground cashews/almonds
5 fl oz/150ml/⅔ cup milk, diluted
with 15 fl oz/425ml/2 cups water
salt and freshly ground black pepper

1 Heat the oil, and cook the onion covered along with the bay leaves for 10 minutes.
2 Add the garlic, cook a further minute, then blend in the yeast extract and oregano.
3 Stir in the flour/nuts, then remove the pan from the heat.
4 Slowly add the diluted milk, stirring all the time to avoid any lumps forming.
5 Return the pan to the heat, and bring to the boil, stirring continuously until the sauce thickens, then season.

Serving Suggestion
Stir in 1 tbsp of shoyu for a more savoury sauce. Serve as prepared, or place in a food processor or liquidizer/blender, and blend until smooth; eat with nut loaves, burgers, bakes, pies, pancakes/crêpes, etc. It also makes a delicious casserole base, simply add cooked vegetables, pulses/legumes, nuts/seeds, etc, depending on the meal structure.

| S or (P) or (A) | Ⓥ |

Pine kernel sauce

This is a truly delicious sauce – a great favourite of mine with its lovely rich flavour.

Imp/Metric	Serves 6	American
1½oz/40g	butter/margarine	3 tbsps
2oz/50g	whole wheat flour	½ cup
	(to convert to P or A, use 4oz/100g/1 cup ground cashews/almonds)	
4oz/100g	pine kernels – ground (they will turn to a sticky paste)	1 cup
	5 fl oz/150ml/⅔ cup milk diluted with 15 fl oz/425ml/2 cups water	
	salt and freshly ground black pepper	

1 Melt the butter/margarine, and stir in the flour/ground nuts to form a 'roux'.
2 Take the pan off the heat and mix in the pine kernels.
3 Very slowly add the diluted milk until evenly distributed, stirring all the time to avoid any lumps forming.
4 Return the pan to the heat, and bring to the boil stirring continuously until the sauce thickens – this may take a while, – then season.

Serving Suggestion
Serve with nut loaves, burgers, bakes, pies, pancakes/crêpes, etc. Excellent as a savoury alternative to a cheese or white sauce in lasagnes/moussakas, etc, and as a protein-rich vegetable topping.

Ⓥ

S or (P) or (A)

Savoury brown sauce

A delicious alternative to gravy.

Imp/Metric	Serves 6	American
1½ tbsps	olive or sunflower oil	1½ tbsps
4oz/100g	onion – finely chop	⅔ cup
4oz/100g	celery – cut into strips, then thinly slice	1 cup
4	fresh bay leaves	4
1	garlic clove – crushed/minced	1
2 tsps	low-salt yeast extract	2 tsps
1 tsp	finely chopped fresh thyme	1 tsp
1 tsp	finely chopped fresh rosemary	1 tsp
1½oz/40g	whole wheat flour	½ cup
	(to convert to P or A, use 4oz/100g/1 cup ground cashews/almonds	
1½ tbsps	shoyu	1½ tbsps
	5 fl oz/150ml/⅔ cup milk diluted with 15 fl oz/425ml/2 cups water	
	salt and freshly ground black pepper	

1 Heat the oil, and fry the onion and celery covered for 5-10 minutes until soft, stirring occasionally.
2 Add the bay leaves to the pan along with the garlic, and cook for a further minute uncovered.
3 Blend in the yeast extract, and add the herbs.
4 Stir in the flour/ground nuts, then remove the pan from the heat.
5 Slowly add the shoyu and diluted milk, stirring all the time to avoid any lumps forming.
6 Return the pan to the heat, season and bring gently to the boil, stirring continuously until the sauce thickens, then remove the bay leaves.

Serving Suggestion
Serve as prepared, or place in a food processor or liquidizer/blender and blend until smooth. Use to accompany nut loaves, burgers, bakes, pies, pancakes/crêpes, etc.

Tomato and oregano sauce

A beautiful, rich 'Italian-tasting' sauce.

Imp/Metric	Serves 4	American
1½ tbsps	olive or sunflower oil	1½ tbsps
6oz/175g	onion – finely chop	1 cup
2	garlic cloves – crushed/minced	2
1½lb/675g	very ripe tomatoes – skin and chop – or 1 × 14oz/400g tin/can, and 1 × 8oz/225g tin/can chopped tomatoes	4 cups
2 tbsps	finely chopped fresh oregano	2 tbsps
	salt and freshly ground black pepper	

1 Heat the oil, and fry the onion and garlic until soft, then add the tomatoes.
2 Bring to the boil, add the oregano, season, and leave to simmer uncovered, until the liquid has reduced and the sauce thickened.

Serving Suggestion
Serve as prepared, or place in a food processor or liquidizer/blender, and blend until smooth; eat with protein-based dishes, or use as a vegetable topping. This sauce is also delicious flavoured with basil or marjoram instead of oregano.

| P or (A) |

Orange, apricot and pecan chutney

A truly delicious chutney – will definitely be popular with the family!

Imp/Metric	Makes 1¼-1½lb/550-675g	American
3	large oranges – skin and segment, squeeze and save the juice from the empty centres	3
6oz/175g	dried apricots – soak overnight or 8-12 hours in 5 fl oz/150ml/⅔ cup boiling water, drain and save any excess liquid then chop until 'mushy'	1 cup
1 tbsp	concentrated apple juice	1 tbsp
1 tbsp	cider vinegar	1 tbsp
	(to convert to A, use lemon juice)	
½ tsp	paprika	½ tsp
2oz/50g	pecan nuts – chopped into very small pieces	½ cup
	(to convert to A, use nibbed almonds)	

1. Place all the ingredients, including the juice from the oranges and soaked apricots, in a saucepan and combine thoroughly.
2. Bring to the boil covered, then simmer gently uncovered for 10 minutes, or until the liquid has almost all evaporated, stirring occasionally to help break down the orange segments.
3. Take the pan off the heat, leave the mixture to cool and thicken, then place in a jar or airtight container and refrigerate.

Serving Suggestion
Serve as an accompaniment to salads, vegetables and main courses.

S or A

Pear and banana chutney

An unusual fresh-tasting, tangy chutney.

Imp/Metric	Makes approximately 1lb/ 450g quantity	American
6oz/175g	dried pears – roughly chop	1 cup
6oz/175g	dried banana – roughly chop	1 cup
½ tsp	finely grated/shredded lemon rind	½ tsp
½ tsp	finely grated/shredded orange rind	½ tsp

1 Soak the dried fruits for at least 3-4 hours in 10 fl oz/275ml/1⅓ cups boiling water.
2 Drain, save the soaking water, and chop very finely.
3 Place in a saucepan with the soaking water and orange and lemon rind, bring to the boil then simmer gently covered for 5 minutes, adding more water if necessary, but the final mixture should be stiff and free of liquid.
4 Leave to cool, then press into an airtight jar.

Serving Suggestion
Serve as an accompaniment to salads, vegetables and main courses.

Biscuits/cookies and cakes

For treats, special occasions and entertaining on the Hay System, biscuits/cookies and cakes are always a welcome sight! The following healthy recipes should impress you and your guests, and prove that you can be 'wicked' without being too naughty! Some of the recipes are also suitable as desserts.

P or A   Ⓥ

Apricot, nut and seed gateau

A delectable way to eat fruits, nuts and seeds!

Imp/Metric	Serves 10-12	American
8oz/225g	dried apricots – quarter	1½ cups
10fl oz/275ml	unsweetened orange juice	1⅓ cups
4oz/100g	flaked/slivered almonds – toasted	1 cup
4oz/100g	sunflower seeds	¾ cup
2oz/50g	sesame seeds	½ cup
2oz/50g	pumpkin seeds	½ cup
5oz/150g	ground almonds	1¼ cups
5oz/150g	ground hazelnuts	1¼ cups
4oz/100g	hazelnuts – chop very finely	¾ cup
6oz/175g	raisins – lexia if available	1 cup
1 tsp	vanilla essence	1 tsp
	Decoration	
	extra apricots and toasted flaked/ slivered almonds/pumpkin seeds	

1 Soak the apricots overnight – or 8-12 hours – in the orange juice.
2 Grease a 7in/17½cm round spring-release tin/springform pan and line the base with a piece of greased baking parchment.

3 Mix all the dry ingredients except the raisins together in a large bowl.

4 Place the soaked apricots, soaking juice, raisins and vanilla essence in a food processor or liquidizer/blender, and blend until well chopped, but still retaining some texture.

5 Add to the dry ingredients, and combine thoroughly to a sticky consistency.

6 Transfer to the prepared tin/pan, and press down using a potato masher.

7 Cover with baking parchment, place a weight on top and refrigerate for 6-8 hours.

8 Release the sides of the tin/pan, turn the gâteau out onto a serving plate, and ease the base away.

9 Slice the extra apricots in half through the middle, and use to decorate the top, along with the flaked/slivered almonds and pumpkin seeds.

Serving Suggestion
Serve as a rich cake, or as a dessert topped with cream, yoghurt or ice-cream.

Carob cookies

Extremely 'moreish'!

Imp/Metric	Makes 8-10	American
3oz/75g	butter/margarine	⅓ cup
1 dsp	honey/maple syrup	2 tsps
	1 tbsp milk diluted with 1 tbsp water	
½oz/15g	dark carob powder	2 tbsps
8oz/225g	ground whole wheat digestive biscuits/	2 cups
	Graham crackers	
	Optional	
	carob bar and drops for decoration	

1 Line a 7in/17½cm round cake tin/pan or similar with foil.
2 Melt the butter/margarine in a large saucepan over a low heat.
3 Blend in the honey/maple syrup.
4 Take the pan off the heat, mix in the diluted milk and the carob powder, then add the ground biscuits/crackers.
5 Combine thoroughly to a sticky consistency.
6 Press the mixture firmly into the base of the tin/pan using a potato masher, leave to cool, then cover and refrigerate for 6-8 hours to set.
7 Turn the hardened mixture out onto a board, cut into biscuits/cookies and store in a refrigerator – or decorate with melted carob pieces or drops. Place some boiling water in a saucepan, rest a bowl on top making sure it lies above the surface of the water, add the carob and leave to melt slowly, stirring occasionally. Brush each biscuit with this melted carob and place a carob drop in the centre, leave to cool and set, then store in an airtight container in a refrigerator. They will keep for 2-3 weeks – if you can hide them from the children! (and adults, too!).

Serving Suggestion
Serve as a healthy alternative to chocolate biscuits/cookies, or use as a dessert base (without the melted carob), top with mashed banana or 'starch' or 'neutral' fruit of choice, and serve with cream/ice-cream and hot carob sauce. It also makes an alternative starch base for cheesecakes.

S

Date and orange slices

These are absolutely delicious – so be prepared to make another batch!

Imp/Metric	Makes 24	American
1lb/450g	dates – dried and stoned/pitted	3¼ cups
1 tsp	finely grated/shredded orange rind	1 tsp
12oz/350g	porridge oats	3 cups
8oz/225g	whole wheat self-raising/ self-rising flour	2 cups
2oz/50g	sesame seeds	½ cup
6oz/175g	butter/margarine	¾ cup
6 tbsps	malt extract	6 tbsps
1oz/25g	sunflower seeds	¼ cup

1 Set the oven to 375°F/190°C (Gas 5).
2 Grease and line a 9in × 12in/23cm × 30cm (inside measurement) Swiss roll tin/jelly roll pan with a piece of greased baking parchment, large enough for the paper to come up above the sides.
3 Place the dates in a saucepan, and add just enough water to cover them.
4 Bring to the boil, then simmer covered for approximately 15 minutes, or until soft and 'mushy', and the water has evaporated.
5 Leave to cool, then stir in the orange rind.
6 Mix the oats, flour and sesame seeds in a large bowl.
7 Place the butter/margarine and malt extract in a saucepan over a low heat, and melt together.
8 Pour the hot melted ingredients into the oat mixture, and combine quickly and thoroughly to form a sticky consistency.
9 Put 8oz/225g of this mixture to one side, and press the remainder firmly into the base of the lined tin/pan using a potato masher.
10 Spread the date and orange mixture over the oat base.
11 Add the sunflower seeds to the remaining 8oz/225g oat mixture, mix in well and sprinkle over the top of the dates.
12 Press down by rolling over the surface with a rolling pin, then bake for 15-20 minutes until firm and browned.

Serving Suggestion
As a sweet serve hot or cold with cream/ice-cream, or leave to cool completely in the tin/pan and cut and eat as biscuits/cookies.

Variation: for a 'chocolatey' version add 1 tbsp dark carob powder to the flour and oat mixture. 1oz/25g/⅓ cup desiccated/shredded coconut can also be added to the topping as an alternative. Dried pears can be used instead of the dates – place these in a food processor or liquidizer/blender, and blend until smooth before using as a filling.

Gingercake

A truly delicious gingercake, which becomes even better with keeping – if you can hide it for long enough from family and friends, that is!

Imp/Metric	Makes one 8in/20cm square/ 9in/22½cm round cake	American
8oz/225g	whole wheat flour	2 cups
1½ tsps	bicarbonate of soda/baking soda	1½ tsps
1½ tsps	ground ginger	1½ tsps
1½ tsps	mixed spice	1½ tsps
4oz/100g	butter/margarine	½ cup
6 tbsps	clear honey/maple syrup	6 tbsps
6 tbsps	blackstrap molasses	6 tbsps
2oz/50g	crystallized ginger pieces – rub off	½ cup

any excess sugar, then place in a food processor
or liquidizer/blender and blend to a paste
2 fl oz/50ml/¼ cup milk diluted with
3 fl oz/75ml/⅓ cup water

| 2 large | eggs yolks, beaten | 2 extra large |

(to convert to V, use 1 tbsp chick pea/
garbanzo flour mixed with 1½ tbsps water)

1 Set the oven to 325°F/160°C (Gas 3).
2 Grease and line the base and sides of an 8in/20cm square or 9in/22½cm round cake tin/pan with a double layer of greased baking parchment.
3 Sieve/sift the flour, bicarbonate of soda/baking soda and spices into a large bowl, adding back any separated bran.
4 Put the butter/margarine, honey/maple syrup, molasses and

ginger paste in a saucepan over a low heat.

5 Use a wooden spoon to break down the ginger paste, and stir the mixture until all the ingredients are evenly distributed.

6 Pour the hot melted ingredients into the flour mixture, and add the diluted milk.

7 Mix well, then beat in the egg/garbanzo flour mix, combine thoroughly, and pour the mixture into the tin/pan.

8 Bake for 45-50 minutes until set and springy to the touch.

9 Cool for 5-10 minutes in the tin/pan, then transfer to a wire rack to cool completely. Peel away the side layers of baking parchment, but leave the base layers and remove once the cake is cold.

Serving Suggestion

This cake can be eaten straightaway, or wrapped in baking parchment and foil and left 3-4 days to become 'sticky'.

 ⟨V⟩

Hot cross buns

A lovely Easter treat.

Imp/Metric	Makes 16	American
1oz/25g	fresh yeast – or 1 tbsp dried yeast/	2½ tbsps
	1 sachet easy blend yeast – use according	
	to the instructions on the packet	
	7 fl oz/200ml/¾ cup warm water (5 fl oz/	
	150ml/⅔ cup cold water, mixed with	
	2 fl oz/50ml/¼ cup cold water)	
1½lb/700g	100% strong whole wheat flour	6 cups
2 tsps	mixed spice	2 tsps
½ tsp	ground cinnamon	½ tsp
½ tsp	ground nutmeg	½ tsp
½ tsp	salt	½ tsp
1½ tbsps	maple syrup	1½ tbsps
2oz/50g	butter/margarine	¼ cup
3oz/75g	currants	½ cup
3oz/75g	sultanas/golden seedless raisins	½ cup
2oz/50g	mixed peel	⅓ cup
8 fl oz/225ml	diluted milk	1 cup
3oz/75g	pastry (if liked – see Steps 7 and 9)	3oz
1½ tbsps	malt extract	1½ tbsps

1 Mix together the yeast and water, then add to 4oz/100g/1 cup of the flour, leave for 15-20 minutes, or until frothy.
2 Sieve/sift the remaining flour, spices and salt into a large bowl, adding back any separated bran, and rub/cut in the butter/margarine.
3 Add the currants, sultanas/golden seedless raisins and mixed peel and maple syrup.
4 Pour the frothed-up flour mix into the dry ingredients, then add the diluted milk, and combine to form a dough.
5 Knead for 10 minutes, or until smooth, then place in a large bowl, cover with a damp cloth or cling film/plastic wrap and leave in a warm place until double in size – approximately 1-1¼ hours.
6 Knock back/punch down and knead for 5 minutes, then divide into 3oz/75g pieces.
7 Shape into rounds, place on greased baking sheets, then cover with a damp cloth or cling film/plastic wrap, and leave to rise for approximately 30-40 minutes, or until double in size. (If you do not want the extra work of making 'crosses' (see below) gently score a cross on top of each bun with a knife – this will open up slightly on rising and produce a 'cross' effect).
8 Set the oven to 425°F/210°C (Gas 7).
9 Make crosses by rolling out the pastry and cutting into thin strips, dampen with water and place on the top of the risen buns.
10 Bake 5 minutes or until browned, then turn the oven down to 375°F/190°C (Gas 6), and cook for a further 10-15 minutes, or until the bases sound hollow when tapped.
11 Mix the malt extract with 1 tbsp water in a small saucepan and heat gently until dissolved, then as soon as the buns come out of the oven brush with the glaze, and leave to cool on a wire cooling rack – or eat warm with melted butter/margarine.

Serving Suggestion
This recipe need not be kept solely for Easter, but can be served as 'spicy buns' at other times of the year (but without the crosses). I often divide this recipe into 2 large rounds which I then gently press in the middle to make a hole, and 'snip' or score around the edges in 5 places – these 'snips'/scores will open up on cooking to give an attractive finished appearance. Glaze as for the smaller buns above.

S   (V)

Rich fruit cake/Christmas cake

A beautifully moist cake, perfect for special occasions such as Christmas and birthdays – or everyday indulgence!

Imp/Metric	Makes an 8in/20cm square or 9in/22½cm round cake	American
4oz/100g	dried figs	¾ cup
4oz/100g	dried dates, pitted	¾ cup
4fl oz/100ml	water	½ cup
1½ tbsps	molasses	1½ tbsps
6oz/175g	butter/margarine	¾ cup
4 large	eggs yolks, beaten	4 extra large
	(to convert to V, use 2 rounded tbsps chickpea/ garbanzo flour mixed with 3 tbsps water)	
8oz/225g	sultanas/golden seedless raisins	1½ cups
2 tsps	mixed spice	2 tsps
8oz/225g	golden seedless raisins	1½ cups
8oz/225g	raisins	1½ cups
8oz/225g	currants	1½ cups
4oz/100g	glacé cherries – naturally coloured – quarter	¾ cup
2oz/50g	flaked/slivered almonds	½ cup
2oz/50g	ground almonds	½ cup
1 tsp	finely grated/shredded lemon rind	1 tsp
3 tbsps	brandy	3 tbsps
	Optional	
	extra brandy	

1 Place the figs and dates in a saucepan with the water and cook covered until they are soft and all the water has been absorbed. Leave to cool.

2 Preheat the oven to 325°F/160°C (Gas 3).

3 Grease and line the base and sides of the cake tin/pan with a double layer of greased baking parchment, leaving a 2-3in/5-7½cm height above the top of the tin/pan.

4 Tie a double layer of brown paper around the outside of the tin/pan.

5 Cream/beat the figs, dates, molasses and butter/margarine together until light and fluffy.

6 Gradually add the beaten egg/chickpea/garbanzo flour and water, mixing until smooth, then sieve/sift together the flour and mixed spice and stir the mixture in.

7 Add all the remaining ingredients and combine thoroughly to achieve a moist consistency – mix in a little water if required.

8 Press into the prepared tin/pan and bake for approximately 1¼-1½ hours, or until a knife when inserted into the centre comes out clean.

9 Leave to cool in the tin/pan, then remove, wrap in greaseproof/waxed paper and foil, and store in a cool place until needed. This cake can be made and kept 4-6 weeks before eating for the flavour to mature. For an even richer cake add extra brandy – prick the base with a fork every 2-3 weeks, gently dribble 1-2 tbsps over the surface, leave to soak in, then re-wrap in the paper and foil until required.

Serving Suggestion
As a Christmas cake, top, or cover completely, with almond paste. A healthy alternative to icing is to sprinkle the top with lightly crushed flaked almonds.

 Ⓥ

Scones

Always a welcome sight at the tea table – especially when piled high with honey and cream!

Imp/Metric	Makes 12	American
8oz/225g	plain/all-purpose whole wheat flour	2 cups
4 tsps	baking powder	4 tsps
pinch	salt	pinch
2oz/50g	butter/margarine	¼ cup
	2 fl oz/50ml/¼ cup milk diluted with 2 fl oz/50ml/¼ cup water	
	Optional	
	1-2 tbsps honey/maple syrup*	

1 Set the oven to 425°F/220°C (Gas 7).
2 Sieve/sift the flour and baking powder, adding back the

---

* I usually make my scones sugar-free: then one has the option of eating them with sweet or savoury spreads. However, if you prefer a sweet scone, add 1-2 tbsps honey/maple syrup and adjust the liquid content accordingly, or add a little extra flour.

separated bran, and salt into a large bowl, then rub/cut in
the butter/margarine.

3 Add the diluted milk, stir in using a fork, then bring the
mixture together to achieve a firm but moist dough.

4 Roll out on a floured surface to ¾-1in/2¼-2½cm thickness,
and cut into rounds with a 2in/5cm scone/cookie cutter.

5 Place on a lightly greased/non-stick baking tray/sheet, and
bake for 12-15 minutes until risen and browned.

6 Cool on a wire rack.

Serving Suggestion

Serve with starch or neutral spreads/toppings – and cream, of
course! For a quick version, shape the dough into one large
circle, score across into 8 wedges, then bake as described – these
score marks will open up on cooking to produce an attractive
'scone ring'.

Variations: for two delicious and unusual variations, replace
4oz/100g/1 cup whole wheat flour with 4oz/100g/¾ cup
cornmeal flour/fine polenta or buckwheat flour – these
mixtures will not rise as much as the 100% whole wheat scones.

S   (V)

Sponge cake

A quick 'mix altogether' sponge.

Imp/Metric	Makes 1×7in/17½cm cake	American
8oz/225g	plain/all-purpose whole wheat flour	2 cups
4 tsps	baking powder	4 tsps
	(or substitute 8oz/225g self-raising/	
	self-rising flour with 2 tsps baking powder)	
1-2 tbsps	clear honey/maple syrup	1-2 tbsps
4 fl oz/100ml	sunflower oil	½ cup
2 large	egg yolks, beaten	2 extra large
	(to convert to V, omit and use an extra	
	2 fl oz/50ml/¼ cup water	
6 fl oz/175ml	water	¾ cup

1 Set the oven to 350°F/180°C (Gas Mark 4).
2 Grease and line the base of 2×7in/17½cm sandwich cake tins/pans with greased baking parchment.
3 Sieve/sift the flour and baking powder into a bowl, adding back any separated bran.
4 Add the honey/maple syrup, oil and egg yolks/water, and enough of the water to produce a thick, batter-like consistency.
5 Pour into the prepared tins/pans, and bake for 20-25 minutes until golden brown and the centre springs back when lightly pressed.
6 Turn out onto a wire cooling rack and remove the baking parchment.

Serving Suggestion
Sandwich together with a starch filling such as mashed banana, chestnut purée, cooked mashed dates, carob cream, etc.

Variation: add 1 tsp of vanilla/almond essence for a vanilla/almond-flavoured sponge; 1-2 tsps orange/lemon rind for an orange/lemon-flavoured sponge; 1 tbsp dark carob powder for a 'chocolatey' flavour. One of my favourites is almond and carob.

Almond paste

A luxurious almond paste which will probably not reach the cake without some secret 'nibbling'!

This quantity is sufficient to top an 8in/20cm square or 9in/22½cm round cake. Make double the quantity to cover the sides as well.

Imp/Metric	Makes 8oz/225g	American
2oz/50g	butter/margarine	¼ cup
7oz/200g	ground almonds	1¾ cups
1½ tsps	almond essence	1½ tsps
4 tbsps	maple syrup	4 tbsps

1 Melt the butter/margarine in a large saucepan.
2 Remove the pan from the heat, add the remaining ingredients.
3 Mix to a moist paste, adding more ground almonds if over moist.
4 Leave to cool – this mixture will become firmer as it cools – then roll out, or shape as desired.

Serving Suggestion
This almond paste can also be shaped into balls and coated in chopped/ground nuts/seeds/carob powder to make petits fours/sweets.

S or A		Ⓥ

Mincemeat

A delicious, fruity mincemeat.

Imp/Metric	Makes 6lb/2¾kg	American
12oz/350g	stoned/pitted dried dates	2½ cups
4oz/100g	dried banana – roughly chop	¾ cup
4oz/100g	dried pears – roughly chop	¾ cup
15fl oz/425ml	water	2 cups
1lb/450g	raisins	3 cups
1lb/450g	sultanas/golden seedless raisins	3 cups
1lb/450g	currants	3 cups
4oz/100g	nibbed almonds	1 cup
6oz/175g	margarine/grated/shredded white vegetable fat	¾ cup
1 tsp	finely grated/shredded lemon rind	1 tsp
1 tsp	finely grated/shredded orange rind	1 tsp
½ tsp	ground cinnamon	½ tsp
½ tsp	ground nutmeg	½ tsp
1 tsp	mixed spice	1 tsp
5-10 fl oz/150-275ml	brandy or red grape juice, or mixture of both to achieve a moist but stiff consistency	⅔-1⅓ cups

1 Place the dates, banana and pears in a saucepan with the water, cover and bring to the boil, then simmer gently until the banana and pears are tender, the dates 'mushy', and all the water is absorbed. Leave to cool then chop very finely.
2 Combine thoroughly in a large bowl with all the remaining ingredients to form a moist but stiff mixture.
3 Cover, then leave to stand in a cool place for two days, stirring two to three times daily, and adding more liquid if required.
4 Press firmly into glass containers, leaving a 1in/2.5cm space at the top.
5 Cover with jam/jelly pot covers, or screw-on lids, and store in a cool, dry place. It will also keep for a year without freezing if well sealed.

Serving Suggestion
Mincemeat is best left to 'mature' for 4-5 weeks, then use to make mince pies, or as a filling in tarts, cakes, etc. Refrigerate once opened.

Crackers (savoury starch-free)

As I have already mentioned, there are numerous excellent savoury starch-based crispbreads/crackers available, and I did not feel it necessary to provide others. I developed the idea of starch-free crackers when looking for something other than raw vegetables to eat with dips, pâtés, spreads, etc – or with cheese. I found that ground nuts and seeds treated in a similar manner to flour made excellent substitutes. You can try varying the types of nuts and seeds used for different flours.

The recipes provided are all egg-free, allowing them to be eaten, if compatible, with a starch or alkaline meal. You may wish to use egg as a binding ingredient in some of the recipes to facilitate rolling out, in which case a little beaten egg yolk will still ensure their compatibility with all meals; the addition of beaten whole egg or egg white will cause them to be classed as protein.

[N]

Almond and poppy seed crackers

Delicately flavoured crackers with a 'melt-in-the-mouth' texture.

Imp/Metric	Makes 15-20	American
7oz/200g	ground almonds	1¾ cups
4 tsps	poppy seeds	4 tsps
1 tsp	baking powder	1 tsp
½ tsp	almond essence	½ tsp
1oz/25g	butter/margarine – melted	2 tbsps
	2-3 tbsps diluted milk	
	extra ground almonds for rolling out	

1 Set the oven to 375°F/190°C (Gas 5).
2 Combine the ground almonds, poppy seeds, baking powder and almond essence in a bowl.
3 Mix in the butter/margarine, then add the diluted milk and stir in using a fork.
4 Bring the mixture together with your hand to achieve a firm but moist dough.
5 Roll out to ⅛-¼in/3-6mm thickness on a surface sprinkled with some of the extra ground almonds – the mixture is fairly easy to handle, but if it is too sticky, sprinkle the top with some extra ground almonds.
6 Cut into rounds with a 2-2½in/5-6cm scone/cookie cutter and use a palette knife/narrow spatula to lift carefully on to a non-stick/lightly greased baking sheet.
7 Bake 8-12 minutes, or until lightly browned and firm in texture, leave to cool and harden on the sheet for a few minutes, then transfer to a wire cooling rack, to cool completely.

Serving Suggestion

Serve as a semi-sweet cracker, as an alternative to bread crispbreads, oatcakes with pâtés, soups, cheeses, etc, or with savoury/sweet spreads for a snack/breakfast meal. They also make an ideal base for canapés at buffets.

Variation: serve as a sweet accompaniment with ice-creams, fools, etc, by using 1 teaspoon of almond essence instead of ½ teaspoon, and cutting the dough into fingers as well as rounds.

S or P

Caraway and sunflower crackers

The simple addition of caraway seeds to these crackers gives them a delicious flavour.

Imp/Metric	Makes 15-20	American
2 tsps	caraway seeds – roughly chop, or grind in a pestle and mortar	2 tsps
4oz/100g	ground sunflower seeds	1 cup
4oz/100g	ground cashews	1 cup
1 tsp	baking powder	1 tsp
1oz/25g	butter/margarine – melted	2 tbsps
2-3 tbsps	diluted milk*	2-3 tbsps
	extra ground sunflower seeds for rolling out	

1 Set the oven to 375°F/190°C (Gas 5).
2 Combine the caraway and sunflower seeds, cashews and baking powder in a bowl.
3 Mix in the butter/margarine, then add the milk and stir in using a fork.
4 Bring the mixture together with your hand to achieve a firm but moist dough.
5 Roll out to a thickness of ⅛-¼in/3-6mm on a surface sprinkled with some of the extra ground sunflower seeds – the mixture is fairly easy to handle, but if too sticky sprinkle the rolled-out surface with some of the extra ground sunflower seeds.
6 Cut into rounds using a 2-2½in/5-6cm scone/cookie cutter, and use a palette knife/narrow spatula to lift carefully on to a non-stick/lightly greased baking sheet.
7 Bake for 10-15 minutes, or until browned and firm in texture, leave to cool and harden on the baking sheet for a few minutes, then transfer to a wire cooling rack to cool completely.

---

* the dough is easier to work if combined with a little egg white/beaten egg/egg yolk – but with careful handling it can be made using diluted milk if preferred.

Serving Suggestion

Serve as an alternative to bread/crispbreads/oatcakes with pâtés, soups, cheeses, etc, or with savoury/sweet spreads for a snack/breakfast meal. They also make an ideal base for canapés at buffets.

P   Ⓥ

Cheese crackers

A delicious cheesy base for savoury toppings and spreads.

Imp/Metric	Makes 15-20	American
8oz/225g	ground sunflower seeds	2 cups
2oz/50g	finely grated/shredded Cheddar/ New York Cheddar soya/soy cheese	½ cup
1 tsp	baking powder	1 tsp
2-3 tbsps	milk	2-3 tbsps
	extra ground sunflower seeds for rolling out	

1 Set the oven to 400°/200°C (Gas 6).
2 Mix together the seeds, cheese and baking powder.
3 Add the milk to form a dough.
4 Roll out to ⅛-¼in/3-6mm thickness on a surface sprinkled with some of the extra ground sunflower seeds – the mixture is fairly easy to handle, but if too sticky, sprinkle the rolled-out surface with some extra ground sunflower seeds.
5 Cut into rounds using a 2-2½in/5-6cm scone/cookie cutter, and use a palette knife/narrow spatula to lift carefully on to a non-stick or lightly greased baking sheet.
6 Bake for 10-12 minutes, or until firm and lightly browned.
7 Leave to cool and harden on the baking sheet for a few minutes, then transfer to a wire cooling rack to cool completely.

Serving Suggestion

Cut into small shapes and use as savoury nibbles, or form into cheese straws.

N

Hazelnut and almond crackers

The sweet, delicate flavour of hazelnuts makes these crackers rather special.

Imp/Metric	Makes 15-20	American
3oz/75g	ground hazelnuts	¾ cup
5oz/150g	ground almonds	1¼ cups
1 tsp	baking powder	1 tsp
1oz/25g	butter/margarine – melted	2 tbsps
2-3 tbsps	diluted milk	2-3 tbsps
	extra ground hazelnuts/ground almonds for rolling out	

1 Set the oven to 375°F/190°C (Gas 5).
2 Combine the nuts and baking powder in a bowl.
3 Mix in the butter/margarine, then add the diluted milk and stir in using a fork.
4 Bring the mixture together with your hand to achieve a firm but moist dough.
5 Roll out to ⅛-¼in/3-6mm thickness on a surface sprinkled with some of the extra ground hazelnuts/ground almonds – the mixture is fairly easy to handle, although if too sticky sprinkle the rolled-out surface with some extra ground almonds.
6 Cut into rounds with a 2-2½in/5-6cm scone/cookie cutter and use a palette knife/narrow spatula to lift on to a non-stick/lightly greased baking sheet.
7 Bake 10-12 minutes until lightly browned and firm in texture, leave to cool and harden on the baking sheet for a few minutes, then transfer to a wire cooling rack to cool completely.

Serving Suggestion
Serve as an alternative to bread, crispbread, oatcakes with pâtés, soups, cheeses, etc, or with savoury/sweet spreads/toppings for a snack or breakfast meal. They also make an ideal base for canapés at buffets.

Variation: serve as a sweet accompaniment with ice-creams, fools, etc, by adding ½ tsp of almond or vanilla essence.

Sunflower and sesame crackers

Lovely nutty-flavoured crackers.

Imp/Metric	Makes 15-20	American
7oz/200g	ground sunflower seeds	1¾ cups
1oz/25g	sesame seeds	¼ cup
1 tsp	baking powder	1 tsp
1oz/25g	butter/margarine – melted	2 tbsps
2-3 tbsps	diluted milk*	2-3 tbsps
	extra ground sunflower seeds for rolling out	

1 Set the oven to 375°F/190°C (Gas 5).
2 Combine the seeds and baking powder in a bowl.
3 Mix in the butter/margarine, then add the diluted milk and stir in using a fork.
4 Bring the mixture together with your hand to achieve a firm but moist dough.
5 Roll out to ⅛-¼in/3-6mm thickness on a surface sprinkled with some of the extra ground sunflower seeds – the mixture does tend to become rather sticky yet crumbly and there may be some difficulty in rolling out, it will help if extra ground sunflower seeds are sprinkled on top*.
6 Cut into rounds and use a palette knife/narrow spatula to lift carefully on to a non-stick/lightly greased baking sheet.
7 Bake 10-15 minutes until browned and firm in texture, leave to cool and harden on the sheet for a few minutes, then transfer to a wire cooling rack, to cool completely.

Serving Suggestion
Serve as an alternative to bread, crispbreads or oatcakes with pâtés, soups, cheeses, etc, or with savoury/sweet spreads for a snack/breakfast meal. They also make an ideal base for canapés at buffets.

---

* this mixture is easier to work if combined with a little egg white/beaten egg/egg yolk – but with careful handling it can be made using diluted milk if preferred.

Bread

There can be nothing more enticing than home-made, freshly-baked bread straight out of the oven. If you do have the time (and energy) bread and yeast baking is a most rewarding culinary occupation – and very therapeutic too!

Bread recipes are numerous and varied, and with the exception of soda bread are almost always starch-based. You will find that most cook books have large bread sections with recipes in line with the Hay principles and these can be used accordingly. No book, however, on the Hay system would be complete without Doris Grant's 'Grant' Loaf and this is set out below.

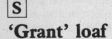

'Grant' loaf

A beautiful, moist bread, quick and easy to make, with no lengthy kneading!

Imp/Metric	Makes 2 × 1lb/450g loaves	American
18oz/500g	strong 100% whole wheat flour	4½ cups
1 tsp	salt	1 tsp
1 tsp	blackstrap molasses	1 tsp
1oz/25g	fresh yeast – or 1 tbsp dried yeast/	2½ tbsps

1 sachet easy blend yeast, use according
to the instructions on the packets
15 fl oz/425ml/2 cups warm water (10 fl oz/
275ml/1⅓ cups cold water mixed with 5 fl oz/
150ml/⅔ cup boiling water)

1 Lightly grease 2 × 1lb/450g bread tins/pans.
2 Place the flour and salt in a bowl.
3 Mix together the molasses and fresh yeast until they turn to liquid, then add 5 fl oz/150ml/⅔ cup of the water.

4 Leave in a warm place for 5 minutes, or until the surface is frothy.

5 Add to the dry ingredients, along with the remaining water, and combine to form a smooth dough, adding more flour/water if necessary.

6 Knead until the dough takes on a uniform smoothness, divide it into two, then shape and fit into the prepared tins/pans.

7 Set the oven to 400°F/200°C (Gas 6).

8 Cover the tins/pans with a damp cloth or cling film/plastic wrap and leave in a warm, draught-free place for 20-30 minutes, or until the dough is within ½in/1¼cm of the top of the tins/pans.

9 Bake for approximately 30 minutes, or until the bases sound hollow when tapped.

10 Turn out onto a wire cooling rack and leave to cool completely.

SERVING SUGGESTION

This bread can be prepared in a 2lb/900g loaf tin/pan, but a better loaf is produced when made in 2 × 1lb/450g quantities as described above. If making one large loaf, however, it will need a longer cooking time – approximately 40 minutes. As it is so moist, this bread will remain fresh for several days (if family/friends have not already eaten it all!), and it is delicious toasted. For a 'nutty' finish you can sprinkle the surface of the dough, before leaving it to rise, with sesame/sunflower/poppy seeds/kibbled wheat – pressing these down gently so that they do not roll off once cooked.

Variation: replace 1½oz/40g/⅓ cup of the flour with an equal quantity of bran, or replace 1oz/25g/¼ cup of the flour with an equal quantity of medium oatmeal (this version enhances the lovely nutty flavour of the bread and increases its moisture-keeping quality).

Desserts and treats

Desserts

Dr Hay considered desserts superfluous to a perfectly adequate meal, their place at the end of a meal merely acting as a temptation to over-indulge – as we all know!

Strictly speaking, desserts on the Hay System should preferably not exist, or if they do should be based on fresh/dried fruits, or some similar healthy dish, but we all need occasional indulgence! (see Treats below).

Therefore, rather than ban desserts completely, the option of selection must be left to the discretion and digestive comfort of the individual. Eaten occasionally in moderation and using sense and care in their selection, they are acceptable.

If you do wish, though, to eat a dessert I would recommend eating less of the first course/s of the meal. All dessert recipes are made with whole foods, and are free of added sugar – so one can indulge without too much conscience-pricking!

Treats

Never feel that you are not allowed any 'treats' or 'frills' when 'Haying'. A treat now and then is preferable to abandoning the Hay System as a whole later. Dr Hay never intended to create a punishing regime, and indulgences *do* have their place! So – if you and your feelings really yearn for a cheese sandwich it is far better to satisfy that craving than feel so deprived and unhappy that you ignore the principles totally and eat two cheese sandwiches followed by apple pie!

Likewise, if eating at a friend's house and you wish to 'indulge' or have no polite alternative but to eat an incompatible meal, do not feel guilt-ridden for doing so. No awful damage can be done.

Apple tofu 'cheesecake'

One of my favourite desserts, a light and refreshing end to a meal.

Imp/Metric	Serves 6-8	American
2oz/50g	butter/margarine	¼ cup
1 dsp	maple syrup	2 tsps
4oz/100g	ground hazelnuts	1 cup
4oz/100g	flaked/slivered almonds – crush into very small pieces	1 cup
1¼lb/550g	very firm tofu	2½ cups
4 fl oz/100ml	concentrated apple juice	½ cup
1½ tbsps	lemon juice	1½ tbsps
1 tsp	vanilla essence	1 tsp
	Decoration	
	apple slices	
	extra lemon juice	

1 Set the oven to 375°F/190°C (Gas 5).
2 Grease a 7-8in/17½-20cm spring-release tin/springform pan, flan/quiche dish or similar.
3 Melt the butter/margarine and maple syrup together in a saucepan, stir in the nuts to form a moist mixture, then press into the base of the prepared tin/pan/dish.
4 Place the tofu, apple juice, lemon juice and vanilla essence in a food processor or liquidizer/blender, and blend until smooth.
5 Spoon on to the nut base and smooth over.
6 Bake for 15-20 minutes until firm and very lightly browned.
7 Bake for 15-20 minutes until firm and very lightly browned.
8 Leave to cool, then remove from the tin/pan (if using), and chill for 3-4 hours before serving.
9 Very thinly slice some apple, brush with lemon juice, and decorate the top of the cheesecake – I usually alternate red and green apple slices for an attractive finish.

Cannot be Frozen

Serving Suggestion
Serve with whipped/heavy or pouring/light cream, or vanilla ice-cream.

S   Ⓥ

Banana, pear and sultana cobbler

A very popular family dessert – the pear and banana flavours blend beautifully with the delicate flavour of cloves.

Imp/Metric	Serves 4-6	American
3oz/75g	dried pears – cut into slivers	½ cup
2oz/50g	sultanas/golden seedless raisins	⅓ cup
2	cloves	2
4fl oz/100ml	boiling water	½ cup
6oz/150g	whole wheat self-raising/self rising flour	1½ cups
¼ tsp	salt	¼ tsp
1½ tbsps	honey/maple syrup	1½ tbsps
	1½ tbsps milk diluted with 2 tbsps water	
1 tbsp	sunflower oil	1 tbsp
2lb/900g	bananas – ripe and well-speckled	2lb
	Glaze	
	beaten egg yolk/diluted milk for glazing	
	Garnish	
1 dsp	sesame seeds	2 tsps

1 Set the oven to 400°F/200°C (Gas 6).
2 Place the pears, sultanas/golden seedless raisins and cloves in a saucepan, add the boiling water, bring back to the boil and simmer for 3-4 minutes.
3 Take the saucepan off the heat and remove the cloves.
4 Sieve/sift the flour and salt into a mixing bowl.
5 In a separate bowl place the honey/maple syrup and gradually whisk in the diluted milk.
6 Add the oil and mix again.
7 Cut the bananas into slices, combine with the pears and sultanas/golden seedless raisins and place in the bottom of a 2 pint/1 litre dish.
8 Pour the honey/maple syrup mix into the flour mix and form into a dough.
9 Roll out the dough to ¾in/1½cm in thickness and cut into rounds with a 2-2½in/5-7½cm ring/cookie cutter.
10 Place the dough rounds overlapping on top of each other around the edge of the dish on top of the fruit mix, leaving the centre empty.

11 Brush the top with the glace and sprinkle with sesame seeds.
12 Bake for 20-25 minutes until the 'cobbler' topping is crisp
and browned.

Serving Suggestion
Serve hot with Polenta 'custard' (page 248), pouring/light
cream, or ice-cream. This dish is also tasty cold; the bananas
will tend to discolour on keeping and, although this will not
adversely affect the flavour, it is a good excuse to finish the
whole thing!

Carob and almond ring

*A very special dessert – the moist almond topping and the sticky
carob base create a delectable feast!*

Imp/Metric	Serves 6-8	American
	Topping	
1½oz/40g	butter/margarine	3 tbsps
2oz/50g	chick pea/garbanzo flour	½ cup
3 tbsps	maple syrup	3 tbsps
	1½ tbsps milk diluted with 1½ tbsps water	
4oz/100g	ground almonds	1 cup
1 tsp	almond essence	1 tsp
	Base	
2½oz/65g	butter/margarine – melted	⅓ cup
3oz/75g	lexia raisins	½ cup
3fl oz/75ml	water	⅓ cup
8oz/225g	almonds – chop *very* finely in their skins	1⅔ cups
½oz/15g	dark carob powder	2 tbsps
	Decoration	
	leaves made from melted carob (optional)/	
	blanched almonds	

1 Thoroughly grease a 8in/20cm corrugated ring mould/tube
pan.
2 To make the topping, melt the butter/margarine, stir in the
garbanzo flour and combine well.
3 Take the pan off the heat, add the maple syrup, diluted milk,
ground almonds and almond essence, then combine well and
leave to cool.

4 Press the mixture into the base of the ring mould/tube pan shaping it to come slightly up the sides, then put to one side.

5 Now make the base. Place the raisins in a saucepan with the water, cook for 15 minutes uncovered, or until the water has been absorbed, then put the raisins into a food processor or liquidizer/blender and blend until smooth. Mix the raisin purée with the melted butter/margarine.

6 Stir in the almonds and carob powder and combine thoroughly to produce a sticky mixture.

7 Press on top of the almond mix in the ring mould/tube pan and smooth level, leave to cool then place in a refrigerator to set for 6-8 hours.

8 To remove, release the sides of the tin/pan and then run a sharp knife around the central metal ring to loosen it slightly.

9 Invert the mould so that the carob base is facing downwards, and rest the central metal ring on a serving plate.

10 With both hands supporting the underneath of the carob base, very carefully ease the almond topping down and away from the moulded tin/pan, until it loosens and can be levered gently down on to the serving plate – use the point of a knife to help if it sticks a little.

11 Decorate with the carob leaves and blanched almonds if liked.

Serving Suggestion
Serve chilled accompanied with cream or ice-cream. For a simpler version press the base mixture into a 7in/17½cm flan/tart ring/pan/dish, top with the almond mix, decorate with flaked almonds and/or grated carob/carob leaves, and serve as a gâteau.

S

Christmas pudding

A delicious, moist pudding – a perfect ending to the Christmas meal!

Imp/Metric	Makes one 2pt/1 litre/5 cup or 2 × 1pt/500ml/2½ cup puddings	American
2oz/50g	dried figs – chop very finely	½ cup
2oz/50g	dried dates – chop very finely	½ cup
4oz/100g	raisins	¾ cup
4oz/100g	currants	¾ cup
4oz/100g	sultanas/golden seedless raisins	¾ cup
2oz/50g	flaked/slivered almonds	1½ cup
2oz/50g	butter/margarine	¼ cup
1 tbsp	molasses	1 tbsp
4oz/100g	finely grated/shredded carrot	⅔ cup
1 tsp	finely grated/shredded lemon rind	1tsp
1 tsp	finely grated/shredded orange rind	1 tsp
2oz/50g	whole wheat breadcrumbs	1 cup
2oz/50g	self-raising/self-rising whole wheat flour	½ cup
1 tsp	mixed spice	1 tsp
1 tsp	ground cinnamon	1 tsp
5 fl oz/150ml	brandy	⅔ cup

1 Thoroughly grease a 2pt/1 litre/5 cup pudding basin, or 2 × 1pt/500ml/2½ cups pudding basins.
2 Mix all the ingredients together in a bowl – sieving/sifting together the flour, mixed spice and cinnamon – to form a moist but stiff mixture – add extra flour if it is too sloppy.
3 Press into the prepared basin/s and smooth over.
4 Place a layer of greased baking parchment, pleated in the centre, on top of the basin/s, cover with foil, then secure tightly with string.
5 Place in a steamer or pan of boiling water with the water level reaching approximately half way up the side of the bowl, and leave to simmer for:
8-9 hours – 2pt/1 litre/5 cup pudding
4-5 hours – 1pt/500ml/2½ cup puddings
Alternatively, pressure cook the puddings:
3 hours – 2pt/1 litre/5 cup pudding
1½-2 hours – 1pt/500ml/2½ cup pudding
Once cooked they will be dark in colour and firm.

6 Leave to cool, then cover with fresh baking parchment and foil, and store in a cool, dark place until required – the flavour will 'mature' and improve with keeping. To reheat:

Steam   3 hours – 2pt/1 litre/5 cup pudding
        2 hours – 1pt/500ml/2½ cup pudding
Pressure Cook 1½ hours – 2pt/1 litre/5 cup pudding
        1 hour – 1pt/500ml/2½ cup pudding

Serving Suggestion
For a spectacular pudding, flame with brandy, then serve hot with brandy butter, custard or cream. Also delicious eaten cold.

Creams
Cream is a welcome addition to cakes and desserts. Below are some dairy-free alternatives, but the variations suggested can also be applied to dairy creams.

Tofu creams
For a basic tofu cream see the Tofu 'custard' recipe (page 249), using half the quantity to serve 4-6 people.

   Ⓥ

Orange cream

A tangy refreshing cream.

Imp/Metric	Serves 4-6	American
10oz/275g	firm silken tofu	1¼ cups
1 tbsp	sunflower oil	1 tbsp
3 tbsps	maple syrup	3 tbsps
4-5 tbsps	unsweetened orange juice	4-5 tbsps

1 Place all the ingredients in a food processor or liquidizer/blender, and blend until smooth.
2 Chill for 3-4 hours before serving.

Cannot be Frozen

Serving Suggestion
Serve as a topping for fruit, desserts, ice-creams, etc.

Variations:

Almond Orange Cream – add ½-¾ tsp almond essence to taste (my favourite!)

Citrus Cream – use a mixture of lemon and orange juice

Lemon Cream – use lemon juice to taste instead of the orange juice

Vanilla Cream – omit the orange juice and add ½-1 tsp vanilla essence to taste

Vanilla Orange Cream – add ½-1 tsp vanilla essence to taste

Nut creams

Almond cream

This mixture makes a delicious, thick, non-dairy cream.

Imp/Metric	Serves 4	American
4oz/100g	ground almonds	1 cup
2 tbsps	sunflower oil	2 tbsps
¼ tsp	vanilla essence	¼ tsp
1 tbsp	maple syrup	1 tbsp
5 fl oz/150ml	water	⅔ cup

1 Place all the ingredients in a food processor or liquidizer/blender and blend until very smooth – adding more vanilla essence/maple syrup to taste.
2 Chill.

Cannot be Frozen
It will keep 2-3 days in a refrigerator.

Serving Suggestion
As for tofu creams above, you can vary the flavouring agents used. Alternatively, make with different nuts. Ensure always, though, that they are *very* finely ground – otherwise a rather 'gritty' cream results! This cream is also excellent used as a cooking cream – without the vanilla essence/maple syrup.

| S |

Polenta 'custard'

A delicious custard – very quick and easy to make – far superior to the 'packet' varieties!

Imp/Metric	Makes 1pt/570ml/2½ cups	American
6 tbsps	polenta	6 tbsps
2 tbsps	honey/maple syrup	2 tbsps
4 tsps	vanilla essence	4 tsps
	5 fl oz/150ml/⅔ cup milk, diluted	
	with 15 fl oz/425ml/2 cups water	

1 Place the polenta, honey/maple syrup and vanilla essence in a large bowl, and combine.
2 Place the diluted milk in a saucepan and bring almost to boiling point.
3 Slowly pour over the polenta mix, stirring all the time so that the mixture is evenly distributed, pour this mixture back into the saucepan and return to the heat, stirring constantly until a smooth 'custardy' texture results – adjust the vanilla essence/maple syrup to suit your taste.

Cannot be Frozen

Serving Suggestion
Serve hot over starch-based puddings or fruits, or leave to go cold for a blancmange-type consistency. While still hot you can stir in some chopped dried fruits, currants, raisins, sultanas/golden seedless raisins and toasted chopped nuts, and eat as a chewy, crunchy custard, or leave to go cold for a more set 'pudding' mixture. Delicious used as a trifle topping.

Variation: prepare with 1pt/570ml/2½ cups Almond milk (page 84).

Tofu 'custard'

Although not the 'real thing' – I think this is a very good custard alternative, and excellent for use at protein meals.

Imp/Metric	Makes 1pt/570ml/2½ cups	American
1¼lb/550g	firm tofu	2½ cups
2 tbsps	sunflower oil	2 tbsps
3-4 tsps	vanilla essence	3-4 tsps
4 tbsps	maple syrup	4 tbsps

1 Place all the ingredients in a food processor or liquidizer/ blender and blend until smooth – adjust the vanilla essence/maple syrup to suit your taste.

Cannot be Frozen

Serving Suggestion
Serve cold as a 'custard' topping on protein-based trifles, etc, or heat through and serve hot like custard – delicious!

Fruit galette

An impressive dessert – perfect for special occasions.

Imp/Metric	Serves 8	American
9oz/250g	ground almonds	2¼ cups
3oz/75g	ground hazelnuts	¾ cup
1½ tsps	baking powder	1½ tsps
1½oz/40g	butter/margarine – melted	3 tbsps
3-4 tbsps	milk	3-4 tbsps
	Cream	
10oz/275g	firm silken tofu	1¼ cups
3 tbsps	maple syrup	3 tbsps
1	kiwi fruit – approximately 3oz/75g in weight	1
1 tsp	finely grated/shredded orange rind	1 tsp
½ tsp	almond essence	½ tsp
	Fruit filling	
3	large oranges – skin and segment	3
3	kiwi fruits – peel and cut into thin slices	3

1 Set the oven to 375°F/190°C (Gas 5).
2 Grease one 8in/20cm and one 6in/15cm loose-bottomed flan ring/springform tart pan, and line the bases with baking parchment.
3 Combine the nuts and baking powder in a bowl, then mix in the butter/margarine.
4 Add the milk and stir in using a fork.
5 Bring the mixture together with your hand to achieve a firm but moist dough.
6 Press 5oz/150g of the mixture into the base of the 6in/15cm tin/pan, and the remainder into the base of the other tin/pan.
7 Mark both rings gently with the back edge of a knife into eight sections.
8 Bake 10-12 minutes, or until firm and lightly golden.
9 Leave to cool in the tin, then carefully turn out.
10 Place all the ingredients for cream in a food processor or liquidizer/blender, and blend until smooth.
11 Spread just over half of the cream on top of the larger base.
12 Arrange the orange segments and kiwi slices over the surface.
13 Place the smaller base on top, cover with the cream, then decorate with the remaining fruit.

Base only is Suitable for Freezing

Serving Suggestion
Serve with a little extra cream if desired and try different fruits and creams.

S

Banana, raisin and vanilla 'ice-cream'

A friend of mine suggested this recipe might be extra special with the addition of a touch of rum . . .

Imp/Metric	Serves 6	American
4oz/100g	raisins – lexia if available	⅔ cup
4fl oz/100ml	water	½ cup
8oz/225g	ground cashews	2 cups
2lb/900g	bananas – select very ripe ones	2lb
scant tsp	vanilla essence	scant tsp
	Decoration	
	extra raisins and slices of banana	

1 Place the raisins in a saucepan with the water, bring to the boil and simmer for 15 minutes uncovered, or until they are soft and all the water is absorbed. Leave to cool, then place the raisins cooked in a food processor or liquidizer, and blend until smooth.
2 Add the ground cashews, and blend again.
3 Slice the bananas, add to the raisin and cashew mix and blend until the mixture is smooth.
4 Finally, blend in the vanilla essence.
5 Pour into a plastic container, and freeze overnight or 8-12 hours.
6 Remove from the freezer half-an-hour before serving to soften, and decorate with slices of banana and raisins.

Serving Suggestion
Serve on its own or with sweet almond biscuits and hot carob sauce – delicious! – or as an accompaniment to other sweet dishes. You can make individual portions by pouring the mixture into small plastic containers, then freezing (I save my empty margarine containers for this purpose). Remove from the freezer and leave to soften slightly, then turn upside down and press the base – the 'ice-cream' will then pop out.

Variations
Date, almond and banana 'ice-cream'
Prepare as above but replace the raisins with dates. Replace
4oz/100g/1 cup ground cashews with ground almonds, and the
vanilla essence with almond essence.

Coconut, date and banana 'ice-cream'
Prepare as recipe above but replace the raisins with dates. Omit
the vanilla essence, and dissolve 4oz/100g creamed coconut in
2 fl oz/50ml/¼ cup boiling water to form a thick cream, then
blend along with the other ingredients – a truly luxurious
'ice-cream'!

P or A   Ⓥ
Peach 'ice-cream'

Imp/Metric	Serves 6-8	American
12oz/350g	dried peaches	2½ cups
	10 fl oz/275ml/1⅓ cups milk diluted	
	with 15 fl oz/425ml/2 cups water	
4oz/100g	ground almonds	1 cup
1 scant tsp	almond essence	1 scant tsp

1 Soak the peaches in the diluted milk overnight or 8-12 hours,
  then place the mixture in a food processor or
  liquidizer/blender, and blend until smooth.
2 Add the ground almonds and almond essence, and blend
  again.
3 Freeze overnight or 8-12 hours, then remove from the freezer
  30-45 minutes before serving to soften.

Serving Suggestion
Serve sprinkled with toasted flaked almonds and accompanied
with cream or yoghurt.

Variation: make with dried apricots or other dried fruits of
choice.

Petit fours/sweets
Delicious 'after-dinner bites' or healthy sweets/nibbles.

P or A	

Apricot and almond

Imp/Metric	Makes 25-30	American
6oz/150g	dried apricots – roughly chop	1 cup
2oz/50g	ground almonds	½ cup
1-2 tbsps	boiling water	1-2 tbsps
1oz/25g	sesame seeds	4 tbsps

1 Place the apricots and ground almonds in a food processor or liquidizer/blender, and blend until well combined.
2 Blend again with enough water to achieve a smooth, moist consistency.
3 Shape as desired and roll in the sesame seeds until coated.
4 Store in an airtight container in a refrigerator, or cool place.

S or A	Ⓥ

Date and raisin

Imp/Metric	Makes 20-30	American
4oz/100g	dates – roughly chop	⅔ cup
2oz/50g	raisins – lexia if available	⅓ cup
1oz/25g	desiccated/shredded coconut	⅓ cup

1 Place the dates and raisins in a food processor or liquidizer/blender, and blend to form a sticky paste.
2 Sprinkle the coconut on to a piece of baking parchment, and roll the date and raisin paste on top into a 6in/15cm square, turning it over so that the other side is also coated.
3 Cover with a piece of baking parchment.
4 Place between the two layers of paper on a plate and cover with another plate.
5 Put in a refrigerator for 3-4 hours to become firm.
6 Cut into strips, and then into diamonds/squares.
7 Store in an airtight container in a refrigerator, or cool place.

Hazelnut and ginger

Imp/Metric	Makes 20-25	American
4oz/100g	hazelnuts – toast, then grind	¾ cup
1½oz/40g	crystallized/candied ginger pieces	⅓ cup
1oz/25g	hazelnuts – toast, then very finely chop	3 tbsps

1 Place the ground hazelnuts and ginger in a food processor or liquidizer/blender, and blend to form a smooth, sticky paste – add 1-2 tsps honey/maple syrup if not quite sticky enough.
2 Shape as desired.
3 Store in an airtight container in a refrigerator, or cool place.

Carob and nut clusters

Imp/Metric	Makes 20-30	American
6oz/150g	carob bar or drops	¾ cup
4oz/100g	finely chopped nuts of choice	¾ cup

1 Pour some boiling water into a saucepan, and rest a bowl on top, making sure it lies above the surface of the water. Add the carob and leave to melt slowly, stirring occasionally.
2 Once melted, stir in the nuts and combine thoroughly.
3 Place a rounded teaspoon of the mixture into paper cases.
4 Leave to cool, then store in a refrigerator.

Variation: add 1 tsp peppermint essence to the melted carob.

| S – or N if the cherry is omitted! | |

Almond and cherry

Imp/Metric	Makes 20-30	American
1½oz/40g	butter/margarine	3 tbsps
5oz/150g	ground almonds	1½ cups
3 tbsps	maple syrup	3 tbsps
1 tsp	almond essence	1 tsp
10-15	glacé cherries – naturally coloured – halve	10-15
	(to convert to N, omit)	

1 Melt the butter/margarine then remove the pan from the heat.
2 Add the ground almonds, maple syrup and almond essence and mix to a moist paste.
3 Leave to cool and firm, then shape into little balls and top with half a cherry.
4 Store in an airtight container in a refrigerator.

Variation: make the above with ground hazelnuts and vanilla essence instead of the ground almonds and almond essence. Both types are also delicious coated in poppy seeds.

Serving Suggestion
Serve as 'petits fours' following a meal, or as a healthy alternative to sweets for children (and adults!)

Curried cashews

These make a delicious snack, or pre-meal nibble.

Imp/Metric	Makes 4oz/100g	American
4oz/100g	whole cashews or cashew pieces	1 cup
1 dsp	mild or medium curry powder – depending on personal taste	2 tsps
1 dsp	water	2 tsps

1 Dry roast the cashews in a saucepan until well browned – this will take quite a time.
2 Meanwhile, mix the curry powder and water together.

3 Take the pan off the heat, wait a moment, then add the curry
mix and stir in very quickly.

4 Leave to cool, then store for 2-3 days in an airtight container
to allow the flavours to mingle.

Serving Suggestion
Serve as nibbles, or add to vegetable dishes, salads, etc.

Tamari toasted seeds

*A very savoury way of preparing seeds – far superior to the usual
salted peanuts!*

Imp/Metric	Makes 4oz/100g	American
4oz/100g	sunflower seeds	1 cup
4oz/100g	pumpkin seeds	1 cup
2 tbsps	tamari	2 tbsps

1 Dry roast the seeds in a saucepan until well browned – this
will take quite a time.

2 Take the pan off the heat, wait a moment, then add the
tamari and stir in very quickly.

3 Leave to cool, then store in an airtight container.

Serving Suggestion
Serve as nibbles, or add to vegetable dishes, salads, etc.

S

(V)

Spicy bulgar wheat pudding

A lovely winter pudding – an up-market version of bread-and-butter pudding.

Imp/Metric	Serves 4-6	American
3oz/75g	bulgar wheat	½ cup
1½pt/825ml	almond milk – see recipe, page 84 – or 10 fl oz/275ml/1⅓ cups milk, diluted with 1pt/570ml/2½ cups water	3¾ cups
½oz/15g	butter/margarine	1 tbsp
2 tbsps	maple syrup	2 tbsps
1 tsp	cinnamon	1 tsp
1 tsp	mixed spice	1 tsp
1oz/25g	desiccated/shredded coconut – lightly toast under the grill/broiler	⅓ cup
3oz/75g	raisins – lexia if available	½ cup
3oz/75g	hazelnuts – toast, remove the skins, then grind until a sticky pulp	⅔ cup
1 tsp	ground nutmeg	1 tsp

1 Preheat the oven to 325°F/170°C (Gas 3).
2 Place all the ingredients, except the nutmeg, in a saucepan and bring gently to the boil.
3 Simmer for 3-4 minutes, stirring occasionally.
4 Transfer the mixture to a 2pt/1 litre/5 cup ovenproof dish.
5 Sprinkle with the ground nutmeg, and bake in the centre of the oven for 20 minutes.

Serving Suggestion
Delicious hot on its own, or with a little pouring/light cream. Also good cold!

S ⃞   Ⓥ

Dried fruit and almond trifle

A delicious trifle mixture – always enjoyed by family and friends.

Imp/Metric	Serves 6	American
	Fruit base	
3oz/75g	dried dates	⅔ cup
3oz/75g	dried pears	⅔ cup
1oz/25g	dried banana	¼ cup
1oz/25g	lexia raisins	½ cup
15fl oz/425ml	water	2 cups
½ tsp	lemon rind	½ tsp
½ tsp	orange rind	½ tsp
	½ × quantity sponge cake recipe (page 229)	
½ ts	almond essence	½ tsp
	Topping	
	1 × quantity Polenta 'custard' recipe (page 248)	
	Decoration	
	toasted flaked/slivered almonds	
	cream	

1 Soak the fruit overnight, or 8-12 hours, in 15 fl oz/425ml/2 cups water. Drain, reserving the liquid.
2 Roughly chop, add the lemon and orange rind and combine.
3 Prepare the sponge cake as in the recipe, adding the almond essence.
4 Slice the sponge in half through the middle, then arrange pieces to line the base and sides of a glass bowl, reserving the remainder.
5 Spoon some of the reserved soaking liquid over the surface, then top with half the fruit mix.
6 Arrange the rest of the sponge on top, and top with the remaining fruit and juice.
7 Make the Polenta custard as in the recipe, then pour over the top of the sponge and fruit mix.
8 Leave to cool and set, then refrigerate for 3-4 hours.
9 Just before serving, decorate with the toasted almonds and whipped cream or just serve with cream.

Cannot be Frozen

Serving Suggestion
Serve with ice-cream, yoghurt or extra pouring/light cream.

Variations: use fresh starch fruits.

Trifle – protein-based
A protein trifle can be prepared using fresh/dried fruits, and sweet Almond and poppy seed or Hazelnut and almond starch-free crackers instead of the sponge. Top with 1 × quantity of Tofu vanilla custard (page 249), and decorate and serve as above.

Bibliography and further reading

Burkitt, Dr Denis *Don't Forget Fibre in your Diet* (Martin Dunitz Limited, 1983)

Cannon, Geoffrey & Einzig, Hetty *Dieting makes you Fat* (Century, 1983)

Chaitow, Leon *Candida Albicans – Could Yeast be your Problem?* (Thorsons, 1985)

Colbin, AnneMarie *Food & Healing* (Ballantine, USA, 1986)

Cowmeadow, Oliver *Introduction to Macrobiotics* (Thorsons, 1987)

Diamond, Harvey and Marilyn *Fit For Life* (Bantam Books, 1987)

Diamond, Harvey and Marilyn *Living Health* (Bantam Books, 1987)

Elliot, Rose *Rose Elliot's Vegetarian Cookery* (Collins, 1988)

Elliot, Rose *Vegetarian Slimming* (Chapmans, 1991)

Graham, Judy *Multiple Sclerosis – A Self-Help Guide to its Management* (Thorsons, 1987)

Grant, Doris *Your Daily Bread* (Faber & Faber Limited, 1944) (Out of print but available from secondhand book shops)

Grant, Doris and Joice, Jean *Food Combining for Health – A New Look At The Hay System* (Thorsons, 1984)

Hodgson, Joan *A White Eagle Lodge Book of Health and Healing* (The White Eagle Publishing Trust, 1983)

Kenton, Leslie *The Biogenic Diet* (Arrow, 1987)

Kenton, Leslie and Susannah *Raw Energy* (Arrow, 1987)

Lidolt, Erwina *The Food Combining Cookbook* (Thorsons, 1987)

McGee, Harold *On Food and Cooking – The Science and Lore of the Kitchen* (Allen & Unwin, 1986)

Macintyre, Dr Anne *ME Post-Viral Fatigue Syndrome – How to Live with it* (Unwin Paperbacks, 1989)

Mackarness, Richard *Not All in the Mind* (Pan, 1990)

Nicol, Rosemary *Coping Successfully with your Irritable Bowel* (Sheldon Press, 1989)

Paul, AA and Southgate, DAT *McCance & Widdowson's The Composition of Foods* (HMSO, 1985)

Peterson, Vicki *The Natural Food Catalogue* (MacDonalds, 1984)

Robertson, Laurel, Flinders, Carol and Godfrey, Bronwen *Laurel's Kitchen – A Handbook for Vegetarian Cookery and Nutrition* (Routledge & Kegan Paul, 1979)

The Royal Society of Medicine Family Medical Guide (Peerage Books, 1988)

Schauss, Alexander *Diet, Crime and Delinquency* (Parker House, Canada, 1980)

Sharon, Dr Michael *Complete Nutrition* (Prion, 1989)

Smith, Esther L. *Good Foods that Go Together* (Pivot, Connecticut, 1975)

Sweet, Amanda *Vegan Health Plan* (Arlington Books, 1987)

Szekely, Edmond Bordeaux *Essene Gospel of Peace* (C W Daniel, 1976)

Walker, Caroline & Cannon, Geoffrey *The Food Scandal* (Century, 1984)

Weitz, Martin *Health Shock* (David & Charles (Publishers) Limited, 1980)

WHO Technical Report Series, No 797 *Diet, nutrition and the prevention of chronic disease – Report of the WHO Study Group 1990* (HMSO)

Wright, Celia *The Wright Diet* (Piatkus, 1986)

Yudkin, John *Pure, White and Deadly* (Penguin Books Limited, 1986)

The following books by Dr Hay and those written on his system of eating are now out of print, but can be found in secondhand bookshops, or made available through inter-library loan.

Boyer, Josephine and Cowdin, Katherine *Hay Dieting Menus and Receipts for all Occasions* (Charles Scribner's Sons, New York, 1935)

Grant, Doris *The Hay System Cookery Book* (Harrap, London, 1936)

Grant, Doris *The Hay System Menu Book* (Harrap, London, 1937)

Dengel, Edward H *Hay System Pocket Guide* (Harrap, London, 1936)

Hay, Dr William Howard *Health Via Food* (Sun Diet Health Foundation, New York, 1929)

Hay, Dr William Howard *Superior Health through Nutrition* (1937), facsimile copy available from The Society of Metaphysicians, Hastings

Hay, Dr William Howard *Some Human Ailments* (Harrap, London, 1937)

Hay, Dr William Howard *The Medical Millennium* (1927) facsimile copy available from The Society of Metaphysicians, Hastings

Hay, Dr William Howard *Weight Control* (Harrap, London, 1936)

Hay, Dr William Howard *A New Health Era* (Harrap, London, 1935)

Osborne, Mabel *Hors-D'Oeuvres for Hay Dieters* (Harrap, London, 1938)

Osborne, Mabel *Meatless Dishes for Hay Dieters* (Harrap, London, 1937)

Index
General index

Meal type index

A Medical Comment
Dr MHS Bound MA, MD, FRCGP

In recent times, there has been an upsurge of interest in 'holistic' medicine, which focuses attention on the whole person – each of us seen as a physically-based personality with a spiritual destiny – living in a particular environment. This is encapsulated by Jackie Le Tissier's approach to the Hay system.

Jackie's research into Haying, and her great commitment to it, has come about from her own illness, a severe form of arthritis. She now appears cured and has led a full, satisfying and active life, both physically and intellectually for several years. Her book is a well written, practical and helpful modern update of Dr Hay's work.

The value of the Hay diet in treating disease has always been controversial. Jackie's conclusions may well be challenged by medical doctors and scientists who find them 'unscientific'. But Jackie believes, as I do, that science and intuition need each other – and that the proof of the pudding (if Haying allows it) is in the eating.

I believe that if Dr Johnson were still alive he would greatly enjoy banqueting with Jackie, and would be a lot fitter for it.